Josephine

A drawing of Josephine, from the record sleeve of "Encores Américaines,"
Columbia record Fl 9543.

Josephine

BY
JOSEPHINE BAKER
AND
JO BOUILLON

TRANSLATED FROM THE FRENCH BY
MARIANA FITZPATRICK

PARAGON HOUSE PUBLISHERS
New York

First paperback edition, 1988

Published in the United States by

Paragon House
90 Fifth Avenue
New York, NY 10011

Originally published under the title *Joséphine* by Editions
Robert Laffont-Opera Mundi. Copyright © 1976 by Opera Mundi.

Reprinted by arrangement with Harper & Row Publishers, Inc.

Library of Congress Cataloging-in-Publication Data

Baker, Josephine, 1906–1975.
  Josephine.

  Reprint. Originally published: New York : Harper
& Row, c1977.
  Includes index.
  1. Baker, Josephine, 1906–1975. 2. Dancers—
France—Biography. I. Bouillon, Jo, 1908–
II. Title.
GV1785.B3A3 1988   793.3'2'0924 [B]   88-2534
ISBN 1-55778-108-7 (pbk.)

Manufactured in the United States of America

10 9 8 7 6 5 4 3

Contents

Introduction

Our evening customers were beginning to arrive when the telegram reached Le Bistro, the restaurant I run in central Buenos Aires, aided by my Korean son, Akio, the oldest of our twelve adopted children.

I stood there stricken, telegram in hand. The wire, signed "Gaby," came from Paris. Its sender, my older brother Gabriel Bouillon, the conductor and virtuoso, adored Josephine. Our separation had in no way dimmed his affection for "Bird," as he called her, or lessened his respect for her voice. I sensed that Gaby was hiding something. He was obviously worried.

"What is it, *Papa?*" asked Akio.

"Your uncle says that *Maman* is very ill. He wants me to telephone Dr. Thiroloix. Keep an eye on the customers."

Akio had joined me in Buenos Aires two years earlier. It was the kind of thing that happens in the best of families, even when they're not composed of bits and pieces like ours. Josephine had insisted that Akio assume his responsibilities as the oldest child at an early age and had taught him to stand up for his beliefs. Therefore it was not surprising that after a squabble with his mother he decided he was old enough to pack up and leave home. With the help of his Finnish brother, Jari, he scraped together enough money for passage to Argentina, arriving on my doorstep with nothing but a dinner jacket in his suitcase. Before taking him shopping for more practical clothes in which to earn his keep, I telephoned Josephine to reassure her of his whereabouts.

This was not the first time since I had left Les Milandes, the renovated château which had become our family home in the Dordogne, that we had conferred about the children. Josephine made a point of contacting me each time there was an important decision to be made concerning their welfare. And it was for their sake, since they bore my name, that Josephine and I refused to divorce. Our problems were those of adults faced with the realities of daily life and had nothing to do with the children. Josephine was unique, and, like all exceptional beings, a difficult day-to-day companion, yet together we had realized her dream, which some called madness, proving that children of different colors, races and religions could live together as brothers, seed of a common species, man.

I placed a call to Dr. Thiroloix in Paris. The Thiroloixes, father and son, had taken care of the Bouillons for years. Paul had been at Josephine's side in 1946 during a three-hour operation, which she had survived largely thanks to her amazing vitality. His son Pierre, a cardiologist, had been following her closely ever since the first of her three heart attacks.

"What did Thiroloix say?" Akio asked anxiously.

"She's in a coma."

"Her heart again?"

"No. This time it's some kind of vascular trouble."

"She'll be all right, won't she? She's pulled through so often."

It was true. Josephine had survived half a dozen abdominal operations and several hospitalizations for her heart and for nervous exhaustion. Her strength was astonishing. "You never do anything halfway," I used to tease her. "Either you're dying or you're killing everyone around you." Josephine would smilingly agree, her warm laughter spilling forth like water welling from the earth.

"I'm taking the next plane to Paris."

At five o'clock the following morning, I received a call from the radio station Europe 1. In spite of the fact that it was 9 A.M. in Paris, I hung up in their faces as politely as possible. The French capital, which Josephine had yearned to reconquer, was clearly concerned about her welfare.

The report of her triumph at the Bobino Theater, broadcast over Argentine television only forty-eight hours earlier, had obviously been accurate. Once again Josephine had fought her way back into the public eye. Now she was faced with the ultimate challenge, the struggle for her life, a battle she had almost lost so often. . . . I tried to forget the anxious note in Thiroloix's voice.

I spent the day dealing with the red tape involved in leaving Argentina if you plan to return. There was no further word from Paris, which I considered a hopeful sign. Akio was greeting Le Bistro's evening guests as my plane took off from Ezeiza airport.

It was impossible to sleep. As we flew through the night, memories of the fifteen years Josephine and I had shared washed over me in ripples, eddies, waves. . . . My impossible, marvelous Josephine. She drew people to her like a magnet wherever she went—in the street, in shops, in nightclubs, in orphanages and above all on the stage. Her willfulness was exhilarating, her courage a perpetual challenge. Sweet, tough Josephine, never on the sidelines, always in the fray. We had met as the lightning and thunder of war were abating and hope rose anew like the sun. It seemed natural that we should fall in love, that we should want to face this rebirth together. We sensed that we shared similar feelings, tastes and dreams. Another common bond was our profession, indispensable to Josephine not as a pedestal but as a trampoline from which to soar toward her ultimate goal.

Along with the return of peace came the realization that Josephine had never abandoned her fight against the hydra of fascism. I had married an Amazon . . . but since I was probably a less selfish and headstrong, more understanding companion than my predecessors, I was able to remain with her long enough to share in the creation of the Rainbow Family she so passionately wanted. Josephine, woman of a hundred faces.

These faces rose before me as I traveled through the darkness to Josephine's side. And with them came the beloved faces of the children. Akio, almond-eyed, sensitive, serious; Jari, with his Nordic fairness and stamina; Jean-Claude, our blond Frenchman, blessed with an innate equilibrium; Mara, a full-blooded Indian, who hoped to become a doctor because they are lacking in his native Venezuela; Janot, the Japanese, whose love of plants and flowers points toward a career in horticulture; Brahim and Marianne, found abandoned under a bush in the midst of the

Algerian war, he the son of an Arab, she a colonial's granddaughter; dusky Koffi from Abidjan, with his purity of spirit; Luis, the Colombian, wed to a girl from Lille and father of little Stephanie; Moses, also married and beginning a career in hotel management; Noël, abandoned on the holiday eve that lent him its name, and Stellina, the last of our children, adopted after I had left Josephine but brought by her to Buenos Aires so that I could meet the second Miss Bouillon. All their faces were overshadowed by images of Josephine, friend of the rich and the poor, the unknown and famous. Her long hands kneading dough or wielding a spade at Les Milandes, opening like lacquered flowers under the stage lights, caressing an animal or the cheek of a child, giving, offering, giving again, with fingers unused to keeping score. Josephine, her eyes bright with enthusiasm, imagination, joy, love and occasionally anger. Josephine the star, swathed in feathers, covered with diamonds. Heroic Josephine in uniform. Josephine the militant, speechmaking, organizing. Maternal Josephine, watchful, demanding, generous. I had known them all, a collection of lives in one.

It was broad daylight when our plane touched down at Roissy. Two o'clock on a rainy afternoon. I glimpsed Gaby in the crowd and nearby saw Jari's white-blond hair. His eyes were masked by dark glasses.

"She's dead, *Papa,*" he whispered.

Dead. So many words described the different Josephines, but this was not one of them. During the car ride to the Salpêtrière Hospital, I tried vainly to visualize her cold, still body, that body which even in repose had an animal grace, a boundless vitality. She would fall asleep whenever and wherever exhaustion overcame her, sinking down on a seat, a rug or even a bed, although she liked the last solution the least. After a brief rest she would be good as new, refreshed and ready for anything. The thought of seeing her body rigid on its deathbed sent shivers down my spine.

As it turned out, my apprehension was in vain.

When we arrived at Salpêtrière, we were directed to the hospital morgue. Sorry, she's not here, they told us. Look in the viewing rooms in that building across the way. We finally found her in a little curtained room overlooking a side street, in easy reach of the hearses.

Josephine was already in her coffin. The lid had been closed.

Invisible? So soon? The reason for this, we were told, was to forestall the hordes of photographers, who would have done anything to snap a final picture of Josephine.

"She looks so beautiful," murmured her sister Margaret. "Lélia, Jacqueline and I dressed her in the ivory-colored gown she wore to the after-theater party last Tuesday. . . ."

That reception celebrating Josephine's triumph had been attended by two hundred celebrities, including Princess Grace and the actress Jeanne Moreau. Josephine always introduced Lélia as her niece, but Lélia and her son Julio were really members of the Abatino family, relatives of Pepito Abatino, who had launched Josephine on her arrival in Paris. Pepito had even been taken for Josephine's husband, a rumor she never bothered to deny. After all, she was the object of so much gossip! She had been deeply attached to Pepito and loved his family like her own to the very end. Jacqueline is Jacqueline Cartier, the journalist, one of Josephine's closest friends during the last years of her life.

"On her deathbed, with her face scrubbed clean of makeup, she had the calm beauty of a woman of forty," Jacqueline told me.

Forty years old . . . Josephine's age when we met. In exactly fifty-one days I had planned to send her a telegram for her sixty-ninth birthday, in spite of all that had come between us. During a trip to Buenos Aires seven months earlier, she had neglected to visit me for the first time. Had she been too busy with her own affairs? Or perhaps unwilling to share them with me as she had in the past? Now that the children were older did she no longer feel the need for my presence, distant though it was? I knew that she had recently begun to consider divorce. At our last meeting, when she was appearing at the Rugantin in Buenos Aires, I had said half-jokingly, "We'll divorce when all the children are of age." Three of them are still minors, Stellina only twelve. As I stood before Josephine's coffin I thought how fortunate it was that although they had lost their mother so cruelly, their father was still there.

Flowers arrived by the armload. They were followed by heartbroken friends. Josephine had the gift of making herself loved, indeed adored, at first sight. Or never. Most of the mourners were new friends, strangers to me. I felt like an intruder. After all, I was no longer part of her life. How could these newcomers comprehend the strains and strengths that had bound us together? Their role had been to engineer Josephine's final triumph.

Josephine, like other entertainers, felt the need to be constantly surrounded, loved, protected, in order to succeed. "We're like pretty little clouds," she once told me. "It takes a strong wind to move us. Be my wind.

It's made of love." She had always managed to find the breezes necessary to further her career.

After winning one battle, she would move on to the next, often with new allies in tow. Past struggles were forgotten in the excitement of the impending fray. Josephine's ability to forget was astounding and to some shocking. When she greeted with open arms friends "forgotten" for twenty years, she was baffled by their coldness. Time had no more importance to Josephine than to a child. Her focus was the future, not the past.

During what was unfortunately to be the final period of her life, she confided her three main goals to her close friends the actor Jean-Claude Brialy and André Levasseur, writer-producer of her revue *Joséphine* at the Bobino. These aims were to write her autobiography, to film her life and to establish a Josephine Baker museum in order to "leave something of myself behind and provide for the children." The success of her new revue had led to hopes for an international tour and enough income to solve her money worries. On Tuesday, April 8, 1975, news of her triumphant gala performance appeared in the press around the world. She alerted her friends that she planned to begin work on her pet projects the following Monday. But on Thursday the tenth, Lélia found Josephine in a coma. She died two days later without regaining consciousness.

"It's best this way," Thiroloix insisted. "Can you imagine a woman like Josephine totally helpless, perhaps even blind?"

When I reached the apartment on the fashionable Avenue Paul Doumer where Josephine had prepared for her final challenge, the stage comeback of a woman near seventy, I found her desk drawers crammed with folders labeled in blue in her large, bold hand: "For the book." The folders bulged with notes, reflections, documents, old programs, press clippings and three hundred pages of the rough draft of an autobiography begun fifteen years earlier. I remembered how she had set it aside because "It's too soon to write my memoirs. I have too much living still to do."

I would study this material later. My first job was to console our stricken children.

I was well aware that the children had given Josephine some difficult moments during their adolescence. But in spite of their rebelliousness, thoughtlessness and youthful need for self-assertion, her death had left them stunned.

Once a semblance of order had been restored, my thoughts returned to Josephine's projects and particularly to what I knew was her fondest hope, ensuring the survival of our Rainbow Family. If I did my job well, I could guarantee our children's future, at the same time recreating their mother's extraordinary personality.

And so I set to work, sorting through those overflowing folders, turning up mementos, outlines, anonymous letters, correspondence with celebrities. . . . Josephine scribbled on everything: stationery from the deluxe hotels she visited on tour, scraps torn from bistro tablecloths, bits of newspaper, printed pages. Gradually everything fell into place, reconstructing an intriguing, unpredictable, sometimes disconcerting being whose fate was determined from childhood by a guiding light. Or was the quality of the guiding light determined by fate?

Wherever there was information lacking, I turned to Josephine's friends, her sister Margaret, our children and my own memory to fill the gap.

And that is how Josephine's book was posthumously born.

Josephine

CHAPTER 1

―――✦―――

Childhood
in St. Louis

My happiest childhood memory? I really don't know, but I can tell you which was the worst. It marked me, first unconsciously and later all too consciously, for life. I think in ancient times they used to call it the power of destiny.

The year was 1917, the place St. Louis, Missouri. I was eleven and lay sleeping in the one-room shack my family called home. It wasn't much more than a heap of dilapidated boards connected by an uneven floor. To keep out the cold, Daddy had lined the walls with pages torn from newspapers and magazines, gaily colored scraps of paper which blended into a crazy quilt of overlapping images. How I used to love to look at them! What on close inspection turned out to be a seed advertisement, a woman's fancy hairdo and a view of the Sunday parade, at a distance became a fabulous animal. I thought our walls were so beautiful that I was sure my father must be a famous artist.

Actually, he was on relief. But to my young eyes, the home he had made for us was a palace.

Earlier that evening my brother, my two sisters and I had gathered around the stove Daddy had made from an oil drum. While the kerosene lamp sent shadows flickering over the walls, my father told us story after story. They all ended alike, with whites and blacks living together in peace since we are all God's children. Daddy had learned those stories from his parents. They had been slaves but we were free. That meant we were lucky even though our dinner that night had been rotten potatoes stolen from a rich man's garbage pail. . . .

Suddenly Mama shook me awake.

Throwing back the threadbare patchwork quilt that covered the bed I shared with my brother and sisters, she pulled us to our feet. An ominous humming sound filled the air. It seemed to be drawing nearer. "Is there a storm coming, Mama?" my brother Richard asked. "No, not a storm, child. It's the whites. Hurry!" "Wait, Mama, I have to get my babies." Two tiny black-and-white puppies shared the bed in which we children huddled together for warmth. I had discovered them half dead in a trash can while I was sorting through garbage. They barely had the strength to whine. Knowing that Mama would be furious, I still had brought them home. After all, they hadn't cost anything and I would somehow manage to feed them . . . which I did, sharing my ration of bread and Sunday treat of milk. Gathering my "babies" up, I hurried along behind Mama, who had picked up little Willie May and was pushing Richard and my sister Margaret out the door.

What I saw before me as I stepped outside had been described at church that Sunday by the Reverend in dark, spine-chilling tones. This was the Apocalypse. Clouds, glowing from the incandescent light of huge flames leaping upward from the riverbank, raced across the sky . . . but not as quickly as the breathless figures that dashed in all directions. The entire black community appeared to be fleeing like ants from a scattered antheap. "A white woman was raped," someone shouted, and although I didn't understand the meaning of his words, I knew that they described the ultimate catastrophe. The flames drew nearer. As the choking stench of ashes filled the air, I was overcome with panic. Mama threw us to the ground and covered us with her body. I could feel her trembling and pressed my face against my "babies," whose hearts were pounding even faster than mine. There was a rushing of footsteps and I could almost hear the Reverend thundering: "And a terrible earthquake came to pass; the sun grew dark as a bottomless pit. . . . Who can survive the day of His wrath?" I opened my eyes. Nearby a white man, his face contorted with hatred, was savagely beating a figure kneeling before him with what looked like a club. Again and again he struck. The only way I could tell that his victim was black was by his raised hands; the rest of him was wet with blood. Finally he crumpled into the mud like a filthy scarlet rag. Mama quickly turned my face away.

The walk home seemed as long and terrible to me as the Reverend's Apocalypse. An eerie silence had fallen, punctuated by whimpers, sobs and moans rising from the shadows. One of our neighbors, recognizing Mama, clutched hysterically at her skirt: "Carrie! Carrie! Do you know what they did to John? They ripped out his eyes!" A wild-eyed old woman in charred clothing rushed up. "They got Eloise. They cut up her stomach." I knew Eloise, a young woman who had once given me a piece of freshly baked corn bread. I had heard she was expecting a child. ". . . And they tore out the baby!" Then the old woman began howling, a sound that seemed to come from her very guts. Suddenly Mama pointed a finger toward the red-stained sky and cried in a voice I had never heard before: "Look up there. Look. God will avenge us." I raised my head with the others, straining to see through eyes stinging with dust and tears. Mama was right. There in the heavens was a huge white figure with outstretched arms. . . . "It's nothing but smoke," someone muttered. "No, it's our Heavenly Father," another voice insisted. And I knew that the second voice spoke truly, because I had seen God before.

I had been seven then. Mama had explained to me that we were very poor, that Daddy couldn't find work. As the oldest child, it was up to me to help out. A white woman was coming to take me away. I was to call her Mistress and do as she said. In return she would give me shoes and a coat. When Mistress finally arrived she told me how much she loved children. I enjoyed the train trip that took us to her house in the country. Mistress's house was immense and she woke me every morning at five o'clock so that I could finish my work by eight-thirty. There was coal to fetch, the stove to stoke, chamber pots and spittoons to empty, beds to make, wood to cut, the kitchen to clean. . . . At nine o'clock I left for school, where Mistress was obliged by law to send me. Country schools closed at two in the afternoon so that the children could help out in the fields. Instead I washed dishes, refilled the lamps, brought in wood, peeled vegetables, washed the front and back steps, did the washing and once a week laundered my own clothes. At ten o'clock I went down to the cellar, where I slept with the dog.

He was a nice dog, who let me share his bed. I gave him my cold corn pone. He gave me his fleas. It made Mistress angry when I scratched myself in the house. Before beating me she would take off my clothes to protect them from wear. She struck me so hard that welts appeared on my back. Luckily the dog would lick my wounds in the night. I think he must have had some kind of medicine in his tongue, because my back began to heal. He was a kind dog, but in spite of the way he warmed our bed I began to cough. My teacher grew concerned about my condition. One day when I had let the dishwater boil too long and cracked the plates, Mistress became so angry that she plunged my hands into the steaming water. Screaming with pain, I fled into the cellar and collapsed. Through my sobs I prayed to God: "Please let me die! I'm too miserable to live!" The ground swarmed with insects, some of which crawled across my body, but I knew that they, at least, would not hurt me. As I was sinking into unconsciousness, I suddenly saw a light moving toward me. There in the midst of a fleecy cloud, God, dressed in white, stood smiling. Leaning forward, he gently pinned a golden crown to my head with a star. . . .

I woke up in the hospital. A neighbor, hearing my screams, had alerted the authorities. My body was covered with cuts and bruises; it hurt me to breathe; my hands were badly burned and I was shaking with fear. A doctor dressed in white like God himself and several nurses smiling like angels hovered over me, asking: "What's your name, little girl? What do they call you?" "Tumpy." "Tumpy?" "After the poem 'Humpty Dumpty.'" He was fat and round, of course. And I was so terribly thin. But at birth I had been such a plump baby that Mama, who hadn't heard the poem quite right, had said, "She looks just like Tumpy!" and the name had stuck. Although I was really named for "Aunt" Jo, my mother's cousin, nobody called me Josephine. "And what is your mother's name, little girl?" "Mama." The police booked Mistress for maltreating a child and then went out to find Mama. She finally arrived at my bedside, her eyes full of tears. I told her that I would miss my friend the dog and then we left for home.

Home . . . Fortunately ours had not been burned down with the others. Perhaps because it stood in the farthest, poorest section of the colored quarter. Not that there would have been much to destroy, since all our furniture had recently been seized. Daddy had replaced it as best he could by nailing together packing cases.

Where was Daddy? I had not seen him since Mama had pushed us out into the night. Now he lay slumped in a corner, his eyes reflecting the horror he had seen. "Fire and blood," he muttered. "Blood and fire. Why? Why?" "Was a white woman really raped?" Mama asked. "I wish the devil had had her!" Daddy replied. "They say young Tom never did anything but look at her. But we'll never know for sure; Tom's dead." So that was it. Because of a lie, men and women of color had suffered and died. Surely such injustice would someday end since God, although he was white, had said we all were brothers. I swore that day from the bottom of my heart that I, Tumpy, would somehow help to make this change occur. I would remember the massacre all my life.

Margaret: Josephine was born one Sunday morning at eleven o'clock in a St. Louis hospital. She had barely emerged into the world when she slipped from the doctor's hands. He caught her just before she hit the floor. Josephine's entire life was like that. Ups and downs.

As an infant, she was sent to live with Grandma, because of what happened to Carrie, our mother. Mama was the prettiest girl in the neighborhood, neat as a pin in her spotless white dresses. In those days she and Grandma lived with Aunt Elvara, the head of the family. Mama was the most popular girl at the dance hall on Sundays. No one could dance like she could, with a glass of water balanced on her head, never spilling a drop. She was still dancing two months before Josephine was born. What had happened was this: Mama was swept off her feet by a handsome, olive-skinned boy—a "spinach," as we called Spaniards—with disastrous results. His family wouldn't hear of marriage to a black girl. Fortunately things took a turn for the better when Arthur appeared on the scene. A tall, muscular black man, he adored Mama. Arthur had no illusions about what had happened, but because he loved and pitied Mama, he took her in. He would raise Josephine like his own, he said. But when little Richard was born, Josephine was sent off to join Grandma at Aunt Elvara's house.

Josephine: Great-Aunt Elvara was a huge woman—though she may have seemed especially large to me since I was so young. Her skin was the color of copper and she wore her coal-black hair in two long braids. Aunt

Elvara was Indian. I had been told that the ways of her people dated back thousands of years, and when she thundered "Tumpy" in her booming voice, my heart would sink. She spent most of her time weaving striped shawls, but occasionally she would order us out of the house while she danced the wild tribal dances of her Cherokee ancestors, her moccasined feet thumping the floor. Other times she sat cross-legged on her straw mat, smoking quietly.

She and my grandmother frequently quarreled. Apparently this was because Grandma was not a full-blooded Indian and, worse, was more than half black. Why this brought dishonor on the Cherokee nation was hard for me to understand. When I scraped my knee I could see that my blood was as red as anyone's. And the day that Aunt Elvara pricked herself with her needle, her blood looked just as red as mine.

I adored Grandma. She often talked about slave days, telling me tales of her parents and grandparents, brought in chains from Africa, sold in North Carolina and finally settling in Missouri. The songs she sang as she rocked me to sleep praised work and nature and told of the freedom that would someday come. . . . "Oh, wasn't that a wide river."

I spent most of my time wandering around the colored quarter. Unlike Aunt Elvara, who detested our neighborhood, I thought it was terribly exciting. Especially on Saturdays. Everyone seemed to own an accordion, a banjo or harmonica. Those without enough money for real instruments made banjos from cheese boxes. We played music that to us was beautiful on everything from clothesline strung across barrel halves to paper-covered combs. As soon as the music began, I would move my arms and legs in all directions in time to the rhythm or mark the beat with my friends on the treasure we pulled from the trash: tin cans, battered saucepans, abandoned wooden and metal containers. What a wonderful time we had! Sometimes lamplight in a window would indicate that a rent party was in progress. The nickels and dimes collected for the refreshments served at these gatherings helped the needy host to pay his rent. I never had a cent of my own, so could only hope to poke my head through the door long enough to catch a glimpse of an ancient piano someone had dragged in, the piano player's round-tipped yellow shoe, a flash of green sock, the sleeve of his pink shirt and the end of his cigarette, which almost touched the hat brim tilted low over one eye. A woman's voice bawled: "Do one little thing, papa, a long time," but when I skipped into the house

chanting her words Aunt Elvara slapped my face. Since when was it wrong
to sing?

Another place I loved to visit was the grocery store. Its owner was
known to be an accomplished thief. A genius. He was so thin that I
wondered where he could find the strength to steal as much as a pin. From
time to time the police would take him away while his wife shouted,
"Don't worry honey, I'll bring you some biscuits." After a brief stay in
jail, he would be back again, squatting on his heels in the rear of the store,
shooting dice with his friends.

Across the street stood a church. It had once been the home of a friend
of my family's, but after the husband had shot his wife to death the
Reverend took the house over. On Saturdays the building was used to sell
everything from old clothes to baked goods, with the proceeds going to
the desperately poor. Some people thought it was scandalous to worship
God in the home of a murdered woman, but I liked the new church better
than the old one, which had been located in a former grocery store and
had a sign above the door saying: "Those who wash their feet before
entering are God's children." I detested washing my feet. So I preferred
praying in the house of the dead lady. The Reverend was very stern with
my friends and me. "If you don't keep still, I'll smack you on the head
with my Bible," he'd say, glowering. We would slip down the aisle looking
for seats close to where the new converts made their public confessions.
The women wore their Sunday dresses and flowered hats.

"Brothers and sisters, we are all God's children! Live and let live. If you
give our Lord a nickel, he will give you back five!" the Reverend intoned.
Then the collection box was passed. We children never had a cent to offer,
but we feared to dip our fingers into the tempting pile of coins since God
was watching. Suddenly someone was singing and the crowd hummed
along; now feet began to tap and a fat woman in tears was confessing her
sins. The singing and stamping of feet grew louder. A man, shouting that
he was possessed by the devil, rose to his feet, followed by another and
another until the entire congregation was standing, rocking, swaying, eyes
closed in ecstasy. A woman fainted and was revived by a friend while the
worshippers leaped and twirled, kicking up their feet to drive away the
devil, and the Reverend tugged at skirts raised immodestly high. Dizzy
with excitement, I felt the call of the Holy Spirit and threw up my legs
with the others . . . until the Reverend thundered with God-like wrath:

"Everybody out! The service is over. God be with you."

I remember one Sunday when God was not with me. On the way home from church I let out a scream. A rusty nail had punctured my bare foot. Before long my leg grew ugly and swollen. Aunt Elvara wanted to send me back to Mama, but Grandma insisted that Mama had enough to do, with the new baby and the washing she took in. Grandma would nurse me. But the infection quickly spread and my foot soon hurt so much that I was taken to the hospital. I heard a nurse whisper, "That leg will have to go." I, who so loved dancing! "No!" I shrieked. "No! Please don't cut it off!" The doctor hesitated. He would first try to drain the wound. What oozed from my body smelled disgusting, and I could see that my blood had turned *black*. My no-good friend Billie, who had told me that my father was a buckra, had lied. My real daddy was clearly *not* white.

I was delighted when Mama came to take me home. But when I saw Richard and Margaret and baby Willie May, I couldn't believe my eyes, even though I knew that they existed. "As the oldest, it's your job to look out for them," Mama explained.

One day while I was helping Mama with a load of wash, I asked, "Is it true that my father was a buckra? Am I really different from the others?" Mama pushed aside her work and pulled me onto her lap. "Listen carefully, Tumpy. You're just like Richard and Margaret and baby Willie May even though your skin is lighter. Daddy Arthur loves you like his own. So just ignore what people say." And that evening, since it was bitter cold outside and none of us had shoes, Daddy Arthur with his usual ingenuity lined strips of coal sacking with paper and stitched them together with string to make wonderful shoes so that Richard and Margaret and I could play in the snow.

Margaret: We were very poor. Josephine has mentioned how we were forced to look for food in white men's garbage. Mama was pleased when we brought home a chicken head to put in the soup. It was so cold in winter that our school was forced to close. This delighted Josephine, who was constantly in trouble with the teacher for making faces. "Why is it wrong?" she would ask. "If God gave us faces, he meant us to use them." She was very conscious of her responsibilities as the oldest child and constantly looked for ways to earn money. With the rest of us in tow, she would ring doorbells in the white quarter and offer our services. "Would you like us to shovel your front walk, ma'am? Can we wash your steps? Do you need help waxing your kitchen floor?" Doors were often slammed in her face because of her frail appearance. But when she was told, "You're too little to work, child," she glibly lied: "I know I look young, but I'm really fifteen." When we did get hired we earned from five cents to a quarter, depending on our employer's generosity. Enough to buy an occasional doughnut each. Then we'd set off on a coal hunt. Josephine had organized the neighborhood children into a team. Armed with one of the coal sacks Daddy used to make shoes, we'd head for the railroad yard, where Josephine would jump onto a coal car, agile as a cat. "Be careful. The watchman has a gun!" While one of us stood guard, the rest would gather up the coal Josephine threw us to stuff in our sack. She would still be tossing down chunks when the train began humming and throbbing. "Be careful, Tumpy!" Josephine never jumped until the train was in motion. Our sack was full. Now we would try to sell it.

Josephine: Most of our coal was bought by Mrs. Dullie, a hard-headed woman, half of whose face had somehow been horribly burned. She wore her hair in tiny braids that bristled from her head, in order, I assumed, to lengthen her hair. But in all the time I knew her, her hair never grew an inch. Happy or sad, Mrs. Dullie smiled constantly, flashing the gold teeth that proclaimed her wealth. In spite of her riches, however, she held the neighborhood record for prison terms, having served seven or eight. No one except a policeman with a summons dared to cross her, partly because she was a big, strong woman whose shoes were tipped with intimidating "bulldog" toes and partly because she carried a gun in her pocket. Mrs. Dullie was famous for her home-cooked specialties. No one could match her sandwiches filled with hot, peppered sowbelly and sold with a beer chaser. As her supplier, however, I also knew about the putrid chicken parts she slipped into her pot. After soaking these smelly morsels in salted water laced with bicarbonate of soda to eliminate the odor, she cooked them several hours, then rolled them in dough. Mrs. Dullie's hot pies were big Sunday sellers.

I occasionally found work baby-sitting for white families. Every time it was the same. I would be taken to look at my charge, then warned: "Be sure not to kiss baby." It was hard to resist that rosy, delicate, almost transparent flesh. How I longed to have a fair-skinned baby of my own, but I knew that this was one thing that would never happen.

The day came when I thought my life had changed for good. Mama explained that a kind white lady with no children of her own wanted to take me in and raise me like a daughter. In return I would help take care of her beautiful house, so different from our single room. I hated leaving Richard, Margaret and Willie May, but I had no regrets about quitting our new lodgings. Having been evicted yet again, we were now installed in a storeroom behind the kitchen of one of Mama's friends. Daddy said, in his fatalistic way, that "each dog has its day and each cat its night," but our only window lacked glass and he was forced to seal it with newspaper. To make matters worse, we now all shared one bed. Our parents slept with their heads at the top and we children with our heads at the bottom. In comparison, my cozy bed at Mrs. Mason's house was like paradise. I liked both the Masons. My favorite was whichever kissed me most that day. Mrs. Mason sent me to a school that I preferred to my old one because the teacher told us stories about kings and queens. I could almost see them with their diamond-studded crowns and red velvet robes, descending the palace steps or strolling through glittering chambers. I thought history was wonderful.

Every evening Mrs. Mason supervised my homework. I was quite intelligent, she said. After each meal I helped her with the dishes. It didn't seem like work, though, because dishwashing was always preceded by delicious food. Actually, the first thing I remember about my stay at the Masons' was a stomachache. "Poor little thing!" Mrs. Mason exclaimed. "You can tell she isn't used to eating. My Lord, how thin she is! I'm going to fatten you up, child." The day after my arrival, Mrs. Mason took me shopping and bought me pretty dresses and shoes that fit, not like the horrible shoes Mistress had made me wear, boy's boots that pinched my feet, with metal-tipped toes to make them last longer.

Best of all, Mrs. Mason gave me time to play. I was even allowed to invite the neighbor children into her basement, where I had constructed a theater like the one Mrs. Mason had taken me to visit. I couldn't believe my eyes when I saw that stage. The actors were as beautiful as the kings and queens in my history book. I asked Mrs. Mason for some old curtain material, nails and string. Boards set on bricks became seats for the audience. I even had a costume, a fitted, tight-waisted dress of Mrs. Mason's and one of her big hats with a long feather. I felt like a star as

I grimaced, mimicked and danced to my heart's content while my friends clapped and clapped. "There'll be another show tomorrow," I'd say. The next day the audience would be back with more friends. Soon I began charging a safety pin for reserved seats and a straight pin for simple admission. "The way things are going, you'll be able to open a notions shop," Mrs. Mason said, laughing. "Unless I become an actress." And we would both smile. I grew healthy, plump and happy under Mrs. Mason's care. "You're getting very pretty, child," Mr. Mason remarked, taking me on his knee. I found that hard to believe because each time I looked in the mirror I couldn't help making a face.

One morning I asked, "Is Mr. Mason sick?" "No, Tumpy. Why do you ask?" "Because last night he came into my room and stood beside my bed." "Did he speak or touch you?" "No, ma'am, but he was breathing very hard. Could it have been a ghost?" Mrs. Mason didn't seem to like the idea of a ghost wandering through her house at night. "Promise you'll call me if it happens again," she said. "I'll come immediately." "Yes, ma'am, I will. I promise. Thank you, Mrs. Mason." The following night while I was pretending to sleep, I heard my door open. The ghost was breathing as loudly as ever. Although my eyes were tightly shut, I could hear it tiptoeing toward me. Suddenly it slipped back the blanket and slid into my bed. "It's the ghost!" I screamed. Mrs. Mason must have been hiding near the door, because she rushed into the room so quickly that the ghost knocked the lamp from her hand as it dashed by. It was Mr. Mason! I couldn't understand why Mrs. Mason scolded him so. If Mr. Mason was sick and cold and wanted to warm up in my bed, what was wrong with that? Mr. Mason wasn't at breakfast the next morning and Mrs. Mason looked sad and tired. "I'm taking you back to your mother, Tumpy," she announced. "It's not your fault, child, but you can't live here any longer." I was crushed. Was it because of the ghost? "Pack your things, Tumpy." "Can I take my new dresses?" "Of course. Take everything." I crept down to the basement for the last time. Never again would I draw back the musty velvet curtains. Never again would I wear my feathered hat. I would never again be queen. I choked back my tears. Somewhere deep inside me I vowed that somehow I would grow up to be a famous star with beautiful flowing gowns.

When Mrs. Mason kissed me goodbye on the doorstep of our miserable shack, I could feel the dampness on her cheek.

Mama was furious. "What's wrong with you, Tumpy? How could you ruin such a wonderful chance?" When I explained about the ghost, Daddy Arthur burst out laughing. "What a fool you are, child." His words surprised me since Mrs. Mason had called me intelligent and whites seldom compliment colored people. But maybe Daddy was right. I still had a lot to learn about grownups.

Once again my life centered around our one-room shack. Mrs. Mason's house had been filled with delicious smells, but the odors at home made me want to hold my nose. From time to time I visited Grandma at Aunt Elvara's house. She always cooked me a special treat, part of which I would slip into my pocket to take home to "Arthur's children," as she called them with a sniff. One day Aunt Elvara invited me to move back with her. It didn't sound as tempting as my warm little bed at Mrs. Mason's house, but anything was better than Daddy's feet in my face at night. At Aunt Elvara's I would at least have a folding bed of my own. Besides, Aunt Elvara seemed gentler now. Was it because I was bigger or because she had aged? She spoke less sharply; she didn't slap as hard; she seemed very tired.

One night Grandma shook me awake. Tears were streaming down her cheeks. "Run home and fetch your mother, child. Aunt Elvara is dying." I peeked into my aunt's bed. Her face was all twisted and she was breathing like a locomotive. Shaking with fear, I hurried through the night. Was it Aunt Elvara's expression that made me shiver or was it the inky darkness? When I reached home, Daddy told me that Mama was at his sister Emma's house, delivering her baby. Once more I set off through the darkness. "Come quick, Mama. Aunt Elvara's dying," I gasped. "I'll be along as soon as I can, Tumpy. I can't leave the baby. *My place is here right now.*" I could hear whimpering sounds in the bedroom and Mama hurried off to Aunt Emma's side. Was it more important to be born than to die? I set off for Aunt Elvara's with a heavy heart. One look at Grandma's face told me that my aunt was dead. Turning my face to the wall, I began to sob. "Don't you want to see her, Tumpy? Didn't you love your aunt?" Grandma asked. "Yes, but I'm scared." "There's more to fear from the living than from the dead, child." I thought about that contradiction for a long time: the living are to be feared, yet it is more important to live than to die.

Soon afterward, a group of men took Aunt Elvara's body away. When they brought it back a few days later, I barely recognized my aunt. I had never seen her look so young. Her black hair was neatly braided and her body in its open coffin lay under a beautiful lavender coverlet. She was smiling. Friend after friend arrived, bringing flowers. The mourners crowded around the coffin, remembering the days when Aunt Elvara had gaily kicked up her skirts as she danced. Someone began softly singing "Keeping Out of Mischief Now"; my aunt's earthly trials were over and she had nothing more to fear. Later I helped Grandma pour coffee and pass sandwiches, sure that my grief would prevent me from ever sleeping again. But in spite of the singing, which lasted for three days and nights, I collapsed on my folding bed and dreamed it was raining flowers.

As things turned out, Aunt Elvara continued to influence our lives from beyond. Her husband, killed in the Spanish-American War, had left her a government pension and life insurance, both of which she bequeathed to Grandma. When Grandma came to live with us, our luck began to change.

Margaret: In 1918, we left the poorest section of the black quarter for a sturdy cement house with a real cellar. Daddy picked up odd jobs wherever he could and Mama worked in Cousin Josephine's laundry. We children made deliveries for "Aunt Jo" after school in return for the pennies she produced from a pouch beneath her skirts. The rest of the time Tumpy put on shows in our cellar, where she had made a theater like the one at Mrs. Mason's house.

This new theater had an added refinement: candles placed in tin cans to give the effect of footlights. Wearing Grandma's cast-off dresses, Josephine would sweep regally across the stage. "Every show is alike, Tumpy," Richard and I would complain. "We're not coming tonight." Profiting from her age and height, Tumpy would furiously shove us down the cellar steps, snapping, "Get in there and take a seat. If you move, I'll slap your faces." She continued to charge a pin for admission and her friends seemed to like the show, because they kept coming back.

One night the performance ended badly. Tumpy was twirling across the stage when her skirt brushed a candle and her dress caught fire. Screaming with fear, we children rushed upstairs for help. Fortunately a neighbor had the presence of mind to wrap our star in the stage curtain, extinguishing the flames. Grandma's dress was ruined but Tumpy was unharmed. The next day she was out in the street rounding up an audience for the evening show. Dancing was in her blood. "Can't you sit still for a minute?" I'd ask. "This is the best way I know to keep warm," she'd reply.

With fifteen cents of our delivery money we would regularly buy tickets for the Sunday show at the Booker T. Washington Theater, where a vaudeville troupe called the Dixie Steppers performed before a black audience. Every show looked the same to me, but week after week Josephine sat glued to the edge of her seat as chorus girls flashed hints of bare skin, comics made faces and a fat singer in a red wig sang the blues. One day Tumpy announced, "I'm going to talk to the director. Since we're going to have to work someplace, why not in show business? Wouldn't that be fun?" "Not for me," I replied, but Josephine, with an assurance that made me shiver, marched over to the guard at the stage door and announced that she had an appointment to audition. The watchman looked her over from head to toe . . . and let her pass, while I waited trembling outside. A few minutes later, Tumpy was back, beaming and snapping her fingers. "It worked. I'm hired!" I couldn't believe my ears. Just like that? "They were in the middle of a rehearsal," Tumpy explained, "but a nice lady asked what I wanted. 'I'd like to see the director, ma'am,' I replied. She burst out laughing and shouted, 'Bob! You have a caller!' " A very tall, very black man with white hair and a kind face had asked, "What do you want, child?" "Please, mister, could you give me a job?" "But you're much too young." "I may look small, but I'm really fifteen." So Tumpy had pulled her usual trick! Maybe it worked for shoveling snow, but in the theater? . . . "He asked if I knew how to dance." "For once you could tell the truth." "No, I lied to him. I said I couldn't dance a step but I hoped he would teach me." "But you *can* dance, Tumpy!" "Not as well as the chorus line. Anyway, this way he'll have a surprise. I start rehearsing tomorrow."

The next day I followed Tumpy through the stage door, as cool as a nine-year-old could be. Tumpy showed me around as if she had lived backstage for years, pointing out the strips of painted canvas rolled out on the floor and the instruments piled into corners. "Do they know you can play the trombone, Tumpy?" "No, but they hired me anyway."

Tumpy's experience with the trombone had been short-lived. A musician couple, the Joneses, used to perform in our neighborhood restaurants as the Jones Family Band. There were actually three of them: Mr. Jones, who was very small and ugly, his tall, pretty wife and their daughter, Doll, who luckily took after her mother. The Joneses asked Mama if Tumpy could join their act. Her pay would be the free meals the band received from the restaurants in which they performed. My sister was very excited at the idea of learning to play a real instrument, but in spite of the fact that Mr. Jones taught her to play the trombone, she soon was home again, worn out and thinner than ever. The Joneses walked miles a day from job to job and Mr. Jones had made Tumpy carry the property trunk.

We stood in the wings watching the chorus line rehearse. I knew how high Tumpy could kick, but these dancers moved in such perfect lines! "Look at their faces," Tumpy said with a sniff. "Not a single smile. Wait until I get my turn." But it wasn't to be that day. "Come back tomorrow," said Mr. Bob Russell. Was he trying to discourage her? If so, he didn't know my sister. The next day we were there in the wings again. "All right, child, get out there with the others," Mr. Russell ordered. The piano player struck a few notes and Tumpy began to dance, but not at all like the rest. Her body moved as though it were on fire. Mr. Russell clapped his hands to stop the music and I thought that Tumpy was finished for good. Some of the chorus girls were sneering and laughing and pointing at Josephine. But Mr. Russell put a quick stop to that. "I have just the part for you," he said. "You'll be our Cupid. Report for rehearsal tomorrow."

We decided not to breathe a word to our parents. If Mama found out that Tumpy was appearing on the stage with half-naked chorus girls, my sister would get a good whipping. Instead we said we were playing in a friend's basement since the fire had scared us away from our own. Our parents were used to our roaming the neighborhood.

On Josephine's opening night, I sat in the audience, heart in mouth. The curtain rose to reveal two lovers standing on a little balcony. Suddenly Tumpy flitted across the stage, a smiling angel in baggy pink tights, complete with two little wings, a quiver and arrows. I thought she looked beautiful and admired the courage with which she hung suspended from the ceiling, the symbol of romantic love. The audience gasped with delight, but their pleasure quickly changed to concern. Just as the piano player burst into a series of tremolos, one of Cupid's wings hooked onto the backdrop, leaving Tumpy wriggling in space. A stagehand, hoping to help, tried to adjust the scenery but only succeeded in getting Cupid stuck for good. "Raise the backdrop," the director shouted, but to no avail. Love's Messenger continued to wave her legs in the air while the couple on the balcony proclaimed everlasting love.

To my surprise, the audience roared with laughter, slapping their thighs and flashing their teeth, while the wronged husband, right on cue, rushed onto the stage to separate his wife from her lover. . . . It seemed like hours before the curtain finally descended.

I huddled in my seat, mortified. Mr. Russell stood glaring in the wings, Tumpy told me later, but his expression quickly changed when someone rushed backstage to announce that the scene had been a triumph. The audience had never laughed so hard and many of the spectators wanted seats for the next performance. Tumpy, her eyes filled with tears, didn't dare face Mr. Russell. "Don't worry, child," he said gently. "There's another show tomorrow and from now on you'll get stuck *on purpose.*" The theater was full for days.

Josephine was delighted with her success, but as time went on her mood changed. The show would soon be leaving town. One Saturday we set off as usual to buy the family's Sunday fish. I could tell there was something wrong. Finally Tumpy blurted out, "Margaret, before I say another word I want you to cross your heart. Good. Now swear that you won't tell Mama —I'm leaving town tomorrow with the show." "No, Tumpy. You can't." Wrapping her arms around me, Josephine tried to explain. She could never become a famous star if she stayed in St. Louis. And being famous meant earning lots of money, never being poor again, helping the family. It also meant showing whites what blacks could do and proving that we're all God's children. Wasn't that true? Surely I understood. I had to agree, but the thought of Tumpy's absence was hard to bear. . . . Nevertheless, I had crossed my heart. My sister hugged me until I was breathless. When had she become so strong? Then she disappeared into the dusk.

I returned home alone, clutching the fish. Nobody noticed Josephine's absence at first, but when night came, Mama asked, "Where's Tumpy?" "She stopped by Mrs. Dayan's house," I replied. Mrs. Dayan was a family friend who lived some distance away. "Since it's so late, she'll probably stay the night," Grandma said. The next day, however, when Tumpy had still not returned, there was talk of calling the police. From the way I hung my head, Mama knew I was hiding something. I finally burst into tears and confessed. To my surprise, Mama calmed Grandma and quietly said, "She has chosen her path. Let her be." "Perhaps it's God's will," Grandma added.

I thought often of my sister, with a mixture of pain and envy. It was true. She had made her choice: chosen to turn her back on Tumpy and all the rest of her childhood to become Josephine. With nothing for baggage but the dress on her back and one pair of shoes, she had set out to conquer the world. She was thirteen years old.

CHAPTER 2

On the Road

WE LEFT BY THE NIGHT TRAIN. I had never seen curtains as pretty as those in the Pullman car windows. From my seat at Mrs. Russell's side, her cigar smoke pricking my nose, I peered nervously out the window, looking for Mama's angry face, Grandma's reproachful eyes or the stern gaze of Daddy or Aunt Jo. No, Daddy Arthur would already be in bed, so full of beer that nothing could wake him. I was safely on my way. Closing my eyes, I dreamed of sunlit cities, magnificent theaters and me in the limelight.

"At least we can't complain about her baggage," one of the dancers remarked to Mrs. Russell. "She doesn't look too bright, though, and I can't see those beanpole legs on the stage." "Maybe not," Mr. Bob retorted, "but watching her dance makes me laugh. When *you* miss a step all I want to do is cry." So much for her! Mr. Bob turned to me. "You'll be earning nine dollars a week, child. Mrs. Russell will help you to buy a new dress." Mrs. Russell groaned through a cloud of cigar smoke. I doubt she approved of my presence, but when Mr. Russell had said, "Let's take her with us," no one had dared to object. Actually, even Mr. Bob had insisted at first that the road was no place for a child. It took many tears to prove how unhappy I was, how much I needed the money, how badly I wanted to be an actress, how willing I was to do *anything* to get out of St. Louis: be a dresser, wash costumes, sew. . . . The leading lady, overhearing our conversation, jumped at the idea of someone to help her change costumes. "All right, you'll be a dresser," Mr. Bob announced.

Mrs. Russell opened the food hamper and passed out sandwiches. There was one for me and I felt like part of the family. As we ate, the cast chattered gaily and although I missed most of what they said, I enjoyed seeing the way the women laughed and joked with the men, casually smoking cigarettes and crossing their legs. So this was the artist's life! Dizzy with delight and exhaustion, I fell asleep in Mrs. Russell's lap.

Morning. We had arrived! People rushed in all directions, gathering up their belongings. We were in a tiny station in a tiny, dusty town. Mr. Russell seemed to know his way around and led us straight to a boarding-house. Just time enough to freshen up and we were off to rehearsal! The theater, like the town, was small and coated with yellow dust. Three tall candles served as stage lights; a jumble of chairs and benches were being pushed noisily into rows for seats; the hall was heated by sickly charcoal fires. A rickety untuned piano completed the dismal scene.

I couldn't believe my eyes. "Get a move on, child. There's a lot of unpacking to do." "This isn't much of a place, is it?" "It's not New York, but you can't always choose." Once the performers in their colorful costumes stepped onto the stage, however, everything seemed right again in spite of the fact that I was only a humble dresser. My role as Cupid had been eliminated because there was no place from which to suspend me, and I could no longer dance with the chorus because the stage was too small. Still, with two matinees and two evening shows to stage, I never stopped running. "Josephine, fasten my dress." "Josephine, quick. My necklace." "Josephine. Hand me my tights."

Our first performance was marked by a special effect that delighted the audience: rain began pouring through the ceiling, plastering the chorus girls' costumes to their skins. The crowd went wild, shouting obscene remarks and happily tossing peanut shells at the dancers, who haughtily continued their routine.

After the final show it was back on the road again. When the last curtain fell, pandemonium broke loose. Each performer was responsible for folding his costumes and wrapping his makeup box in heavy paper. He then passed his possessions on to a packer, who transferred them to a stagehand to store in enormous boxes and trunks. Finally we all lined up before Mr. Russell's loge to collect our pay. For the first time I heard the words "I owe you . . . nine dollars." "Yessir." "Here, Josephine—one, two, three, four, five. The rest I'm keeping to cover the cost of your clothes." "Yessir." I was ecstatic. I was going to be dressed like an actress!

Once again the station, the platform, a new train to catch, the sandwich basket; once again laughter and joking, but not as loud as before; it had been a long, hard day. One by one the cast dozed off, their bodies rocking with the motion of the train.

The next day a different town, another theater, the same amount of dust, and still no pulley for Cupid. So the love scene was performed without him. Just as the wronged husband surprised the lovers on their balcony, a huge black man, for whom the situation apparently had unhappy associations, stood up in the audience, pulled a razor from his pocket and shouted, "Get your hands off that woman, trash." Several male dancers leaped from the stage to lend a restraining hand, while Mr. Russell shouted, "None of it's real, folks. It's only a play," and members of the audience called, "Come on, let's see the show." Finally convinced that it really was make-believe, the man returned his knife to his pocket, pulled out a wad of chewing tobacco and settled back to enjoy the rest of the performance.

Another town brought a new kind of trouble, this time involving wages. The theater had been packed, yet the take had been meager. There would be two dollars less all around. Amid loud complaints from the cast, Mr. Russell and the cashier tried to explain. The theater had been full of gate-crashers as well as drafts. By simply prying apart a few boards, freeloaders had come pouring in. Mr. Russell signed IOUs all around. "Put that piece of paper in a safe place," one of the dancers whispered, folding hers neatly and sliding it into a purse pinned to her coat lining. The purse was bulging with similar receipts. This had obviously happened before. But Mr. Russell assured us that business would improve when we got to New Orleans.

In the meantime we continued to travel from one cramped theater to another, places too small to let Cupid fly or permit Josephine to dance with the chorus. Was this why the girls treated me more kindly?

My two favorites in the troupe were our leading lady and the piano player. The latter had endless tales to tell and was expert in several musical

styles. He was a master at playing boogie, with its trainlike rhythm so dear
to those who frequently travel the rails. He also knew songs of the old
South and every time the cast celebrated a full house, a birthday, or a
relative discovered on the road, I had my chance to dance and sing. Mr.
Russell, watching me fling myself about, promised to have me back on the
stage as soon as possible.

Clara Smith, our leading lady, was very black, fat and short. The red
wig that was one of her trademarks was gaily decorated with a bow or
paper flowers. Her face was layered with purple powder, her teeth were
yellow from pipe tobacco. She favored short, gauzy dresses worn over pink
tights and was partial to high-heeled shoes. "Did you know that Sophie
Tucker learned her stuff from me, child?" she asked. Everyone had something to say about that Tucker lady, including how she sang in blackface
to hide her ugliness. I found it hard to believe that a white star would
pretend to be black when most black people seemed so unhappy. The
piano player told me how at the end of each performance Miss Tucker
pulled off her wig to show her blond hair. He added that one day when
her trunk had not arrived, she had been forced to come on stage as she
was and had *still* had a huge success. I carefully studied my own face in
the mirror: an egg-shaped blob on a grasshopper's body. Was there any
hope for me at all? Would appearing in whiteface help? "She doesn't
perform in blackface anymore," Clara Smith said, "but she still copies my
singing style." And for good reason. Our star had a magnificent voice that
sent shivers down your spine. But her sweet tooth was her undoing and
it was my job to nurse her through the frequent illnesses brought on by
her gluttony. In return she gave me an alphabet book to study so that I
could learn to form my letters and write correctly. She also lent me
magazines and I was soon able to recognize the faces of all the best-known
performers of the day. How proud I was the time I came across a picture
of Mrs. Clara Smith! It was true, then. She really was a famous figure
among the Negro public. If only she could have said no to sweet potato
pie! "Come on and join me, child. Help yourself," she'd insist. Thanks
to her example, by the time we got to New Orleans my body was less
painfully thin, though my face was as egg-shaped as ever.

New Orleans . . . the Crescent City. Surely I was dreaming. The piano
player had told me that it was a musicians' paradise and he was right; there
was music everywhere. I had never seen so many people, bars and dance

halls. No sooner had we deposited our baggage than we were heading up Canal Street for Congo Square. "This is nothing," the piano player insisted. "You can't imagine how it used to be. One parade after another; bands competing in the streets to prove they were the best. But Storyville's been closed down since the war. It's simply not the same." The war. From everything I'd heard, I hated it without quite knowing why. The broken men with their missing arms and legs and eyes terrified me. Still, I pitied them and hatred for those who had harmed them stirred within me. "Try not to think about it, child," cautioned Mama Smith, and she took me to a restaurant that served delicious portions of crab, rice, corn, tomatoes and a little green vegetable called okra. New Orleans was everything I'd dreamed of and I hoped we would be staying for a while.

The theater we performed in was immense, with a huge orchestra pit and plenty of space for Cupid. But my heart sank when Mr. Russell told me my scene had been cut. Worse, the scene that would replace it had no child's role. Had Mr. Bob lost his faith in me? Perhaps he had noticed that I was growing taller every day without getting any prettier.

I couldn't believe my eyes when the Joneses turned up—complete with trombone and property trunk—among the extras hired for our New Orleans stay. After we had fallen into each other's arms, Mrs. Jones suggested that I move in with them and split the costs. It seemed like a good idea and once more I found myself in a "single room for four." For a brief time we even became four and a quarter, for Doll unexpectedly gave birth to a baby so tiny—it barely weighed a pound—that it died almost at once, to the Joneses' apparent relief. I didn't really like Doll, but group living was cheaper for all concerned. We even had our own bathroom, which seemed to me the height of luxury. Then, just as suddenly, we were reduced to three when Doll left us to live with a vicious little man—a dwarf, in fact—who gave her the beatings she seemed to crave.

Our New Orleans engagement came to an end all too soon. As we were packing up, Mr. Russell broke the terrible news. He no longer needed me. I couldn't believe my ears. He had seemed to like me well enough. "Why don't you stay on with the Joneses?" he suggested. "Since they know your family, I'm sure they'll look after you." This time my pleading fell on deaf ears. In fact, before pushing me out of his loge, Mr. Russell announced that he didn't think I was stage material. I was completely crushed. I didn't want to join up with the Joneses; I wanted to remain with the troupe, which would surely get to Broadway someday.

In the bustle of getting the show on the road, I was completely ignored. Noticing that one of the big shipping crates was unlocked, I cautiously inched back the lid, packed down some dresses and slipped inside. No sooner had I lowered the lid than I heard someone cry, "Hurry up. Here's another one. Let's get it locked and loaded." "You'll have to give me a hand. This one's heavy." "What's in it?" "Costumes." I was picked up, dropped, hoisted into the air again . . . until I finally fell asleep, overcome with fatigue and emotion.

I awoke to the rocking of the train. A moving railroad car erases the past and the Joneses quickly faded away with the rest. Pressing my nose against the side of the crate, I gulped for air. It was lucky our next engagement was only twenty-five miles away. Finally the train stopped and I heard baggage men cursing. Again I was roughly picked up and brutally dropped, by now half unconscious. Then total silence. For the first time I was afraid. Suppose the baggage was left unopened until tomorrow night? Was there a show scheduled for that evening? I couldn't remember and my head began to swim with panic. Smothering and shivering at the same time, I shouted through chattering teeth, "Help! Somebody help me." The louder I called, the weaker and more terrified I became. By now I was sure I would die. At last I heard what sounded like footsteps. "Help!" I screamed and heard a scream in reply, the frightened cry of a woman shouting that there was a ghost in the theater. Footsteps again but all I could do was whimper. "It's a ghost for sure," the woman's voice insisted. "That's ridiculous," a man's voice replied. "Where did the sounds come from?" The footsteps retreated and I promised the good Lord that I would never again hide in a packing case. His will be done. Amen. As I began whimpering again, the footsteps grew nearer. "This way!" A key turned, the crate's lid swung back, and there I was, bruised and tearful, blinking up at the night watchman and his wife. "Poor child. She's frozen. We've got to warm her up."

Before I knew it, I was in the watchman's bed, a hot-water bottle at my feet and a cup of warm broth in my hand, not knowing whether to laugh or to cry. At the sound of Mr. Russell's voice in the next room— he had been summoned from the tiny town's one hotel—I ducked under the covers. "Absolutely not," he growled. "She's useless. Too small for a dresser and not tall enough for the chorus." To my amazement, Mrs.

Russell came to my defense. "But, Bob, she's growing by the minute."
"Well, one thing that *isn't* going to change," Mr. Bob said firmly, "is that
light skin of hers. She'd stick out in the chorus line like a sore thumb!"
As they continued to argue, I shrank further and further under the
bedclothes. My color . . . I hadn't really thought about it since the days
when Billie had called me a buckra's daughter. So that was it! To the
whites I looked chocolate, to the blacks like a "pinky"; there was no place
I belonged. As I lay there sobbing, the sheets were flung back and I found
myself face to face with Mr. Bob. "What a nuisance you are," he growled.
"What do you want, anyway?" "To stay with the show, Mr. Bob." "I
never saw such a stubborn child." "Look, Bob, you can't send her back
to New Orleans," Mrs. Russell intervened. "All right, all right." I jumped
up in bed at his words. "She can stay—until we get back to St. Louis."
The very place I had wanted to leave forever! Mrs. Russell patted my
cheek. Where would I spend the night? she wondered. There wasn't an
empty room in town. The watchman kindly agreed to let me remain in
his family bed until morning.

Mama Smith was pleased to see me the next day, and I thought I
understood what was bothering Mr. Russell. He felt that his leading lady
was monopolizing my time. He wasn't paying me to spend hours in Mama
Smith's dressing room improving my penmanship and learning to read.
I could study at night after the show if I wasn't too tired. At the theater,
I was supposed to pitch in like the others, performers and stagehands alike,
shifting scenery, repairing properties and sewing costumes. I was determined to prove my worth so that Mr. Russell would change his mind
about leaving me off in St. Louis. He seemed as hard a nut to crack as
he had accused me of being. First it had been Tumpy, then Pinky, now
I was teasingly called "hard nut." Would Josephine never be born? While
I waited, I almost died.

As we traveled from city to city, from one fleabag hotel to another, I
was constantly cold and would turn up my gas heater full blast. One
morning they found me on the floor, unconscious. Since I had sealed the
door and window for extra warmth, word quickly spread that I had tried
to kill myself. They all had their own explanation for my desperate act:
I missed my family, I needed more affection, I was overworked. (It was
true that in accordance with my new resolve I never sat still: I sewed,
brushed costumes, polished shoes, ironed, dressed hair, hooked and un-

hooked clothes, fastened, buttoned, unbuttoned, laced, unlaced, hung up, laid out, packed, unpacked.) Quickly realizing that my status as a suicide had earned me the attention and pity of the cast, I made no attempt to set things right. Even the chorus line fussed over me now. Almost losing me had made them love me. I would never forget that lesson. I was no longer Tumpy or Pinky, but Birdy, the troupe's mascot. My efforts were now rewarded with smiles.

One day a dancer took a nasty fall, causing her knee to swell to the size of her head. Quick as a flash I pleaded, "Mr. Bob, let me fill in for her." As it was almost show time, he had little choice. Mrs. Russell quickly sewed me into a spangled costume and I darkened my skin with makeup to avoid standing out on the stage. Since I had never danced with the chorus before, the girls were convinced I would have a bad case of stage fright. Strangely enough, just the opposite was true. It was as though I had swallowed a shot of gin. The whistles, the shouts, the bravos, the laughter, the hundreds of staring eyes, were wonderfully exciting. I returned to the wings, to find Mr. Russell weeping with laughter. "You're a real clown, Birdy. A born comic." I peered at my face in a cracked mirror. My makeup was streaked with sweat and it was easy to see why the crowd had pointed at me, howling with laughter. Well, what was the matter with that? Was it wrong to make people laugh? Not according to Mr. Bob. "I want you to do exactly what you did tonight at every performance," he ordered. We'd see about that! I had heard the same thing after my one and only appearance as Cupid. This time, however, his words turned out to be true. I became the show's "funny girl."

Despite my success, a cloud dimmed my happiness. If only I could dance like the others . . . "Never mind, child," Mama Smith consoled me. "Someday those girls will be copying you." I was also plagued by the fear that when we returned to St. Louis my theater days would be over for good. "When do we play St. Louis?" I asked repeatedly. "It depends on how things go," Mama Smith would reply with a shrug. "We were due there last month, but something better turned up, so we took off in the other direction."

As the days turned into weeks, my self-confidence grew. True, I was still maid of all work backstage, but I was funny girl to the crowd. After the injured dancer's knee had healed, Mr. Russell decided to keep me at the tail end of the chorus line to make people laugh. As quick as a monkey

I had learned that when I rolled my eyes and made the very faces that had earned me a scolding at school, the crowd would burst out laughing. The schoolroom and life were apparently as different as the stage and the audience.

I was now earning ten dollars a week, and since Mr. Russell tried his best to avoid IOUs, after paying my room and board I had something left over to spend on myself. I still looked like a string bean, but I tried to round myself out with skirts and blouses worn with high heels to make me look older. It was important that my success be clearly visible when I got to St. Louis.

Were my worries over? Not really. When we arrived in Philadelphia, Mr. Russell announced that the show would soon be disbanding. The Dixie Steppers were through; it was every man for himself. The cast was plunged into gloom. Except for me. I wasn't afraid of adventure. After all, I was young and strong and full of self-confidence. Rumor had it that a new show called *Shuffle Along*, with an astonishing word-of-mouth reputation, was on its way to Philadelphia. We had heard that the tryout performances were so successful, the show was already booked for New York. And they needed more dancers! A Negro company on Broadway? That was something new.

I met two of the cast members, the Caldwells, at a bar in the theater district. He was a dancer and she was a chorus girl. We liked each other at first sight and they told me more about the amazing show created by Sissle and Blake and Miller and Lyles. I looked at them blankly. The names meant nothing to me. Sissle and Blake were a famous theatrical team, Wilsie Caldwell explained. Eubie Blake, whose father had been a Civil War veteran and an ex-slave, played the piano and composed the scores; Noble Sissle, a minister's son, wrote the lyrics. Together they sang like nobody else on earth. Hadn't I ever heard "I'm Simply Full of Jazz"? she asked. Of course. Well, a few months ago in Philadelphia, Sissle and Blake met Miller and Lyles, two comedians who had built up a comedy act based on Southern humor. The four men decided to create a show that would rival the major white productions. Audiences were getting tired of the conventional, European-style operettas. "They're just full of ideas!" Wilsie exclaimed. "For example, all the chorus girls will be mulattoes." Wilsie was a "pinky" like me. "Do you think you could get me an audition?" I asked her.

Soon afterward I found myself face to face with Mr. Sissle, a thin man with a small mustache and a full head of hair. Mr. Blake, plump and bald-headed, sat at the piano, his nose buried in his music. He never once opened his mouth. Nor did Mr. Sissle waste words. "Too young," he snapped. I began my usual routine. "But I'm seventeen. . . ." "Sorry. Too small, too thin, too dark." By the time I rejoined Wilsie at the stage door I was boiling with rage. "Too *dark?* Mr. Russell says I'm too *light!*" Wilsie tried to explain. Mr. Sissle wanted his chorus to look like the Tillers, a highly successful white company, so he was hiring only the lightest-skinned dancers. "He's ashamed of his kind," I sniffed. "Not at all, Josephine. It's just the opposite. He's hoping to beat the whites at their own game. Since they prefer blackface shows to real black performers, he's decided to give them white black folks. *Shuffle Along* isn't variety or burlesque. It's a real musical comedy with a plot."

"That's all well and good, but it's no help to me. I think he's horrible." "Josephine, he's really very nice. You can't imagine what he's been through." And Wilsie explained that since the show was all black, no one had wanted to book it. It wasn't until they auditioned their main numbers in front of old John Cort, the famous owner of a chain of theaters, that Sissle and Blake had finally got their chance. Cort couldn't resist the score, but unfortunately he had been wiped out by the recession—1921 wouldn't be soon forgotten—and all he had left was a theater on Sixty-third Street, as run down as he was broke. The company was in the process of rebuilding the stage, but there was no assurance that rain wouldn't fall through the roof. Mr. Cort had given the cast costumes left over from two recent flops and because some of the clothes were Oriental, Sissle and Blake had written an Oriental blues number. The same applied to "Bandanna Blues," some of the leftover costumes being made of cotton. The composers had created *that* number by telephone, Sissle from Boston and Blake from New York. "It's the most wonderful show you can imagine," Wilsie concluded excitedly. "Why don't you apply for a job as a dresser?" "I've *been* a dresser," I replied coldly.

A few days later at the Standard Theater, Mr. Russell's company broke up for good. Goodbye, Mama Smith. When asked about my plans, I pretended I was going to New York. New York . . . the words rang in my head. The Caldwells and *Shuffle Along* were there now, and before leaving, Wilsie had said, "Remember, it's only ninety miles from Philadelphia." Still, it took all my courage to spend my remaining dollars on a ticket north. Was it coal dust or tears that were stinging my eyes?

New York was dazzling, overwhelming. I somehow made my way to Mr. Cort's theater on Sixty-third Street. Everything Wilsie had said was true. The theater itself was very shabby, but there was a long line at the box office. *Shuffle Along* was clearly a hit. "Don't miss it!" "Dynamite!" raved the critics. When the Caldwells found me waiting at the stage door, they were appalled at my appearance. I had been sleeping on park benches for two nights and my cheeks were so sunken, I thought they would force out my teeth. Wilsie insisted that I move into their little rented apartment. The way things were going, *Shuffle Along* would be running for two years. "Is Mr. Sissle any nicer?" I asked nastily. "He's thrilled to death, Josephine. The show is so successful that they're forming a touring company. Cities all over the country are asking for bookings. Why don't you talk to him again?"

This time I was auditioned by the show's manager, Al Mayer. I had taken the precaution of covering myself with Wilsie's lightest powder. Mr. Mayer studied me carefully. Then, without mentioning color, he simply said, "Too young, too skinny." "What about hiring her as a dresser?" Wilsie asked. Mr. Mayer hurriedly agreed, then turned his attention elsewhere; he had a thousand things on his mind. "At least it'll keep you going for a while," Wilsie whispered. "The thing to do is to learn all the songs and dance steps. Someone is sure to get sick."

It was back on the road again. Brush, fasten, unfasten, button, unbutton. The dancers looked discouragingly healthy and it was all I could do to keep myself from wishing for a magic potion that would strike one of them down. Every night I prayed: "Lord, I'm not asking for anything dramatic, but please do *something.*"

My wish was finally granted. Shortly before show time one evening, a member of the chorus fell ill. Through her tears, she confessed that she was expecting a baby. The manager was furious. "Couldn't you have told me in New York?" he shouted. Thank you, Lord and Baby Jesus, I whispered; she would be out of the show for at least four months, beginning tonight. "If it's any help, I know all the songs and dances," I murmured. The manager couldn't believe his ears. There was no talk of "too dark," "too young," "too skinny" now. They had me dressed and ready and out on the stage before I knew it. Once again, when I saw those watching faces a giddiness swept over me and I let the music carry me away. The audience whistled and clapped, apparently loving the song our star, Eva Spencer, was crooning. But once we were back in the wings, Eva burst into tears. "Did you *see* her?" she sobbed, pointing at me accusingly. "She stole the show with her stupid faces. Get rid of her. It's her or me." "O.K., O.K.," said the manager soothingly. "I'll have them send a replacement from New York. Just calm down, Eva."

I was heartbroken. Once again I had had my chance and ruined it. None of the other dancers would speak to me, and since there wasn't an empty bed in town, I was forced to wrap myself in an old dressing gown and curl up in a loge for the night, alone and miserable. I was awakened by the manager's voice in my ear. "On your feet, girl." Cautiously I opened one eye. This was it; he was sending me back to New York. To my surprise, he was waving a newspaper under my nose, but I was too dazed to make out the words. "Listen to what the critics say," he shouted. " 'A revelation' . . . 'Unique sense of rhythm' . . . 'a born comic.' " "But how do you know they mean me?" I gasped. Underlining the words with his finger, the manager read: " 'It's impossible to take your eyes off the *little cross-eyed girl.*' " He looked at me slyly. "Who else could it be?"

Those first reviews were followed by a flood of others like them in the various cities we toured. At the box office, people began asking, "Is this the show with the little cross-eyed girl?" I had become the star of the chorus, much to the disgust of my fellow dancers. "Monkey" they called me, and did what they could to make my life backstage miserable. I finally took to dressing in the bathroom. At least no one bothered me there! One of the dancers even tripped me up one night as we were making our entrance, but I managed to do such a comical nose dive that I received more applause than ever. They didn't try *that* again!

Back on Broadway, news of the little dancer who was triumphing on the road reached the ears of Sissle and Blake. They had just celebrated their 504th performance—an amazing feat—and were ready to take the Broadway cast on a national tour. One day the manager summoned me into his loge. "Josephine, the big bosses want you to join the show in Boston."

Wilsie was waiting for me at the station. I threw myself into her arms. "Has Mr. Sissle seen the reviews?" I asked excitedly. "Every one of them," Wilsie replied with a smile. "Who would have thought you'd upstage us all?" I could barely contain my joy, but when we arrived at the theater and I found myself face to face with my employers, I was speechless. Mr. Sissle broke the ice. "Miss Baker, do you know why I didn't hire you last year in Philadelphia?" "Too small, too thin, too dark," I mumbled. "No. Too *young*. It's against the law to employ anyone under sixteen in New York." I smiled. This was July 1922, so I had just slipped in under the wire. I felt like Sleeping Beauty when she woke up a hundred years old, yet as young as ever.

We were booked in Boston for two weeks, but our engagement was so successful that we stayed for fifteen. Still, my heart sank the first day when I saw nothing but black faces at the box office. I remembered how my employers had hoped to attract a white audience. As it turned out, however, the line was composed of servants who were buying tickets for their bosses. As far as my *own* bosses were concerned, my exposure to Sissle and Blake helped teach me the technique of using entertainment as a way to open white eyes to the black world.

From Boston we headed west: Milwaukee, Des Moines, Peoria, Indianapolis and—at last—St. Louis.

My homecoming was everything I'd dreamed of. I was now earning thirty dollars—as much as the Caldwells. We arrived on a snowy December day and headed straight for the theater—not the Booker T. Washington, for blacks only, but a handsome building in the main part of town.

"Where are you planning to stay?" Wilsie asked. "At home, of course. I can't wait to see my family." "Just be sure you're not late for the show." The other dancers looked at me curiously. "Where exactly *is* your house?" I didn't reply, and to throw them off the track circled the theater several times before hailing a taxi. "Bernard Street, please." The driver looked at me with amazement. "A well-dressed young lady like you wants to go to that part of town?" The words "well-dressed" delighted me, because I was wearing my very best clothes—a cloche hat and a blouse that tied at the throat. I could feel my fur coat collar caressing my neck. Still, the driver was right. It *was* a bad neighborhood. I told him to leave me off at the corner.

It was easy to see that things had deteriorated during my absence. The family was now crowded into a basement room, having relinquished the ground floor to other tenants. Daddy Arthur was lying in bed—this had apparently become his chief occupation—and Grandma was sitting on her mattress in the corner. The only trace of happier days was a large portrait of Aunt Elvara hanging opposite the air shaft. The curtains were black with soot, heat blasted from a rickety stove, but most of the room was freezing.

Margaret, Richard and Willie May greeted me joyously. They couldn't get over my clothes and took turns running their fingers over the fabric and playing with my necklace. "You look beautiful," they gasped. "Anyone can see that you're a star." I made no attempt to disillusion them. It was just like old times and they happily made space for me in the corner where the three of them slept. I had grown used to electricity and a bathroom, and here I was with a kerosene lamp, a bucket and dipper, and a communal washtub. There were dirty dishes under the bed. . . . I was ashamed of my own mother.

Christmas would soon be here and I bought what I could to make it a festive one. But when I got home from our Christmas Eve performance Mama was waiting up, stern as a judge. "I was at the theater tonight," she said grimly. My heart sank. Had she been disappointed to discover that I wasn't a star but was merely a funny girl in the chorus? Before I could ask how she had liked the show, she had slapped me so hard that I thought my neck would snap. "My own flesh and blood up there with naked women!" I was stunned. "But, Mama, they're not naked! All you can see is their legs." "And everything else," she sobbed, sinking into a chair. How could she be so unfair? I was ready to walk out of the house for good.

But Grandma saved the day. "Be fair, Carrie. If Tumpy was doing wrong, Elvara would have told me. She paid me her usual visit last night. In fact, she came *twice*. Once to tell me that she's still watching over us and again to say how happy she is that Tumpy is home." I had noticed that every night at a certain hour my aunt's portrait would begin to glow and her face seemed to soften. Each time this happened, Grandma would put down her knitting and thank the Lord for keeping her sister near. I had also observed that Elvara's visitations coincided with the nightly return by lantern light of our neighbor across the court. What's more, when he was ready for bed and snuffed out his lamp, Aunt Elvara would abruptly leave us. I would never have dreamed of sharing my suspicions with Grandma, however. She counted so much on those visits. Throwing her arms about me, she whispered, "Don't run off mad, Tumpy. It's

Christmas." She was right. This was a time of forgiveness. I had all sorts of treats prepared for the little ones. It would be our first true Christmas.

The next day the entire family gathered, including Aunt Jo, in a flowered dress, and cousins I had never seen before. I had helped Margaret and Mama—who never breathed another word about the show—to scrub the house. And after my final performance we had a real celebration. I had bought some whiskey and we all joined Grandma in an old-fashioned reel.

From the moment I arrived home, I was anxious to explore our old neighborhood. It had changed amazingly in two years. Roads were being built everywhere; Aunt Elvara's house was now a pile of rubble; Billie had disappeared and her mother, wrapped in rags, lived alone in squalor. One day I set out to find my friend Mary, a gentle, delicate girl who had been a faithful spectator at my basement performances. She now lived in a strange-looking house with her mother, whose hair had somehow turned red. Several men were lounging about, smoking and chatting with a group of girls as scantily dressed as some of our dancers. Mary led me into an upstairs hallway, where we could make ourselves heard over the music and laughter. "Your mother lets you live in a place like this, Mary?" She gave a strange laugh. "*Lets* me? She brings me home men." Her eyes were like bottomless wells and I could smell whiskey on her breath. Willie May's face suddenly floated before my eyes. She was gentle and delicate too. . . . In a way I was happy that Mama had slapped me. I never saw Mary again.

Margaret: When Tumpy announced that she would be moving on with the show, we were crushed. Especially Willie May, who clutched at her big sister's skirts, begging to go along. For a moment I thought Josephine might give in—which would have meant swearing me to secrecy again, since Mama would never have approved.

I could tell that Tumpy was worried about Willie May's future. "If only she wasn't so young I'd take her. But at her age the director would never allow it. Promise me you'll look after her, Margaret." I gave her my word. "Work hard, Willie May," she insisted. "Learn to write as fast as you can so you can tell me what you're doing." Josephine promised Mama she would send home fifty dollars a month to cover Willie May's clothes and education. "You'll see how wonderful school is; you'll learn about kings and queens. And if you're a good girl, I'll be back to see you next Christmas."

The following month fifty dollars arrived in the mail; it continued to come regularly for two years. Then in 1924 the postman brought us a hundred dollars all in one bundle. I still remember Daddy and Mama sitting up half the night as they counted out bills. "That makes ninety." "No, Arthur, a hundred." "Let's count it again." "Now I get a hundred and three." "One more time . . ." Soon afterward the sum became two hundred dollars monthly. We were rich! But Josephine's instructions remained unchanged. "Fifty dollars a month is for Willie May's schooling." Although I continued working at the laundry daytimes, I too went to school—at night. We had everything we needed. Daddy regained his will to live and Mama even managed to set something aside. In 1929 Josephine sent us enough to buy a comfortable house. But in spite of her generosity, she had broken part of her promise. She didn't come back the next Christmas, or the next, or the next. . . . In fact, it was fourteen years before we saw her again. By then, despite the finest care, little Willie May was dead.

Josephine: Toledo, Grand Rapids, Detroit, Buffalo, Rochester, Philadelphia, Atlantic City . . . Wherever we went we brought down the house, playing to mixed audiences in neighborhoods where blacks had never before performed. Sissle and Blake were tireless. Although we were giving ten performances of *Shuffle Along* weekly, they had found the time to put together a new show, *In Bamville.* Not only was I in it; they had written a special part for me.

March 10, 1924. My first opening night and the first tryout performance of *In Bamville,* at Rochester's Lyceum Theater. I had become a veteran of all-night rehearsals, endless cups of coffee, anxiety, doubt, cries of "It simply doesn't work. Take it out," and "I like it. Let's try it again." Scenes had been taken apart and reconstructed. There were moments of self-hatred brought on by exhaustion and spells of self-love. The stage is a fragile ship which must be ready to weather rough sailing. But this time we hoped for sunshine. After all, *Shuffle Along* had brought so many of us happiness: Freddie Washington, the exotic dancer; Elida Webb, now a choreographer; Katerina Yarboro, headed toward an operatic career; Florence Mills, triumphing at the Plantation; Paul Robeson, fresh out of college and a last-minute replacement when one of the show's Harmony Kings had been called to his mother's bedside; and above all, me. At $125 a week, I was the best-paid girl in the chorus. All because I could cross my eyes!

We were in Pittsburgh when we received the terrible news that our manager, Al Mayer, was dead at forty-five. Sissle and Blake took the night train to New York to pay Al their last respects and the rest of us shared their grief. It was common knowledge that without Al, *Shuffle Along* would never have seen the stage. Somehow he had managed to find the necessary funds. What had happened in Burlington was typical. As Al paced worriedly up and down the train platform, a fellow passenger had approached him. "Did you see that black company last night?" "Yeah." "Aren't they terrific?" "Thanks. I'm managing the show." "No kidding. Congratulations. What a gold mine." "Could be, but I don't have the cash to get to our next booking." The astonished stranger excused himself and rushed off to the station house, returning with train tickets for everyone. He owned the railroad!

Could *In Bamville* survive without Al? I could tell that there were money problems by the anxious faces around me. One crisis followed the next and when the show finally opened in New York on September 1, its name had been changed to *Chocolate Dandies*.

Compared to *Shuffle Along*, which had been staged on a shoestring, *Chocolate Dandies* was a superproduction with lavish sets. *Shuffle Along*, with its sixty performers, had operated on $7,500 a week, but we now numbered 125, not counting three flesh-and-blood horses for the race track scene. Mr. Blake lived in a constant state of nerves—"Unless we can net $16,000 we're through"—and everyone else except me seemed to share his anxiety. Wanting nothing but the best, Sissle had hired a top director from the *Ziegfeld Follies* and the dazzling costumes were a far cry from the hand-me-downs we had worn at the Cort. Dressed in a clinging silk dress with a slit skirt, I sometimes played the vamp opposite our male lead, Lew Payton. More often my role was slapstick—a grinning girl with outsize shoes, a dress cut up to my thighs, a sash with a huge bow, and all the silly faces I could think of.

We spent opening night waiting anxiously for the reviews. They were disastrous. "This is pale-face stuff, not black magic." "Lacks the spark of *Shuffle Along.*" Blake and Sissle looked grim. Who could ask for a prettier tune than "God bless the Dixie moonlight, God made the night for you," or a livelier one than "Have a goody goody goody good, have a goody goody good good time"? Yet the critics and their following felt the special charm of *Shuffle Along* had been lost; *Chocolate Dandies* looked too *successful.* In spite of the reviews, our nightly audiences seemed to love us, but rumors flew that we were losing money. We would just have to hold on for as long as we could.

I prayed for our luck to change. I've always been superstitious and to this very day I make sure to look over my left shoulder with a coin in my hand on evenings when the moon is in its last quarter. Back then I slept with a good-luck penny under my pillow. Was that why a messenger knocked on my dressing-room door one morning? "A letter for you, Miss Baker." I couldn't believe my eyes. It was an offer to appear at the Plantation, the Broadway nightclub that had launched Florence Mills and was currently starring Ethel Waters!

CHAPTER 3

———————⌁∽⌁———————

First Love

I HAD NEVER SEEN ANYTHING as magnificent as the Plantation. It looked like paradise, with its bright lights and starched tablecloths. What's more, it welcomed black *and* white customers.

The performers were "white" blacks, in accordance with the vogue for light-skinned entertainers. The waiters were not only white but *French*. I found them charming, especially the way they spoke to me as if we were all one color. *"Rigolote,"* they called me. "Fun-ny." I was still in the chorus and might well have passed unnoticed except for my bobbed hair gleaming with oil and my eyes, which I was learning to roll in all directions. In fact, I practiced making faces daily before the mirror, with amazing results. "Keep it up and you'll soon be using your tongue as a scarf," said one of my friends, laughing. I spent the rest of my time memorizing Ethel Waters's songs. I enjoyed it, and after all, you never knew.

As I walked into the dressing room one evening, a flash of color caught my eye. There on the makeup table stood a little bunch of violets. "They're for you," announced one of the dancers, handing me an envelope addressed to Miss Josephine Baker. I quickly pulled out the card. It was signed "Henry," but that was the only word I could read, partly

because of my excitement (this was the first bouquet I had ever received)
and partly because although Clara Smith's lessons and my own efforts had
taught me to puzzle through the newspapers—especially the headlines—
I couldn't read longhand. My fellow dancers collapsed with laughter.
"Josephine has a boyfriend," they mocked, "but she's so stupid she
doesn't know what he's saying." "He'll be waiting for you at the stage
door," said Bernice, one of the kinder girls, fingering the card. "Yes, but
what for?" someone asked. "She's so innocent she wouldn't know a
ding-dong Daddy from a Romeo." Let them tease me all they wanted; I
didn't care. When I buried my nose in my violets I could smell woods in
springtime.

During our Charleston number the girl beside me gave me a vicious
pinch. "I'll bet it's that fat guy over there. The one with the red tie and
the potbelly!" and as we returned to the dressing room, another dancer
hissed, "What a funny idea to send flowers to the ugliest girl in the show.
He must be some sort of pervert!" When the show was over, the chorus
girls removed their makeup as slowly as possible. They were going to wait
around to see "Josephine's sweetheart" if it took all night. Bernice came
to my rescue. Slipping out the door, she found my suitor and told him
to wait for me up the street. When I finally emerged from the theater,
I heard jeers of "Josephine's been stood up." "He's already jilted her."
Head high, I sailed up Broadway, my violets pinned to my coat. Suddenly
I heard a voice behind me murmur, "How nice of you to wear my flowers."
I stopped dead in my tracks, afraid to turn my head. Suppose it was the
man with the paunch?

He was slender, very young, and as nervous as I was. His eyes were as
blue as the sky; his hair like the setting sun. And he had freckles.

"Freckles? You mean he's white?"

Those were the first words I heard the next day as I stood at the dressing
room door. Bernice had obviously let the cat out of the bag. When I
entered the room, there was total silence. A bouquet of violets sat on the
dressing table at my place. Then suddenly there was a burst of questions:
Where had we gone? Had he kissed me? Had I gone home with him? Had
he come to my place? "Don't be silly," one of the girls interrupted.
"Visited her in *Harlem?*" She was right. No white man would ever make
it to my shabby apartment, since it meant passing my landlady's door.

How many times had she told me: white men pay us compliments so they can go to bed with us, then once they get us pregnant they disappear because it's against the law to marry us no matter how much they like to touch our skin. Judging from my color, my mother could tell me a thing or two about that! Always the question of color. Only the other day a white producer had visited our show looking for someone to use in a film, but none of us would do. He wanted someone extremely dark-skinned to play the part of a harem girl. Our girls, who were the most beautiful café-au-lait color imaginable, were furious. Some of them even had blue eyes and naturally blond hair, due to their mixed blood. I was gradually learning that there was discrimination between blacks as well: the darkest versus the lightest, pale skin versus black. It made me want to turn and run. Wasn't there any place in the world where color didn't matter?

Thank goodness for Henry. He seemed to be above such things. He had taken me to Greenwich Village, the artists' quarter, since there was no question of going to a Broadway restaurant. Blacks couldn't eat in places where there were white customers, although they were considered fit to work as waiters, cooks or entertainers. In the soft light of the Village bar where we sat talking, Henry's eyes semed full of little stars. He told me that I had beautiful hands, that he was a student, that he liked the way I danced because it looked so natural and unschooled.

Unschooled was right! And I reminded myself that I would have to begin to work on my reading so that I could decipher Henry's cards if he continued sending me violets.

As we were saying good night at the front door, my landlady spotted Henry. Shrugging her shoulders, she turned away. But the next morning when she saw me she muttered, "Poor little fool."

Bernice seemed worried too. "You have long *talks?* About what?" It was hard to explain: about everything and nothing, about our shared belief that someday the barriers between blacks and whites would disappear. But for the moment, I felt so ignorant beside him. Henry insisted that this was not the case. I simply lacked instruction. I could learn very quickly if I tried. Why didn't we go to a tearoom the next afternoon instead of taking our nightly trip to the Village?

I was terrified. What should I wear? Bernice offered to lend me her silk blouse and some of her pungent toilet water, which I splashed on nervously. Henry obviously cared more about grooming than I did. In my family, too much attention to personal appearance was considered indulgence in the sin of pride.

Henry was waiting at the stage door after the matinee. Fortunately the tearoom was nearby; Bernice had also lent me her shoes and they were pinching my feet. It was an impressive place, full of fresh flowers and sparkling crystal, but my pleasure was marred by the fact that people began staring the moment we walked in. My green blouse, high heels and layers of white powder attracted the eye and Bernice's perfume seemed to alert the nose. I sat primly on the edge of my chair as we were served tea, toast, butter and jam. It all seemed like a dream, but changed quickly to a nightmare. Hungry and confused, I swallowed a large piece of toast at a gulp and it stuck in my throat. When I tried to wash it down with a mouthful of tea, I spilled some of the burning liquid onto my blouse. To my horror I could feel butter sliding down my chin and I was sure the entire room could hear me chewing. Everyone seemed to be staring, including Henry, who had put down his cup. Cheeks burning, I plunged my knife into the jam pot, not seeing the serving spoon until Henry, his eyes ice blue, placed it in my hand. When I tried to spread jam on my toast, I realized I had taken too large a portion and most of it stuck to my fingers. Where had my napkin gone? There it was on the floor. I furtively licked my fingers, drained my cup at a gulp and began coughing and sputtering loudly in the now silent room.

"Where in the world did he find her? In a zoo?"

"She could use another coat of whitewash."

"Where will it end if we let them into places like this?"

I heard every word and was sure that Henry had too, although I didn't dare to look at him. As he placed a dollar on the table, I stumbled to my feet, teetering on Bernice's shoes, which I had half slipped off to relieve the pain.

No matter what anyone said, black or white—we were *not* alike. There were places where my people weren't welcome. Henry walked along beside me in silence. What was there to say? I wanted to die on the spot.

"It's a real joy lending you things," grumbled Bernice when I returned her spattered blouse. "Pig."

I don't know how I managed to dance the Charleston that night.

The next evening brought more violets. This time the card read: "I'll be waiting at the stage door. I love you. Henry." No man had ever said those words to me before! My feet never touched the stage all evening.

"Excuse me for taking you to that snooty place."

"Forgive me for not knowing how to act."

He gave me a dazzling smile. "Everything can be learned, Josephine."

Everything. I recognized a jam spoon now and I knew all Ethel Waters's songs by heart—luckily, because Ethel arrived at the theater one night with a pondful of frogs in her throat. She managed to get through the evening like a true professional, but the next morning she sent word that she had lost her voice completely. I knocked at the director's door. "I can sing all her numbers." He looked at me with amazement. "You're kidding. Show me." It's not easy to perform in an office in front of a man who stares at you as if you're some sort of bug. But ever since Henry had said that he loved me, nothing seemed impossible! I threw myself into the current hit "Dinah," Ethel's greatest success. "You're on," said the director. "Starting tonight."

When I returned to the dressing room after the show, the girls were buzzing with excitement. "You were sensational. Did you hear them clapping for 'Dinah'?" "Dinah" 's success didn't much impress me. I could have been a canary for all it mattered. The song was so popular, it practically sang itself. What *did* please me was having added a few songs that appealed to *me*. "Ukulele Lady" for one and "Charleston," which brought down the house even though I didn't sing as well as Ethel—I'd never been taught to do *that*, either.

"You were spectacular!" Henry reported. "You have a real future."

I was finally beginning to think so myself. How badly I had needed someone to encourage me. But the next evening I found violets in the dressing room and Ethel on the stage. I couldn't believe my eyes. She had been ordered to bed for two weeks.

"Your success cured her fast," snapped Bernice.

"It's not fair," I complained to the director. "You promised—"

"I didn't promise anything."

"You told me after the show that they liked me better than Ethel because I made them laugh."

"Not *better*. The same. Anyway, she's *lighter* and prettier."

It was back to the chorus again. When I ran into Ethel in the wings she gave me a furious look. That was the last straw. "Back so soon?

Too bad for the show," I snapped. Ethel was so startled by my rudeness that she muttered something like "Stupid darky." I'm sure she would have pulled my hair if it hadn't been so short. I was ashamed of us both.

After the performance Henry took me to our Village bar and tried to cheer me up. Didn't I understand? What had happened with Ethel and in the tearoom was more a question of class warfare than of race. One-hundred-percent whites didn't get along together, either. Why was it all so complicated, I wondered, when life could be so simple? I looked lovingly at Henry's freckles. At least the two of us were proof that whites and blacks could truly love each other, perhaps for a lifetime. I asked him question after question about his parents and his childhood, so different from mine. If only I could meet his family . . .

"All right. I'll arrange it."

"You'll bring them to the Plantation? When?"

"How about tomorrow night?"

I couldn't believe my ears. He had told them about his black friend. My dreams of meeting Henry's parents were going to come true. I tossed and turned all night. How should I address them? *Another* thing I'd never learned. Would I be able to carry on a conversation? I mustn't appear overly friendly at first, no matter how much I liked them—and I *knew* I was going to love them. Suppose we went out together after the show and I dropped my napkin again? But his parents would certainly refuse to go to Greenwich Village . . . and where else could they take a colored girl? My heart sank, but the thought of Henry's reassuring blue eyes made my spirits rise again.

The next day brought another bunch of violets, but all through the first part of the show I searched the audience in vain for Henry. Had something gone wrong? Had he told them I was a chorus girl? Had they refused to come? Were they planning to arrive for the second part of the performance? If they weren't in the audience after the intermission I simply *couldn't* dance the Charleston.

A knock on the door. It was Henry. Alone.

No. He was carrying two cages. A parrot sat in each.

"You don't get the joke? These are who I live with. I tell them about you every night."

No, I didn't get the joke.

"I want you to have one. I want us to share *everything.*"

I took the cage, trying to smile.

"Isn't it cruel to separate them?"

"Heavens, no. They're beginning to have lovers' quarrels."

We didn't go down to the Village that evening. Instead we went our separate ways to put our birds to bed. Poor lonely creatures! Like me. But what had I really expected? That love would conquer all? Not only the difference in our colors but the class barriers Henry had talked of yesterday . . . He liked me enough to give me Toby but not enough to introduce me to his parents. And would I have dared to take him home to mine? How I wished that Henry had been *forced* to present me to his family. "We want to meet your Miss Baker, Henry. We'd be *honored*. Ask her if she'll do us the *kindness* of coming to tea."

I burst into tears.

"To be or not to be," squawked Toby.

They were the only words he knew.

"Miss Baker?"

A beautiful young woman stood at my dressing room door. Her clothes were exquisite, her hands freshly manicured. I was struck by her forthright manner. "My name is Caroline Dudley. I'm looking for black performers for a show I'm taking to Paris." "Paris? *The* Paris?" "Yes; Paris, France."

She smiled at my confusion. France . . . I had dreamed of going there ever since Albert, one of the waiters at the Plantation, had shown me a photograph of the Eiffel Tower. It looked very different from the Statue of Liberty, but what did that matter? What was the good of having the statue without the liberty, the freedom to go where one chose if one was held back by one's color? No, I preferred the Eiffel Tower, which made no promises. I had sworn to myself that I would see it one day. And suddenly here was my chance at the very moment that I felt like tossing over everything. Things couldn't be worse. Or could they? Mrs. Dudley reassured me. "Paris is the most beautiful city in the world. Think it over. I'll be back."

What should I do? Part of me wanted to stay with Henry, yet another wanted to get as far away from him as possible. In New York I was nothing but a "darky" to people like Ethel, but in Paris I would be treated like a white girl, or so Albert said. When Mrs. Dudley returned she offered me $150 a week. I hesitated. "Suppose they don't like me. I'll be stuck there on the other side of the ocean." "They'll *love* you."

A freckled face passed before my eyes, but love, like a mirror, is best when it's intact, and ever since Toby's arrival a little corner had been chipped away from mine. Later that evening I told Henry about Mrs. Dudley's proposal. According to backstage gossip, she was immensely rich and worldly. She knew Paris well and had decided to stage a black revue there partly for fun and partly because she had been informed that the time was ripe. My redheaded friend made a face. I could tell he was upset, but remembering the evening with the parrots, I couldn't resist giving him a little dig. "In France I can go wherever I please. I'll be accepted in *the best families*. Being black is taken for granted there." "Do you really believe that?" Henry exploded. "Yes." "Another proof of your ignorance," he said nastily. My heart fell. Silence. Then:

"I'm taking Toby home with me. Sarah misses him. Only those without hearts can endure separations."

It hurt to see him go, but I would have to do without him in order to succeed. When Mrs. Dudley offered me two hundred dollars, I accepted.

"But what do you want me to *do*, Mrs. Dudley?" "Dance the Charleston." "That's easy enough. It simply means throwing up your arms and legs as if you were flinging your heart and soul away. The way my grandmother used to do when she was happy. Just like back in South Carolina."

"You've got plenty of spirit, but nothing to wear," Mrs. Dudley remarked. And she gave me a handful of bills to spend on a dress.

I had never seen so much money. Fortunately I knew a seamstress in Harlem and I hurried to her workroom. She would have to work fast, I explained. I was about to leave for Paris. Paris? She couldn't believe her ears. I would need something *really* special. Yes, but at the same time suitable for traveling, because it was a long journey. We buried ourselves in fashion magazines and five days later, after endless arguments and indecision, she had completed a truly remarkable outfit. Even in Harlem people turned to stare as I walked by in my new pearl-gray golf pants, which clung to my buttocks then flared down to my ankles, a belted orange jacket and a jaunty silver lamé hat. Not to mention my new green shoes . . . My seamstress assured me that I looked gorgeous. No comment from Mrs. Dudley when I showed up for rehearsal. She simply scribbled the name of her dressmaker on a slip of paper and placed it in my hand.

She was sending me to a real couturier. I was as surprised as they were when they found me standing at their door. Before I knew it, I had been whisked into a dressing room and told to wait there.

My trip was off to a fine beginning! I should have known enough to realize that since Mrs. Dudley's dressmaker had a white clientele I would have to be kept out of the salon while the models were being presented. Just as I was about to march out the front door, the house director stuck her head through the curtain, blinked at the sight of my trousers and hissed: "It's Mrs. Dudley's protégée!" The salesgirl smiled at me thinly as the directress hurried away. There was a sudden commotion at my fitting room door, and in swept a tall, slender blonde in a filmy dress. A single twirl and she was gone, to be followed by another mannequin in an even more revealing gown. Since I couldn't appear in the salon, the models would come to me! It seemed I should be grateful for this attention, but I was furious, first because the girls obviously would have turned up their noses at me had they dared—and *held* them, since I had borrowed Bernice's perfume again—second because of the humiliation of my exile. In spite of the fact that Mrs. Dudley had insisted, "Order whatever you like and charge it to me," I said haughtily, "Nothing appeals to me," and stalked away in my green shoes.

I had never seen such beautiful clothes.

Mrs. Dudley's troupe was unmistakably black. We were twenty-five in all—dancers, singers, musicians, most of us extremely dark-skinned. Mrs. Dudley did not share New York's infatuation with "white," blond-haired Negro girls. She wanted the real thing, Charleston-style. I had a solo part now. The troupe's leading lady was Maud de Forest, a hefty "mama" with a ringing voice, but my own favorite was the jazz band. Hearing it made me want to jump up and dance with happiness. I could feel the music in my very bones.

Our departure date was drawing near. I had bought myself a trunk for seventeen dollars and marveled at its velvet lid, the iron and ironing board it contained and of course my wardrobe—a rather flashy collection of clothes which I had finally bought in Harlem, hoping for the best. At this point Mrs. Dudley was more concerned about my legal status than my appearance. She had ordered a copy of my birth certificate to be sent from City Hall in St. Louis. Sensing my tendency to lie about my age in order to get work, she not only doubted I was twenty but feared that I might not yet be eighteen. Were that the case, I could not leave the country without my parents' consent. If I should be obliged to get my mother's permission, I had no doubt of the reply. A resounding no! The certificate arrived at last. Yes, I *had* been born on June 3, 1906. I was nineteen. Now it was off to the passport office, where I had earlier certified that I was twenty. Would I be sent to prison? Fortunately Mrs. Dudley had connections. She told the clerk that she would vouch for me and thanks to her name and fortune, my passport was promptly issued.

What a relief! I was ready to sail for France.

The *Berengaria* terrified me on sight. The huge transatlantic liner bore no relationship to our Mississippi paddle boats. As I shrank back from the gangplank, Mrs. Dudley slipped her arm around my shoulders. She always seemed to know what I was thinking.

I quickly grew accustomed to shipboard life in spite of the fact that since the *Berengaria* flew the American flag, she followed the American practice of confining black passengers to certain parts of the ship. At least I was sailing toward freedom! No sooner had we set sail than talk turned to the traditional ship's gala. Would our troupe be willing to perform? I immediately volunteered to sing. "You'll be sorry," warned Mrs. Dudley. What did *she* know? Hadn't I successfully replaced Ethel Waters? I couldn't wait to feel the excitement mounting in the room at the sound of my voice. Besides, I wanted to show the white passengers what a "darky" could do. I decided on two sentimental numbers: "Brown Eyes" and "If You Hadn't Gone Away." After one rehearsal I was sure of my success.

Before the show I stood looking over the rail. The sun was sinking into the sea for the second time since we had left New York. The sky was aflame. And I would soon be entertaining the first-class passengers. Yes, I would always remember September 16, 1925. The date of my first real performance—and my first resounding flop.

I couldn't seem to find the beat. Was that why no one listened? When they *did* listen, it was even worse. They clearly didn't like what they heard. My voice began to crack. In quick succession I produced three off-key notes, which the orchestra tried to drown out.

Utter humiliation.

"They hate me! Why did I ever come? I want to go home."

Mrs. Dudley listened calmly. "All right, Josephine. But you'll have to be patient. We're in the middle of the ocean."

I tried to swallow my tears and my pride. I should never have left New York. At least in Harlem they accepted me! Would the voyage never end? Luckily Mrs. Dudley had promised I could go back whenever I liked. That meant the instant we touched shore. No, not quite. I'd go as far as Paris so I'd have something to talk about when I got back to Harlem.

Mrs. Dudley did her best to comfort me, explaining that my mistake had been to sing torch songs. My talents lay in the dancing I loved, the livelier the better.

On September 18 there was a mine scare. The passengers were ordered to put on their life belts and gather around the boats. There would probably be a boat for our deck if there were enough to go around, but we would be the last to leave ship. We could hear the first-class passengers shouting. Children were crying. Gathering by the railing, we began to sing. The same songs our ancestors had sung on the slave ships that carried them to America. A musician called Sidney picked up his clarinet. He played so softly and sweetly that tears came to my eyes. Why had I ever left home? I buried my face in my hands. Suddenly I realized that Sidney had stopped playing. He was standing at my side.

Sidney was the only musician who hadn't made fun of me after my disastrous rendition of "Brown Eyes." Ten or so years my senior, he was café-au-lait, like me. Born in that musical mecca New Orleans, he was one of nine children, almost all of whom were musicians, including the shoe-maker father. He had a French name. Bechet. Sidney Bechet.

Sidney had traveled widely. Four years ago he had performed in London and Paris, appearing at the Alhambra Theater in a show starring Mistin-guett, the queen of French music hall. My spirits lifted when he talked about Paris. I shouldn't be afraid, he said. Parisians didn't notice people's skins. The city glowed like a pearl in an emerald setting, he continued. The green part was the suburbs, where gay little houses with red tile roofs sat by the water's edge. There were wonderful places to fish. "If I ever have the money I'm going to buy me a house there," he confided. "I love fishing."

Together we gazed at the sea. Not a mine or a cloud in sight.

CHAPTER 4

•‣∞‣•

The "Revue Nègre"

LE HAVRE . . . IT WAS RAINING. Welcome to France!

"Will you be taking the next boat back, Josephine?" Mrs. Caroline asked slyly. "I'll tell you my plans when I get to Paris," I replied, with more confidence than I felt. Mrs. Dudley handed me a pocket dictionary.

"Bonjour, ma cocotte," called a smiling Frenchman at the Le Havre station. What did *that* mean? When I was seated in our cozy compartment—so different from the unpartitioned carriages back home—I consulted my dictionary. *"Cocotte*—black cast-iron receptacle used to stew food." I burst into tears. Here I was, just off the boat, and they were calling me a *pot*—black, of course, and undoubtedly ugly. Mrs. Caroline tried to explain. The way he was using the word wasn't in the dictionary. It meant something like "cutey."

We were a wide-eyed, bewildered group, except for Sidney and the dancer Louis Douglas, who had performed in Paris before. Mrs. Caroline and her secretary propelled us toward the *wagon-restaurant.* In America, Negroes were always told the dining car was full if there were white passengers eating. Here we were smilingly welcomed. We couldn't believe our eyes. "It's like this everywhere," Douglas explained. "Not just in the restaurants. You can buy the best seats in the theater if you like." "It sounds like paradise." "And you're going to *love* eating snails!" "Snails?" I gasped. *"Dee*-licious," commented Sidney. I could feel my stomach churning.

One look at Paris and I felt as good as new. The thing that impressed me most was the honking taxi horns. At home, automobile horns were heard only in bands or on New Year's Eve. I was also struck by the women's clothes. In New York I had heard that Parisiennes wore corsets and leg-of-mutton sleeves. Not at all. Their bodies moved freely, their sleeves were closely fitted, their heels were extremely high and the little hats they wore perched on their heads looked like the dots on an *i.* Everyone seemed to be bursting with life. And most surprising of all, I saw couples *kissing* in the streets. In America you went to jail for that! It was true—this *was* a free country. France was a wonderful place!

André Daven (director of the Théâtre des Champs-Élysées): It was raining that morning in 1925. The Gare Saint-Lazare was teeming with its daily ration of pale, grim-faced commuters. Suddenly the bustling crowd froze. An excited, noisy, gaudy knot of people had just stepped off the Le Havre–Paris train. They were carrying strange-looking instruments and laughing uproariously. Their rainbow-colored skirts, fuchsia jeans and checked and polka-dot shirts lit up the gray platform. Unbelievable hats —cream-colored, orange, scarlet—dipped over their darting, laughing eyes. . . .

A tall, willowy girl in black-and-white-checked gardening overalls and an amazing hat detached herself from the group. "So this is Paris," she cried. These were Josephine's first words about the city she was to conquer.

Two dangers threatened this collection of innocents: the night spots of Montmartre, ready to corrupt the kings of the Charleston at ruinous cost, and alcohol. This was the era of Prohibition in America and our new-found friends were not acquainted with champagne. It seemed advisable to delay this encounter for as long as possible. We therefore rented an entire hotel on the Rue Campagne-Première [in Montparnasse] and in-stalled our theater's bouncer as the troupe's watchdog. His braided uni-form and fancy cap obviously impressed them. A tourist bus was also hired to ferry the cast back and forth from the theater. During rehearsals, while the gifted Douglas supervised the dancing, Paul Colin sat sketching the faces and bodies that were to make his name. "They're breathtaking," he exclaimed. [*Les Nouvelles Littéraires*, May 28, 1959]

Paul Colin: The success of the poster I designed to launch the *Revue Nègre* was probably linked with Josephine's triumph. . . . At ten o'clock one morning I watched a colorful, raucous group swarm toward the theater, devouring their latest find—croissants from a bistro on the Avenue Montaigne. Harlem was invading the Champs-Élysées Theater. Leaping onto the stage like children at play, the troupe broke into a frenzied tap dance. . . . With their bright neckties, dotted pants, suspenders, cameras, binoculars and green-and-red-laced boots, who needed costumes? What style! The stagehands stood open-mouthed in the wings and from our seats in the hall, Rolf de Maré, the theater manager, André Daven, the director, and I sat gaping at the stage. The contortions and cries, the sporty, perky breasts and buttocks, the hairdos, the boaters, the brilliant cottons, the Charleston, were all brand-new to Europe.

A great deal remained to be done to organize the show. My role was to design the posters and work on the scenery. Unfortunately the leading lady, Maud de Forest, looked like a washerwoman, but I spotted a girl in the chorus who had a beautifully proportioned body. "What a pity *she's* not the star," I sighed. Daven agreed. When we were done, the show had been polished down to three-quarters of an hour—forty-five minutes which would be remembered for fifty years! Maud was left to her spirituals while we focused the projectors on the slender dancer.

I lost no time in asking the young woman to pose in my studio. Since she didn't speak French, we communicated through little drawings. Her name was Josephine. In spite of her magnificent body, she was extremely modest. I couldn't seem to make her understand that I wanted her to pose *nude!*

Josephine: It was the first time I had ever been in an artist's studio. All those windows made me feel like a storefront dummy on display. "There's no such thing as modesty among artists," Monsieur Rolf had explained. I did my best to understand. It had already been decided that I would reveal more of my body in the show than had been originally planned. Whatever they said! But this was different. Two thousand people were nobody, but undressing in front of a single man . . . ? The mere sight of my jacket lying on Monsieur Colin's footstool made me feel faint. Stalling for time, I examined the paintings that filled the room, laughing nervously. Monsieur Colin gave me time to collect myself, then led me to a little washroom attached to the studio. I reappeared in my bra and panties. I didn't usually wear a bra, but today I had known that I would have to get undressed. I avoided Monsieur Colin's eyes. With a sudden gesture, he reached over and undid my hooks. Oh, *no!* I wanted to dash through the door and down the stairs, but I was glued to the spot. Monsieur Colin calmly began to draw.

As he worked, he smiled at me from time to time. I gradually grew more relaxed. He obviously saw me as an object; not a woman but something to be painted. Suddenly he threw down his paintbrush and shook his head violently. What was the matter? What was he trying to say? I really *must* learn to speak French! He finally handed me a little sketch of myself completely nude. *"No!"* I gestured, and for the rest of the evening I managed to hold on to my panties. Monsieur Colin told me to come back the next evening.

Had he discussed my behavior at the theater? The next day several people drew me aside to explain that I would never be anything without the poster, that I would not be the first person or the last to undress in front of Paul Colin, that artists had certain rights and I as a mere beginner had certain *duties.* Just think—my likeness would be plastered all over Paris! Yes, but *naked!* What would they say in St. Louis?

That night I removed all my clothes.

As time passed, I began to feel increasingly comfortable with Paul, as I now called him. I spent many happy hours in his quiet studio. Paul gave me self-confidence. For the first time in my life, I felt beautiful.

The morale of the rest of the troupe was not as high as mine. We had thought our show was marvelous and Monsieur Rolf's verdict—"Catastrophic"—struck us like a thunderclap. But he was an able and agreeable taskmaster and we did what he wanted although it meant working night and day.

As opening night approached, our rehearsal schedule grew more and more hectic. Some of the troupe were so disgusted they were ready to take the boat home. Not I. I felt happy and free. Sensing that the organizers liked my work made me blossom like a flower. If it had been December I would have called Monsieur Rolf my Santa Claus. He liked to put his index finger on the top of my head (he was very tall) and twirl me around like a top. When I had stopped spinning he would say in a serious voice: "You're going to be famous, young lady." He seemed to believe it, which made me believe it too. It kept me from sleeping at night.

I gradually learned that Monsieur Rolf was a patron of the arts who had decided to make his mark. It was he who had been responsible for bringing the controversial Swedish Ballet to Paris a few years earlier and last April he had inaugurated a series of stylish music hall shows featuring famous names. Pavlova was one of them: a tiny lady who stood on the tips of her toes. But in spite of such stars, music hall seemed to do poorly in this elegant neighborhood, so one of the painters involved with the Swedish Ballet, Fernand Léger, who had done sets for a *ballet nègre* of his own, called *The Creation of the World*, had suggested that it would be "dynamite" to bring a *real* black troupe from New York. They had contacted Mrs. Caroline and here we were.

André Daven: Opening night was unforgettable. At midnight Parisian café society literally *invaded* the theater, shoving aside the security guards. Because of advance reviews in the press, the air was crackling with tension. Would it be necessary to empty the hall?

At last the curtain rose, revealing a backdrop on which Paul Colin had painted a whimsical skyscraper. Onto the empty stage behind a colorful peddler's cart strolled Sidney Bechet, playing a poignant, tender melody on his clarinet. The pure, spellbinding music filled the air and within thirty seconds the uproar in the hall had ceased. As the last sweet note faded away, the audience burst into thunderous applause. Now it was Josephine whose presence filled the stage, bringing with her a glimpse of another world. As she danced, quivering with intensity, the entire room felt the raw force of her passion, the excitement of her rhythm. She was eroticism personified. The simplicity of her emotions, her savage grace, were deeply moving. She laughed, she cried, then from her supple throat came a song, crystal clear at first, then with a hoarseness that caught at the heart.

Josephine: Driven by dark forces I didn't recognize, I improvised, crazed by the music, the overheated theater filled to the bursting point, the scorching eye of the spotlights. Even my teeth and eyes burned with fever. Each time I leaped I seemed to touch the sky and when I regained earth it seemed to be mine alone. I felt as intoxicated as when, on the day I arrived in Paris, Douglas had given me a glass of anisette.

There was total silence in the hall. Then the crowd began to laugh, to shout, to tap its feet, to whistle. "They like me, they like me," whispered my inner self, which had somehow retained its composure. The music reached me through a wall of cotton. The clamor grew deafening; it was a triumph. The curtain was lowered, then lifted again. I continued dancing. Now it descended for good—and so did I, collapsing in a heap. From miles above I heard "Jo-se-phine," and forcing myself to the surface, found myself eye to eye with Monsieur Daven. Why did he look as if the *Titanic* had just gone down? "They whistled," I whispered ecstatically. "This isn't New York," he snapped. "In France they whistle when they *don't* like the act." His words were like a knife in my heart.

Suddenly a group of young people burst into the wings shouting "Josephine" and grinning from ear to ear. I was propelled onto the stage, the curtain rose again, and although some of the audience whistled, the rest clapped like mad.

After the show Monsieur Rolf gave a magnificent reception. The entire theater was transformed for the occasion. When we had finished the lavish midnight supper, everyone danced.

Before the premiere, Monsieur Colin, insisting that I have a dress worthy of a star, had taken me to the famous couturier Poiret, who had a beard like our Reverend back home in St. Louis but was twice as stout. His piercing eyes instantly demolished my red-and-yellow "made in Harlem" outfit. I was quickly stripped of my clothes by two young women who instinctively sensed their master's wishes. Here I was, nude again. At least I was getting used to it. A third flunky now appeared, carrying a bolt of the most beautiful silvery material I had ever seen. It looked like a flowing river. Monsieur Poiret poured the gleaming torrent over me, rolled me up in it, draped it about my body, pulled it tight, ordered me to walk, then loosened it around my legs. I felt like a sea goddess emerging from the foam. . . .

When I walked into the opening-night reception on Paul's arm, I realized that the guests were all celebrities. They stared at me open-mouthed. Was this the savage they had gaped at on the stage? The women tried to stare me down, but I felt taller than all of them. The men caressed me with their eyes.

"What's *that*, Paul?" I cried. "Caviar." Pulling out his pad, he dashed off a flurry of sketches. A fish. A female fish. The eggs of a female fish. It seemed that the French ate *anything!*

The press couldn't seem to say enough about the *Revue Nègre*. The clippings I collected served as my French textbooks. Whether they liked me or not, the journalists who reviewed me became my language professors.

One of the critics compared our movements to St. Vitus's Dance. "What kind of a dance is that?" I asked. "It's a nervous disorder that makes you tremble and jerk all over." "That's not a sickness," I retorted. "It's the way we act in church back home." "Here in France, God likes us to kneel quietly." Why didn't God demand the same behavior in France as in Harlem? It would make things so much easier.

According to another reviewer I was a "black Venus." It was true that everyone seemed to love me, but I had heard no talk of marriage. Venus, yes. But the black part didn't seem to help. Fortunately, I didn't have much time to think about it; Monsieur Rolf was making changes in the show again. He had decided to add some new dancers. One of them was a West Indian girl named Mathilde Darlin. "If you add a *g* it will sound more like Harlem," I remarked. And since she was even younger than I was, we called her Baby. Baby Darling.

Baby eventually married a black actor, Mr. Legitimus, and started a family. There are now thirty members of the Legitimus clan living in Paris, all of them actors. Ranging in age from two to sixty, they are in constant demand for the stage, television and films. Baby, now a stout matron, recalls the early days:

When I was fourteen, I was taken by friends to one of the first performances of the *Revue Nègre*. "*You* can't dance like that," they taunted. "Let's see you try." I never could resist a dare, so I presented myself to Louis Douglas, who received me in blackface and white lips. "Can you do the Charleston? The black bottom? The cakewalk? O.K., come back tomorrow." The next day he quickly saw that I could do none of them. But he hired me all the same because I had nerve. "I like people with nerve," he confided. And that's how I met Josephine. She was very nice to me in spite of the fact that the other girls were most unkind to her. They resented her for replacing the star. She had her own style of dancing and was constantly making faces. Her beauty was even more startling

because she acted as though she were ugly. I could see trouble coming.
. . . In fact, I saved her life one day. What happened was this. One of
the dancers had been so rude that Josephine had slapped her. The girl ran
off to her musician boyfriend, who had been drinking. He pulled out a
knife with which to "kill Josephine." I ran screaming to the dressing room
to warn her and just as I slammed shut the door, a knife buried itself into
one of the panels! Life was exciting backstage at the Champs-Élysées
Theater. I'll never forget those three months. . . . Perhaps the reason
Josephine liked me was that I was French. She learned the language
amazingly fast, partly because she was in such demand among Parisians.
What was a cocktail party, a reception or a benefit without Josephine
Baker?

Josephine: On October 16 we began the third week of our engagement
at the Champs-Élysées. Monsieur Rolf was still making changes. The
latest was a line of chorus girls, dressed in transparent white sheaths,
parading to the music of tom-toms. On October 23, the newspapers
announced that "the amazing troupe currently brightening the Parisian
scene" had even more surprises in store.

I had moved to a pretty little hotel on the Right Bank. What luxury
to eat breakfast in bed, to wake up to the odor of croissants! Although
neither young nor handsome, the room waiter was the first Frenchman
to truly savor my charms. I'll never forget his face the day he found me
soaking in the tub. He almost dropped the tray.

In spite of my affection for the Hotel Fournet, my many expenses—
pedicurist, manicurist, dressmakers—soon forced me to seek cheaper lodgings. I decided to rent an apartment in Montmartre with Maud and
another dancer, Mamie. That way I could send two hundred dollars home
to St. Louis. Since I didn't understand the postal regulations, I asked one
of my suitors, a charming young journalist named Georges Simenon, to
handle the mailing. He did his job so capably that people assumed he was
my secretary. It hadn't taken long to learn that I couldn't lift a finger
unobserved. Such was the price of fame. Georges vanished one day as
abruptly as he had come. It appeared that he was married. Would there
always be barriers between me and those I wished to love?

Articles in which I barely recognized myself continued to fill the press.
This one from the newspaper *Candide* was typical:

Everyone is talking about the show. Some people have seen it as many as six times . . . others stamp out of the theater before the first curtain. . . . At one point a strange figure in a ragged undershirt ambles onto the stage looking like a cross between a boxing kangaroo and a racing driver. Josephine Baker. Woman or man? Her lips are painted black, her skin is the color of bananas, her cropped hair sticks to her head like caviar, her voice squeaks. She is in constant motion, her body writhing like a snake or more precisely like a dipping saxophone. Music seems to pour from her body. She grimaces, crosses her eyes, puffs out her cheeks, wiggles disjointedly, does a split and finally crawls off the stage stiff-legged, her rump higher than her head, like a young giraffe. . . . Quick as a one-step, she's back again. This is no woman, no dancer. It's something as exotic and elusive as music, the embodiment of all the sounds we know. . . . And now the finale, a wildly indecent dance which takes us back to primeval times . . . arms high, belly thrust forward, buttocks quivering, Josephine is stark naked except for a ring of blue and red feathers circling her hips and another around her neck.

I read such statements with the same astonishment I imagine a child would feel when the ball he has thrown crashes through a window.

Since I personified the savage on the stage, I tried to be as civilized as possible in daily life. A reporter from the newspaper *Comoedia* describes a tea party at Mrs. Caroline's:

Mrs. Dudley's house overlooking the quays is a fifteenth-century marvel. . . . Sidney Bechet in evening clothes lounges at the piano, humming and tapping his foot. Suddenly the rhythm quickens and the words grow loud and clear. . . . Bechet is improvising as usual. The saxophonist and flutist of the Charleston Jazz Band can't read a word of music. If asked when he learned to play the piano, he grinningly replies "at birth." . . . At his side in an elegant pastel suit sits Louis Douglas. He seems to be dreaming.

Would a Parisienne have entered the room any differently than Josephine, with her cherry-colored dress, small hat pulled low on her forehead and blue, ermine-trimmed coat? I doubt it. Only later, when she becomes more relaxed, animated, *herself*, will the distinction be clear. For now, except for the dazzling luster of her hair, her manner seems all too familiar. "Paris is marvelous," she gushes. "And your dressmakers are divine!"

It was true. And I had met them all: Vionnet, Schiaparelli and of course Monsieur Poiret. In fact, he and I had already locked horns. He said blue, I said pink. His fitters listened round-eyed to our quarreling. I thought they would swallow their pins. The finished dress was *pink* and the model became known as the *robe Joséphine*. I was learning the importance of names—having them, making them—but at the same time I sensed the dangers. Recognition was followed by oblivion, a yawning maw whose victims disappeared without a trace.

On November 1 we learned that to commemorate Armistice Day there would be a special matinee starring the *Revue Nègre*. Rolf and Douglas had continued adding new material—a musical crap game, a boisterous takeoff on a black wedding, and for the gala performance a well-known illusionist, Pierre Pradier. "Won't you imitate me, Pierre?" I begged. "Josephine, you're inimitable," he replied with a smile.

We would soon be leaving Paris for Berlin. Leaving Paris . . . I can't describe what a wrench that was for me. Here, for the first time, I had truly felt alive. I had plotted to leave St. Louis, I had longed to leave New York; I yearned to remain in Paris. I loved everything about the city. It moved me as profoundly as a man moves a woman. Why must I take trains and boats that would carry me far from the friendly faces, the misty Seine, the colorful quays, hilly Montmartre, the Eiffel Tower, which seemed constantly ready to kick up a leg?

As I sat despondently in my dressing room, there was a knock on the door. The man who entered spoke dreadful English, but his face was kind. "I was told there was a girl at the Champs-Élysées who was setting the stage on fire. I see that it's true. I'm Paul Derval, director of the Folies-Bergère, Miss Baker. I'd like you to be in my next show."

I couldn't wait to kiss my good-luck penny.

CHAPTER 5

———··✦◦✦··———

From Berlin to the
Folies-Bergère

KIKI WAS A SNAKE I FOUND on the quays. I had heard that "snake" was all the rage, and not realizing that this meant snakeskin, had bought the real thing. He was adorable, just long enough to knot himself around my neck like a collar. He loved to lie there warm and snug and looked just right with my favorite black velvet dress. After the show I was always invited out dancing. I'll never forget my escort's face the first time I took Kiki along, especially since we were doing the Charleston at the time. Only the bravest admirers asked me out twice, which was as good a way as any to choose among them.

Suitors are a special race. Take my little architecture student, for example. He spent night after night in the audience with a single thought in mind: to be seen with me in public. I finally accepted his invitation. But when he pulled out a thousand-franc note, I snatched it away and stuffed it into my handbag. He looked at me with utter dismay: it was his entire month's allowance. "If you want to take out an actress, you have to pay for it," I snapped. That may sound cruel, but I was remembering the colored section of St. Louis and how hard it was to earn money there.

Anyway, my lesson didn't seem to take. The young man camped outside my door until I finally took pity on him. Perhaps success had gone to my head! I invited him up to my room, where I received him reclining on my bed—a remarkable structure which I had mounted on planks and draped with flowing red, white and blue cretonne in an attempt to duplicate Napoleon's royal couch. The delighted student called me his *chou*. Shoe? I reached for my dictionary. "*Chou*—cabbage." A vegetable? I ordered the young man to his knees and planted him by my bedside. Then I left for the theater. Unkind? Perhaps. But looking back on it now, I wonder if the ghost of an African ancestor humiliated by an arrogant plantation owner hadn't been lurking someplace under my well-oiled scalp.

I *had* to succeed. I would never stop trying, never. A violinist had his violin, a painter his palette. All I had was myself. *I* was the instrument that I must care for, just as Sidney fussed over his clarinet. That's why I spent thirty minutes every morning rubbing my body with half a lemon to lighten my skin and just as long preparing a mixture for my hair. I couldn't afford to take chances.

Berlin.

I found it dazzling. The city had a jewel-like sparkle, especially at night, that didn't exist in Paris. The vast cafés reminded me of ocean liners powered by the rhythms of their orchestras. There was music everywhere. Word of our success at the Champs-Élysées had preceded us and we were greeted with great excitement. There were rumors that the show was indecent, an impression I may have strengthened when a reporter asked me to describe my ideal world. One where we can all go naked, as in paradise, I replied. I was quick to add that few of us can *afford* to show our bodies.

I was immediately caught up in a whirlwind of flowers, declarations of love, new acquaintances. One night I was told that the most famous director in Germany was in the audience. I was used to such descriptions by now. Everyone I met seemed to be "the greatest," "the most eminent," "the finest." Perhaps this was sometimes the case, but in my ignorance how was I to know? Fame is a ladder with many rungs and there is one for each of us. Back in St. Louis, everyone knew Mrs. Nichols's cat because one of its ears had been ripped off by a dog! When I politely

murmured, "Everyone says you're the most famous painter [writer/jour-
nalist; the most beautiful woman] in Berlin," my listener's face would
glisten like a flower after the rain. But I quickly realized that the description "famous director" was more than idle chatter. The intensity of his
gaze was like banked fire: he glowed with an inner light. It appeared that
Max Reinhardt was immensely creative, interested in all forms of theater
and completely unconventional. He had staged superb tragedy in a circus
and believed that theater was for everyone. Before I could begin my
"Everyone says you're . . ." he informed me, through an interpreter, that
I had tremendous presence and that the only thing that really interested
him on the stage was an actor's personality. The finest scenery and lighting were mere window dressing for the performer who gave a show its flesh
and blood. That was why he liked the *Revue Nègre* and admired my work.
I seemed oblivious to rules. . . . He appeared to sense my feelings and what
I was trying to do. No one had ever spoken to me about the theater that
way before. "I'd like you to stay here and work with me at the Deutsche
Theater," he announced. "With a few years' study, you could become a
fine comedienne." My eyes filled with tears. "I can't," I stammered. "I've
signed a contract to perform in the Folies-Bergère." Raised eyebrows all
around. "Never mind," the translator said soothingly. "Herr Reinhardt
hopes that another time you'll be free."

Free.
Birds are free. They can fly where they like. If only I could do the same.
Mrs. Caroline had learned about my contract with the Folies and she was
furious. First because I hadn't consulted her, second because she feared
they would turn me into a feathered mannequin, preventing me from ever
"amounting to anything," and finally because it meant the end of the
Revue Nègre.

I felt like kicking everyone in sight. Why couldn't people leave me
alone? If I stayed in Berlin it would be to study with Herr Reinhardt. But
I didn't have much time to think about the future. My days were filled
with parties, receptions, journalists who said I "personified Expression-
ism," whatever *that* meant, faces and more faces, among them a friend
of Monsieur Derval's. "I look forward to seeing you in the Folies," he told
me. "Don't count on it." "What do you mean?" "I may have changed
my mind." "They'll *sue!*" one of the dancers gasped. I shrugged. Law-

suits, contracts—the less I knew about that kind of red tape the better. In St. Louis, we slapped hands to seal a bargain! Anyway, who could make a decision when there was dancing every night and all that wonderful German beer to drink?

A few days later, a Monsieur Lorett visited me in my dressing room. It appeared that Monsieur Derval had sent him. He had three expressions —hurt, angry and charming—which he used alternately. I couldn't *do* this, he insisted. I'd signed a contract and you didn't go back on your word. Poor Monsieur Derval had already hired a number of people because of me. Didn't I realize what the Folies *was?* It took three months to rehearse a show, which involved five hundred people and utilized twelve hundred costumes created by famous designers. They counted on me to be there to inspire the dressmakers and because of me they had built the show around tunes by Spencer Williams and Irving Berlin. . . .

It didn't take long to make up my mind. Herr Reinhardt hadn't mentioned Irving Berlin, whom I adored. Besides, twelve hundred costumes . . . Just as I was about to say yes, I decided to test my worth, since *I* was now introduced in public as the "famous" Josephine. "If you want me to leave Berlin, it will cost you an extra four hundred francs a show." Silence. Monsieur Lorett scurried away—for good, I presumed—but the next day he was back. "Since Monsieur Derval has already invested heavily in the show because of you, he is forced to accept. Please return to Paris at once."

A show, like a love affair, ends in sorrow. During our tearful farewells, we all swore to keep in touch. Sidney was leaving for Moscow with two musician friends. As he kissed me goodbye he murmured, "When I hit my high notes I'll think of you, little bird." "I'll never dance like I did to your clarinet," I replied. "It lifted me right off the ground."

The Folies-Bergère. Monsieur Lorett was right; it *was* incredible. I had never seen such a beehive of activity. A streak of light in the corridor signaled a seamstress dashing by with a spangled dress; hairdressers hurried along carrying fabulous wigs. . . .

The company performed in a handsome new theater built on the site of a former winter garden, which had had a fountain, a canopy as a sky and chandeliers to provide the sunlight. There was even an underground river, they said. "I don't believe it, Monsieur Derval." "It's true, Josephine. And in olden days a monk lived by the riverside. In fact, when the theater's foundations were being laid, I discovered a little stone staircase and a bench by the water's edge where the monk had meditated." I found this particularly moving, since before each performance I liked to kneel on my dressing room floor and bow my head. I believe in the importance of prayer. It's the best way we have to draw strength from heaven. One day as I was praying, someone opened the door. Since I was busy talking to the Lord, I didn't look up. The intruder, who turned out to be the stage manager, lost no time in telling the entire cast that I had been worshipping stark naked. Why not? That was the way God had made me.

I reacted quite differently, however, the day I saw the round eye of a camera peeking from my closet. A photographer! I furiously ripped open the curtains and would have throttled the intruder if he hadn't slipped from my grasp.

The atmosphere backstage was wonderfully alive and busy, very different from New York and the Champs-Élysées. The army of chorus girls was English and they lived like schoolgirls, with an Anglican clergyman who settled their disputes. Unlike American dancers, who had identical long necks, similar proportions and the same weights and heights, as if they were factory made, the English girls were individuals. Monsieur Derval liked variety. "I offer something for every taste," he boasted. The show girls, who paraded around the stage in a series of dazzling costumes, one more revealing than the next, also came in various shapes and sizes, including a voluptuous redhead and a slinky brunette. The redhead showed me a picture of her baby one night. It was for him that she worked.

I returned to my dressing room. There wasn't a single photograph stuck in my mirror. A whimper. I had almost forgotten the two-month-old puppy I had bought the day before. He was plump, white and silky. I buried my face in his warm little body.

Three more days until opening night. We were rehearsing around the clock. Monsieur Louis Lemarchand, who had written the show, had an ingenious last-minute idea for getting me onto the stage. An enormous flowered ball would be lowered slowly from the rafters and settle among the musicians. As if obeying the music, its lid would gradually open, revealing me crouched in the mirrored interior. As the audience gasped with surprise, I would straighten up and begin to dance, half nude.

. . . Then the lid would close and the ball would return to the ceiling. It would be a charming number and Monsieur Derval assured me that even if I couldn't hear the applause from within my ball, it was sure to be deafening.

Rehearsal time. I climbed up the little iron stairway to the rafters and the smiling stagehands helped me squeeze into the ball. After the lid had been carefully closed, I felt myself descending toward the stage. What a delightful idea! I landed with a painful bump and when the lid swung open I heard Monsieur Derval shouting above the music: "Gently! Put her down gently!" As the tempo quickened, the brass section took up the beat, I began dancing on my mirror, not stopping to admire my reflection, sure the effect was marvelous. The cast and the stage crew applauded loudly. When the music had stopped, I crouched back inside the ball and the lid closed over my head. I felt myself rising. The number was sure to succeed. If only they could see me in St. Louis!

Suddenly my heart skipped a beat. Something was wrong. The ball had begun to rock violently. Although the ropes that controlled one of its sides continued moving upward, the other ropes hung slack. As the ball tipped further and further off center, the lid began to slide open. How was I going to keep from falling out? Huddled on the tilting mirror, which was slippery as ice, I hung forty-five feet above the orchestra. The musicians played on obliviously. Too frightened to shout, all I could do was pray.

Suddenly I heard Monsieur Derval cry: "Stop! For God's sake stop!" (That was *his* way of praying.) As the music died away, the dancers raised their heads and everyone began screaming at once. The stagehands in the rafters, who hadn't noticed anything amiss, looked down in horror as the dangling ball gave a final sickening lurch and came to a stop. Someone suggested calling the fire department, but by the time they arrived with their ladder it might be too late. A stagehand offered to lower himself on a rope, gather me up and carry me to safety. Too dangerous.

Fortunately the winch that controlled the lid still worked. "Josephine," called Monsieur Derval from fifteen feet above my head. "Do you think you can climb onto the lid? You'll have to move very slowly and carefully." He enunciated each word as if I were deaf. I said I would try. One false move and the delicately balanced ball might turn completely over. . . . I seized the edge of the lid with one hand, then the other. If only there were something to brace myself against! This was very different from those happy days climbing up coal cars in St. Louis. "I made it," I finally shouted. Monsieur Derval, flat on his stomach in the rafters, sighed with relief. I stood trembling on the lid. He signaled the stagehands to begin turning the winch. "Slowly, very slowly," he commanded. In the silence, the click of the winch could be heard with each revolution. The ascension was agonizingly slow: twelve feet, nine feet . . . The winch, which had been designed to control the lid, was carrying my entire weight. Six feet, three feet, two feet . . . I stretched out my arms to Monsieur Derval, who was half hanging in space, held at the ankles by stagehands. He hauled me onto the platform. Drenched with sweat, we fell into each other's arms. It was like the scene in a Western when the hero rescues the leading lady from the Indian torture pole. My knees were shaking so badly that I could hardly get down the stairs. In the hall, the applause was ear-splitting. Could we do it again on opening night? Certainly not! Embraces, tears. "Call a doctor, quick," shouted the director. "Don't bother. I'm fine." "It's not for you, Josephine. Two of the dancers just fainted."

I knew how they felt.

The ball was a great success. The critics found it "ravishing." But the thing that caused the most comment opening night and for fifty years to come was my banana waistband.

Sixteen bananas pointing comically toward the ceiling were attached to a belt slung low around my hips to accentuate my forward and backward movements.

"Do they like the show, Monsieur Derval?" "They *love* it. I knew it would be a hit because of its title: *La Folie du Jour.* All my shows have thirteen-letter titles. The one time I tried fifteen letters, I ended up with a flop." "Isn't it hard to come up with the right number of letters?" "No, Josephine, I have one hundred and fifty thirteen-letter titles registered with the Authors Guild. So I hope we'll be working together for years to come."

Monsieur Derval couldn't do enough for his star. He told me to buy anything I pleased and charge it to him. I spent hours at the dressmaker's and hairdresser's. I was manicured, pedicured, pampered, perfumed. "Perfect," I murmured, inspecting myself in the mirror. What a wonderful revenge for an ugly duckling!

I now lived in two large rooms in a boardinghouse near the elegant Parc

Monceau. One of the other boarders was a beautiful girl with long chestnut-colored hair. On her birthday, a handsome fair-haired man came to dine at her table, which was close to mine. They were no sooner seated than he handed her a tiny jewel box. I heard her gasp when she opened it. In a flash she had slipped the sparkling ring on her finger. "Let's eat; I'm starving," she cried. I was sure that under the circumstances I would have spent the evening gazing into the eyes of the elegant suitor. Everything about him intrigued me: the way he moved, the way he said goodbye, tenderly kissing her palm, the way he flung his fur-lined cloak around his shoulders. . . . I even dreamed about him that night.

He came to visit her every day, nodding to me politely when we passed in the hall. I learned that he was the owner of an automobile company. Women were mad about cars in those days; we all wanted to drive, including me. I was taking lessons every afternoon and my teacher assured me that I would receive my permit on my twentieth birthday. I couldn't wait until June.

As time went on, something began to bother me. I had noticed that my pretty neighbor had other visitors besides "Marcel." They couldn't all be brothers and cousins! What a pity. I loved to see well-matched couples.

One evening as I prepared to leave for the theater there was a torrential downpour. I was looking in vain for a taxi, when Marcel emerged from my building and offered me a lift. His car stood at the door. Although it was very handsome, it didn't compare with its owner. During the short ride to the Folies, I was so overcome with shyness that I could barely speak. Marcel must have thought I was an ignorant savage. As we said goodbye at the theater door I wanted to kick myself.

The cast threw a party for my twentieth birthday, deluging me with perfume, scarves, bracelets and another puppy. Poor Monsieur Derval. I could see he was worried about my dressing room rug! I smiled and sang and thanked my friends warmly, but my heart was aching. I couldn't help remembering a handsome couple bending over a jewel case.

Four days after my birthday, I received my license. Perhaps *that* would cheer me up. One beautiful June morning I asked Monsieur Derval if I could drive to Deauville. Of course, he replied. It was good for a rising star to be seen in fashionable places. I rented a little Renault convertible two-seater just for me. I wanted to be alone, to speed down the road, free or seemingly so, dizzy with motion. . . .

About twenty-five miles outside Paris, another car caught my eye. It followed me, passed me, slowed down to let me by, overtook me again. How childish! Peering through my windshield, I recognized . . . Marcel! He was alone too. I overtook him and we laughingly started to race. I didn't do badly for a beginner and we were in Deauville before I knew it. I drew up to the Hotel Normandy with a flourish, soaking with perspiration. Marcel stood waiting, relaxed and smiling. Would I care for a cup of tea?

Yes, but . . . The tearoom had a dance floor. And once I was in Marcel's arms I knew he could ask me for anything. He wanted everything.

When we returned to Paris, Marcel resumed his hectic life. Neither of us went back to the Parc Monceau. Instead he set me up on the Champs-Élysées in an apartment I called my "marble palace." I continued to haunt the shops and dressmakers, hounded by photographers, but in spite of the attention I received, couldn't wait to return to my palace at night and rejoin my beloved. I was living a new life, that of a woman waiting for her man. . . . Marcel was seldom free. He had many professional obligations and there was no question of my going with him to business functions. How I hated our separations! When he finally did arrive at my palace door he always brought a surprise: white mice with tiny pink noses, parrots who ate the curtains, and finally a miniature monkey who loved to snuggle against my shoulder. Occasionally after the show Marcel took me to a private dining room or a country inn for a midnight dinner. We were forced to hide our love. There were many men who were more than willing to pursue me in broad daylight, but they bored me so! I preferred to return to my little zoo and my pure-hearted animals.

Yet I wasn't totally happy.

One day I asked, "Marcel, why don't we get married?" Stony silence. I knew I shouldn't insist, but I couldn't help repeating my question, this time adding, "I'd like to have a baby." Still no reply. Then finally a brusque: "I don't want to get married." He didn't mean to be cruel; he was simply making a statement he assumed I would understand. "Is it because I'm a dancer or because I'm black?" I snapped. "Both," he calmly replied. Then he tried gently to explain that he had to consider his family, his position, the circles he moved in. . . . "You can't change the world, Josephine." *"Yes you can and I intend to do so,"* I shouted. "Things *have* to change. There's been enough of your kind of class and racial hatred."

"But, Josephine, *you're* the one who hates *me*. I adore you." "Not enough to have a child with me." I tried to choke back the tears.

The next time Marcel visited the marble palace, he found nothing but parrots, white mice and a monkey.

Theater people are lucky. Our daily encounter with the public allows us to avoid people otherwise. My experience with Marcel made me throw myself into my work harder than ever. I'd show him; I'd show *everyone!*

I was earning a great deal of money but I wanted to earn even more. It wasn't because of the money itself—which ran through my fingers like water—but because of the importance the *world* placed on wealth ("You can't change the world"). All right, then. I would fight with the enemy's weapons. After the show at the Folies, I began appearing at various cabarets, where I danced the Charleston until the wee hours. I quickly became the toast of café society, that group of Parisians whose money flowed like champagne, whose whims made or destroyed reputations.

At dawn I would head home through a murky Paris preparing for work —the Paris of the poor. Collapsing into bed, I would snuggle against my puppies and sleep until the maid awakened me at four. There was always something to do. If a reporter was waiting, I would slip into a slinky negligee. Or it might be time to dress for a cocktail party, benefit or reception, where I would be introduced to a duchess, two or three scholars, a fashionable author or an artist, who would invariably ask me to pose. For these occasions I would put on my latest Poiret or Vionnet creation and stuff my head with as many French words as possible. I was drawn, painted, sketched, caricatured, photographed, filmed. My voice was even recorded. "Not for just an hour, not for just a day, not for just a year, but always." Always . . . *toujours*. In French it rhymed with "love"—*amour* —but for me the word was meaningless. No, not quite. I still had myself in spite of all the faces that had turned away from me during my brief twenty years. But I no longer had time to spare for those who didn't interest me. Let them call me heartless and temperamental if they liked. I had decided to do as I pleased. When I was summoned to a social function to be shown off like a circus animal in fancy dress, I would glue myself to the buffet table instead of joining the expectant guests on the lawn, then quietly slip away.

About this time I adopted two cats, a male and a female. Everyone predicted they would massacre my puppies, but my animals never fight. Loving them equally and raising them together seems to make them happy. And when they're happy, so am I. Monsieur Derval didn't seem to share my pleasure. "You're giving me gray hairs, my young friend," he scolded. It was partly because of his rugs and partly because he couldn't get used to my "disappearances," as he called them. "Monsieur Derval, Josephine's not in her dressing room and it's time for the fifteen-minute call," the stage manager gasped one evening. After searching everywhere, they finally discovered me eating soup with the watchman and his wife; delicious steaming bowlfuls that smelled of the outdoors.

Another time it was: "Monsieur Derval, it's almost show time and Josephine's door is locked." This time the watchman hadn't seen me. Had I perhaps been taken ill in my dressing room? The stage manager rushed off to borrow the firemen's pass key. When they finally opened the door, there I sat, stark naked, calmly eating lobster. Why all the fuss? It didn't take long to put on *my* costume.

I'll never forget that face. How could I? The delicate features, the lively, thoughtful eyes, the glinting monocle, the sensitive, sardonic mouth. We met in a cabaret. "Josephine, I'd like to introduce Count Abatino." A successful administrative career in Rome; a distinguished Italian family. Why couldn't I fall in love with an *orphan?* A frequent visitor to Paris, the Count was known in café society circles as Pepito and his wit and elegance made him a popular member of the nightclub set. How could I have been so stupid as to have danced the tango with him, exposing myself to that ultimate physical test? We can dance it a thousand times, only to find during the thousand and first that we can no longer limit ourselves to dancing. The music has swept us away, two souls who can rejoin their bodies only by fleeing together and making love. . . .

Pepito returned to Rome, his career, his family, his friends. For me it was back to the Folies in spite of my heartbreak. Would I never find happiness? I poured all my misery into my performance on the mirror and tried to exhaust my passion through my banana dance. "You're even better than on opening night," observed Monsieur Derval. "It's good for an artist to suffer."

As I dejectedly entered my bedroom at dawn, an envelope on the

dresser caught my eye. It was postmarked Rome. A letter from Pepito!
Since it was written in French, I couldn't decipher most of it, but I
managed to grasp the important part. He was thinking of me. Life was
worth living again. There was someone to whom I mattered. I began
hurrying home from my cabaret shows to open his daily letters, consulting
my dictionary when necessary. Pepito's messages became the high point
of my existence. My sudden happiness puzzled my friends, who believed
that Count Abatino had discarded me. Why was I so serene? They
searched for a mysterious Prince Charming, never guessing that the
source of my joy was a little white square of paper on my dresser.

Late one night I arrived home to find my dresser top bare. Had the
envelope slipped to the ground? As I bent down to look for it, my heart
pounding, I suddenly heard a voice:

"I wanted to tell you in person."

Pepito! He stood there tall and slim, a teasing look in his eye. But when
he spoke, his voice was full of tenderness: "I can't live without you,
Josephine."

I tried to reason with him. There was Rome, his family, his career.
. . . "No, Josephine, there's only Paris and you." It was thus that Pepito
entered my life for good. "But what will become of you, darling?" "You're
looking at Josephine Baker's new manager."

We were inseparable. Mademoiselle Baker and the Count Abatino
became a familiar pair at receptions, shows, parties, midnight suppers and
cabarets. Pepito took charge of my life. At last I had someone to help me
fight my battles. One day he remarked that instead of spending my
evenings in other people's cabarets, I should open one of my own. He was
right as usual! Shortly before Christmas we launched Chez Joséphine near
Pigalle. The time was ripe. Paris was in a giddy mood, eager for pleasure.
I supplied the amusement it craved, patting my gentlemen customers'
heads and pulling their beards, flattering the women and teaching them
the Charleston. Pepito introduced me to the international set. . . . But
the two of us couldn't wait for dawn, when we could be alone.

On Christmas Day I disguised myself as Santa Claus. An enormous
glittering tree had been set up at the Folies for the children of the Paris
police force. I handed out toys and goodies, a dark-faced Santa as merry
as the children. This was what money was for: to bring happiness. Sud-

denly I noticed a group of expensively dressed young people, wearing patent leather shoes, mingling with the crowd. Friends of the management had brought their children, who already had more toys than they could play with, to see "Josephine as Santa Claus." I was furious. Next time I would buy the toys and distribute them myself to the sick and needy.

CHAPTER 6

On Tour with Pepito

PEPITO HAD EXTRAORDINARY HANDS, finely molded yet immensely strong. To me they symbolized the way his outward charm concealed a will of iron.

One night another pair of hands caught my eye. If only I could have captured the pictures they traced as they fluttered through the air. "It's Jean Cocteau," Pepito whispered. I was fascinated by Cocteau's voice, which ranged from tinkling to velvet smooth, but he spoke so quickly that most of what he said escaped me. The conversation quickly turned to my archrival, Barbette. Cocteau was mad about her. At the end of her highly successful act at the Casino de Paris, she would leap from her trapeze, walk gracefully to center stage, snatch off her wig and reveal . . . that she was a man! "The two of you are total opposites," Cocteau teased. "Barbette hides everything and you show all you've got."

Unlike some of the more intellectual cabarets, Chez Joséphine was completely devoted to fun. I wanted my customers to shed their cares like dogs shaking off fleas. Still, our midnight suppers were among the most expensive in Paris. Forty-five francs for a dozen oysters and almost as much for a dab of caviar. We also offered a specialty called "sybarite soup," which kept our customers going until dawn. "If they want to enjoy the black Venus, they'll have to pay for it," Pepito insisted.

Colette was among our visitors. I would have called her the white Negress had I dared, because of her kinky hair and natural grace. Of all the women I knew, she was the only one who seemed completely open, deeply attuned to animals and growing things, a potential soul mate. She offered to send me a copy of her book about backstage life at the Folies. Did I know a dancer who spent her free time knitting baby clothes? "Of course," I replied. "Is she a friend of yours?" Colette burst out laughing. The girl *she* knew had danced there fifteen years ago. Her baby would be full grown now. Didn't I realize that there was *always* a girl knitting baby clothes backstage at the Folies?

One afternoon Pepito took me to Versailles. As we walked through the gardens I remarked that I would like to play someone like Marie Antoinette one day, a person who had really existed. I was tired of my bananas and so was the press. Even though our latest show had a thirteen-letter title—*Un Vent de Folie (A Gust of Madness)*—one critic had complained that it would take more than a gust, it would take a *cyclone* to make Mademoiselle Baker stop wiggling in the same old way. I was ready for a change and Pepito knew it.

Not that I wasn't successful. My face and rump were famous! I could honestly say that I'd been blessed with an "intelligent" derrière. Most people's were only good to sit on! Yes, I was giving my all on stage, but was I paying my dues in the real world, an obligation we must all assume someday? What about my debt as a human being? I would be forced to face up to these questions sooner than I thought.

May 21, 1927. Since the night before, the eyes of the entire world had been glued to a solitary voyager, a man who had become one with a giant bird named *The Spirit of St. Louis*. Think of it: my own home town. He intended to cross the Atlantic with a single sweep of his wings. The idea seemed incredible. I remembered my uneasiness on the *Berengaria* as I gazed across the seemingly infinite waters day after day. He would be forced to conquer fear, distance and perhaps bad weather, totally alone. . . . New York lay behind him and Paris was waiting. I was amazed to see people in the Folies audience that night. Could I have chosen, I would have been in the street, searching the sky. Suddenly a stagehand rushed into my dressing room. "He's made it. He's here!" Beside myself with excitement, I dashed onto the stage, stopped the orchestra and announced in my best French: "Ladies and gentlemen. Good news. Charles Lind-bergh has arrived!" The audience rose to its feet as one, clapping and shouting. And *I* burst into tears. Here I was, a black American, telling an assemblage of whites what one of their kind had accomplished. The crossing had taken only thirty-three hours and fifty minutes, as if St. Louis were right next door, as if the ocean had become a huge puddle, as if France and America were neighbors, sisters. . . . I saw that plane as a bird of peace, uniting people everywhere. Perhaps there was hope after all! I wanted to throw my arms around Mr. Lindbergh. He was a real hero!

What was a dancer draped in bananas beside him?

I've always loved the cinema, so I was thrilled when a compatriot, Rex Ingram, decided to film our Folies show. But playing in *La Revue des Revues* turned out to be less fun than I'd anticipated. It involved doing exactly what I'd done for the past two years: getting into an egg decorated with marabou feathers, stepping out again, dancing with my bananas. . . . One night soon after the film had been completed, Pepito rushed into my dressing room with exciting news. A well-known French novelist, Maurice Dekobra, had just completed a film script specially for me. He called it *La Sirène des Tropiques* and everyone said that I would love my role.

I played the part of a West Indian girl named Papitou, who longed to come to Paris and was astonished when she couldn't pay her boat fare with beads. A real featherbrain. A "native village" hastily constructed in the studio served as our set. Its freshly built straw huts absolutely glistened. "We could use some manure around here," I remarked to the designer. Film-making involves hours of waiting and I passed the time watching the adjoining set. They were filming a story about the Revolution. The main prop, a guillotine, made my blood run cold. "You're on, Josephine," the director shouted. "It's time for your belly dance." Because naturally Papi-tou danced exactly like Mademoiselle Baker of the Folies. "That's one of the reasons people will come to see the film," Pepito gently explained.

The script called for me to stow away on a steamship. Now came my big moment. Down I tumbled into a coal bin, emerging black with dust. "Roll your eyes, Josephine," the director cried. Next I was pushed into a hold full of flour, which turned me dead white. This apparently was riotously funny.

The finished film brought tears to my eyes. Was that ugly, silly person me? What a total waste of time! "At least it paid well," remarked Pepito tartly. And I received a note from a delighted Monsieur Dekobra addressed to "my tropical fairy and unforgettable siren, in memory of the Parisian jungle."

Jungle was right! "Someday we'll move to the country," Pepito promised, but in the meantime offers were pouring in: Vienna wanted me for two performances at a thousand dollars each; London was willing to book me for whatever price I asked. Pepito began organizing a European tour.

One evening word arrived that a couple named Dalliez planned to celebrate their wedding anniversary at our cabaret. I decided to surprise them with a cake. They turned out to be a charming pair who had seen my show several times and were devoted fans of mine. Before I knew it, I was telling them about my experiences moving from hotel to hotel. Only the other day the management with loud apologies had announced that we would have to give up our suite; there had been a booking error. It was clear to me, however, that the *real* reason they wanted us to leave was that the hotel was crowded with Americans. I had seen their faces when I walked through the lobby. A colored girl? You mean they let *those* people in here now? The Dalliezes were horrified. I reassured them that I felt very much at home in France and realized that the hotel in question was really a tiny offshoot of America. "Why don't you come and stay with us awhile?" Madame Dalliez suggested. "Our house is much too big for us. It's not the country but it's close! Bring Monsieur Pepito with you." We downed a few more glasses in honor of the years of married bliss that lay ahead and at dawn our guests got up to leave. "Is it a promise, Josephine? You'll come?" "It's a promise." They stumbled off into the morning light.

That noon, after his night on the town, Maurice Dalliez, a shoe factory manager, was sipping a cup of strong coffee when the doorbell rang. His wife was still asleep. The maid rushed into the dining room, eyes popping. "It's Josephine, monsieur." And so it was, along with four suitcases, four dogs, a piglet named Albert, my goat Toutoute—the cabaret's mascot— my goldfish and Pepito. "I took you at your word, Monsieur Dalliez." He was stunned but delighted. "Wake up, Marguerite. Josephine's here!" Madame Dalliez came sleepily into the room and we all burst out laughing. "We're leaving in a few days to go on tour," Pepito reassured our hosts. It was true. We wouldn't be inconveniencing them for long. I fell in love with their house on sight. Surrounded by trees and gardens, it looked and felt like a real home. With a thankful sigh, I slipped between the cool sheets in my airy bedroom and fell fast asleep.

The Dalliezes couldn't get over the fact that Josephine Baker was living under their roof. Neither could I; it was the first time I had been part of such a happy family. I tried to enjoy it while I could, because I would soon be departing to dance in all the capitals of Europe. "You were born to dance," Marguerite insisted. She was right. But was that *all* I was good for? I wanted to die dancing, but not on the music hall stage. It was such an artificial life. I would continue performing for a few more years, then I would retire and get married. I wanted a houseful of children and animals. . . . "Pepito loves you very much. I'm sure he'll marry you," Marguerite assured me. I didn't tell her that he'd already proposed. How strange it was; up until now *I* had been the one who pleaded with my lovers to marry me. This time it was just the opposite; I was the one who hung back. I didn't try to analyze my reasons. I loved Pepito. I depended on him. He dealt with all my problems. He handled all my baffling, tedious paper work. He had abandoned everything for me. I was his entire life. His jealousy was enough to prove he loved me. Yet deep down inside me there was something that refused to say "I do."

For some time now, Pepito had been asking me about the old Negro spirituals. I sang him all those I knew. Early one morning when no one was left at Chez Joséphine but us and the Dalliezes, I decided to try a few blues numbers. . . . "I *knew* it," Pepito cried delightedly. "I was sure you had the makings of a blues singer!" Thanks to his encouragement, I screwed up my courage and began performing a few blues numbers nightly.

Soon afterward we left for Vienna.

Our Austrian engagement had been preceded by disastrous publicity. The capital was flooded with leaflets denouncing me as the "black devil." There was no way to bar me from Vienna, but it was made clear that I was the embodiment of moral decadence. A Jesuit priest at St. Paul's Church, near the Johann Strauss Theater, had devoted an entire sermon to the evils of the Charleston . . . and on the day of my arrival in the

Austrian capital, the bells of St. Paul sounded the alarm. Other churches joined in the protest. "They expect you to appear stark naked," Pepito reported. "They may be in for a surprise."

On opening night there were people distributing tracts in front of the theater. I could sense the electricity in the hall. When I walked onto the stage, there was a stunned silence. I was wearing a long gown buttoned to the neck. For a moment I stood motionless under the spotlight, then in a voice trembling with emotion and stage fright, I began to sing. I had chosen one of the blues songs that had moved Pepito—a poignant lullaby dating back to the not-so-distant time when America's black men cringed under the lash: "Pretty Little Baby." My performance made all the papers the following day. I was acclaimed by prudes and libertines alike. Now I could dance anything I wanted, any way I liked, expressing the joy and love which, despite what the priests might say, were surely recognized in paradise.

Partway through our tour, we stopped off for some needed rest at the Dalliezes', where Toutoute was growing fat and sleek from grazing in the garden. I had such stories to tell our friends: how after appearing before a censorship board in Budapest I had been forced to escape the crowd in a hay wagon; about the frightening incident at the Royal Orpheum when a man suddenly stood up in the audience waving a bomb. Fortunately it was filled with nothing more lethal than tear gas, and the spectators who had come to applaud "the scandalous Baker" escaped with a simple case of watery eyes. I shared their good fortune.

Then there was the performance at Prague's Lucerne Theater during which a hundred rabbits' feet rained onto the stage. Somehow the Czech public had got the idea that I possessed a treasured good-luck rabbit's foot which I had received from an old family friend in South Carolina. Thanks to their attention, I have had an ample store of rabbits' feet ever since, to reinforce the powers of my good-luck penny.

And who could forget that evening in Leipzig when three crocodiles, clicking their teeth, slithered into my dressing room? They had somehow escaped from their trainer.

Best of all, for me who worshipped kings and queens, were my appearances before royalty. I couldn't wait to tell the Dalliezes about the night the Swedish royal family attended one of my performances in Stockholm.

Better still, in Copenhagen I was summoned to the palace, where a delightful surprise awaited me. A group of pink-and-gold princesses and their little friends were seated in a circle on plump cushions. I was to dance for them. I'll never forget the shining faces of those royal children. Indeed, all children are kings.

My first appearance in Denmark took place in June 1928 at the Dagmar Theater. It didn't take long for me to understand why the little princesses had not been permitted to attend. The program included a group of Tiller girls, who raised and lowered their legs like mechanical dolls; a dreadful Viennese singer; a second-rate military band and some mediocre acrobats. That was the trouble with the tour. Although I was billed as the star, we had no control over whom the local impresario hired to round out the show. This enraged Pepito. "Next time we'll arrange the entire program ourselves," he insisted. "Mademoiselle Baker deserves the proper setting." In the meantime he concentrated on adapting my act to the city in question. Whereas in Vienna I had been demurely dressed, in Copenhagen I began my performance wearing my bananas. Then while the orchestra played a jazz number, I quickly changed into a green feathered loincloth for my ostrich routine. Another speedy change and I was back in shorts to do my shoeshine-boy act. I finished off the evening in a slinky gown, singing a love song—but never the same one twice. "This is your chance to try out new material for Paris," Pepito insisted. "You can't afford to get stale."

Everywhere I went I bought the local costume. Soon my trunks were bulging with embroidered vests and fancy caps. In Amsterdam I purchased a headdress and enormous wooden shoes. Pepito burst out laughing every time I wore my finery. "You're the most overdressed nude dancer I've ever seen," he teased. Somehow I felt that wearing a nation's costume brought me closer to its people.

From Scandinavia we proceeded to Rumania. The roses were in bloom and the streets were filled with girls carrying enormous basketfuls of petals for preserving. I was booked at the Scarabus in Bucharest, a huge outdoor theater. Every seat was taken, but this did not discourage an extra presence: rain. Since the Rumanian impresario had no intention of reimbursing his audience, the show continued, the spectators huddling stoically under umbrellas. I found an umbrella of my own backstage and danced beneath it as best I could while the orchestra, strings untuned by the rain, played discordantly on and my bananas, swollen with moisture, plopped to the ground like rotten fruit. By the end of the act I felt completely nude. "Charming," muttered Pepito as he carefully gathered up the soggy fruit.

How could I ever forget my second engagement in Budapest? During our travels Pepito had come up with the ingenious idea of establishing a chain of Chez Joséphine cabarets in the cities where I performed. The Budapest club was extremely successful—a full house nightly. Every evening the same young man appeared at the same table. Night after night he sat alone and unsmiling behind his champagne bucket, staring at the show—which meant me. He never said a word. When my engagement at the Royal Orpheum was drawing to a close, I decided to have a farewell party at the cabaret. My Hungarian friends arrived in droves and we drank and danced gaily. As dawn approached and the crowd thinned out, I noticed the mysterious young man. There he sat at his usual table. After the last guests had departed, he rose to his feet. Because I was leaving Budapest the next day and we had never spoken, I followed him into the hall to say goodbye. As I searched for the proper words, he gazed at me somberly. Then he reached into his pocket—for a cigarette, I assumed— pulled out a revolver, pressed it to his temple and pulled the trigger.

It was horrible.

There he lay, dead at my feet.

I could guess what would happen next from the look in Pepito's eyes. HE COULDN'T LIVE WITHOUT THE BLACK VENUS . . . DEAD FOR THE LOVE OF JOSEPHINE . . . SHE LEAVES, HE DIES, the headlines screamed. Pepito's suspicions were the hardest part to bear. Wild with jealousy, he suspected the worst. There had surely been secret meetings. . . .

The next few days were a nightmare. All I could see were the eyes of the desperate youth. How could I have anticipated his action? What had caused it? Why had he dragged me down with him? The gossip columns sickened me with their smut; Pepito's accusations hurt me deeply. He and I finally had a violent quarrel. I had never betrayed him; how dare he question me? How could he hold me responsible for the behavior of a sick man? Pepito collapsed in tears, begging my forgiveness, kissing me, babbling that he loved me too much. . . . It was humiliating and absurd.

The day of our departure, I felt the staring eyes and heard the whispers as I walked down the hotel corridor. I gazed straight ahead, teeth clenched, heart aching. No one ever knew how long I was haunted by the look in that young man's eyes. Not even Pepito.

The first rule of the stage is that the show must go on.

I had just learned this lesson and I would never forget it. The day I missed a performance would be the day I was put in my grave.

Pepito and I continued hopping around the map like fleas. What an exciting way to learn history and geography! I couldn't wait to get to Spain, where we were booked for several months, and the country turned out to be everything I'd dreamed of. We were no sooner over the border than my pulse quickened. The glowing coal-black eyes, the music drifting from the shadows, the mysterious, scented churches, filled me with excitement. Spain was unique: passionate yet pure.

During my engagement in Madrid, I met the famous Gypsy dancer Macarona in one of those dance halls where Gypsies seem to pass their days and nights dancing the way other people breathe. She had extraordinary presence. In spite of her enormous girth, when she began to dance her hulking body was transformed into thunder, violence, flame. All that remained were her arms, her legs, her feet striking the ground with an imperious precision, tapping out a compellingly vigorous, sometimes tender message. I never grew tired of watching her. Macarona's dancing fascinated me; it was so totally different from mine. How had she learned to codify the language of the heart? All dancing is magnificent when it's pure. I bought myself some ankle-strap shoes and tried to execute a zapateado, much to Macarona's glee. I knew I looked like a clumsy monkey beside her. On the day of our departure, she embraced me with special warmth. "What did she say, Pepito? Translate it for me." "She's sure you have Gypsy blood."

Wherever we went, Pepito was presented as my husband. This both pleased him and simplified matters for me. My "husband" was a superb manager; he taught me how to present my calling card to embassies; how to establish good relations with the press. "It's important to get as much publicity as possible," he explained. "Remember, you're the black Venus who drives men mad."

I was made particularly conscious of my powers to inflame one day in Huesca, when the audience began flinging shoes at my feet. They obviously wanted to drive me off the stage, but were seated too far away to give me a boot in the rear. The manager and Pepito burst out laughing at my distress. Didn't I realize that I had been given a toreador's welcome? I was a sensation! I gratefully gathered up the footwear, hats and even a pair of suspenders. The Spaniards certainly had strange ways of showing their enthusiasm. . . . Another memorable incident occurred in Seville. In spite of the hot weather, my blood ran cold when I saw a group of Ku Klux Klanners suddenly march by. "Don't be silly, Josephine. They're penitents observing Holy Week." We rented two folding chairs and settled back to watch them pass. It was an imposing sight, but I couldn't keep from shivering.

One beautiful spring day in 1929 we set sail for South America on the *Comte Verde*. It was very different from the crossing I had made in the other direction almost four years earlier! This time I had a first-class cabin. Fourteen sun-filled idle days, highlighted by the traditional celebration at the equator. . . . A costume ball was planned for the occasion and I overheard two American women passengers mutter, "Naturally Josephine Baker will win first prize with her bananas!" Pepito disguised himself as a pirate, an eye patch replacing his monocle. As for me, I stuffed my cheeks with cotton, blackened my face with a candle, attached pillows fore and aft, slipped on the petticoat of the Gypsy costume I had bought in Spain, stuffed balloons I had wheedled from a child into my blouse, draped myself in shawls and stuck black paper on my front teeth. Barefoot, knock-kneed, fat and gap-toothed, I waddled into the first-class salon. Everyone burst out laughing. The two Americans, one decked out as Cleopatra, the other as a marquise, looked daggers. I knew what they were thinking: She'll do *anything* for attention. And the purser announced: "First prize for the ugliest costume goes to . . . Miss Josephine Baker."

At last the South American coastline came into view: Rio with its towering Christ, imposing bay and Sugar Loaf Mountain! But our journey wasn't over. Our destination was Argentina.

"Press hard with your thumb, Miss Baker." "But that's *ink!*"

"They want your fingerprint, Josephine." "We're off to a fine start. Back home, they only fingerprint criminals."

Pepito's agent in Buenos Aires met us in high spirits, a bundle of newspapers under his arm. "Everyone's talking about you," he cried delightedly. I knew enough Spanish to decipher the words beneath my photograph. "The scandalous Josephine" . . . "The provocative Black Venus."

My heart sank. In the hours that followed I realized that I was being used in Buenos Aires as a banner waved by some in the name of free expression and by others in defense of public morality. The rival political parties were quick to take sides. One faction supported my presence, while the other, headed by President Irigoyen, denounced me in the press. When I arrived at the theater on opening night, it took a police escort to get me through the milling crowd. Once I was safely inside my dressing room, my fear turned to anger. What did I care about Argentine politics? I didn't know the slightest thing about them. How dared they do this to me? "Miss Baker can't possibly perform under these conditions," Pepito informed the manager after a quick look into the hall. "But we're sold out. Still, you may be right. I'm not sure it's safe out there." My back rose. "I don't think you realize who you're talking to, gentlemen. That stage is *mine* and no one can keep me off it!"

Finally the curtain rose. Demonstrators had placed firecrackers under the seats and my appearance was met with a series of explosions. Shouts of "Long live Irigoyen" and "Down with Irigoyen" added to the confusion. The curtain descended. Scuffling in the hall. Up came the curtain again. The orchestra tried valiantly to drown out the hubbub with a series of tangos. Then, as firecrackers gave their last sputters and the police dragged the most violent demonstrators from the hall, I began dancing. When I finally returned to my dressing room, Pepito gathered me in his arms. He had been terrified. So had I.

Chile, Brazil . . . A kaleidoscope of sounds and colors, plains and mountains, riches and sickening poverty. All too soon our tour reached an end and it was time to reembark. We sailed from Rio on the *Lutetia.* Among the passengers was the renowned architect Le Corbusier, returning from a series of South American conferences. He was a modest, fun-loving man and we quickly struck up a friendship. He enjoyed hearing me hum my favorite songs as we walked the deck together and I was fascinated by his talk about cities of the future carpeted in green for the pedestrians, with traffic circulating on ramps overhead. "Never forget, Josephine, that cities are made for men, not the opposite," he cautioned.

This time there were two Josephine Bakers as we crossed the equator.

Le Corbusier appeared at the masquerade ball dressed completely in black with a waistband of feathers. He was wonderfully comical. "What a pity you're an architect, monsieur," I cried. "You'd make a sensational partner."

CHAPTER 7

——⟡——

The Casino de Paris
and Zouzou

I COULD LISTEN TO PEPITO by the hour.

He had a convincing explanation for my success in post-war Paris.

"You were just what people needed after the restrictions of war. They craved something wild, natural, extravagant—you!" I gazed through the bay window at the handsome oaks that gave our property, Beau Chêne, its name. Perhaps it had been foolish to buy this peaceful haven in the Paris suburb of Le Vésinet, but we adored our new home.

"You also represented freedom," Pepito continued. "The right to cut your hair, to walk around stark naked, to kick over the traces, including corsets!" I smiled. Here was Pepito telling me what I had done for Frenchwomen when I was much more concerned with all that he had done for me. He had taught me the mysteries of fish knives and forks, how to dress discreetly, how to speak and stand and act like a lady.

"It helped that the time was ripe," Pepito reflected. "People were beginning to collect *art nègre*, the public was discovering jazz. Five years earlier you'd have been booed off the stage. Five years later—*now*— you've got to come up with something new, Josephine, if you want to stay in the public eye." "I'm sure you're right, Pepito, but *what?*" "You mustn't change *too* much or you'll disappoint your audience. They count on your earthiness and abandon." "Does that mean more bananas?" "No, *cherie*, they've served their purpose. It's time for feathers and charm, sensitivity, songs, wit, feeling. It's time to use everything you've picked up in the twenty-five countries we've visited in the last two years. . . . I think you're ready to do it. Monsieur Varna agrees." *"What?"* "It's all arranged, Josephine. All we have to do is sign."

Henri Varna? The Casino de Paris? I couldn't believe my ears. The Casino was famous as the domain of la Miss—the legendary Mistinguett. Only last year she had triumphed there in *Paris-Miss,* Henri Varna's first show. And now it was *me* he wanted! "He's come up with a marvelous title for your show: *Paris qui Remue.*" "Bustling Paris" . . . Thirteen letters. How could we miss?

Things began moving at a breakneck pace. I could barely find a minute to play with my animals, stroll through my grounds, inspect my truck garden, talk to my hothouse flowers. . . . I was forced to leave my green oasis daily and hurry to the Rue de Clichy and Monsieur Varna's colorful, hectic world.

Henri Varna impressed me on sight. A slender, lively man with piercing yet gentle eyes, he was constantly on the move, experimenting, reworking, improvising: a creative power crackling with ideas.

"Josephine, here's what you'll be wearing." Monsieur Varna handed me a sketch of the costume for my first number, "L'Oiseau des Îles." It consisted mainly of two enormous white wings! How would I be able to move? "And here's a drawing of the set." I gazed at what appeared to be a virgin forest. Into it descended something reminiscent of our Reverend's description of Jacob's Ladder. "What in the world is that coming out of the sky?" "The ramp." "I'll never get down it wearing these wings." "She's right, Henri," a voice agreed dryly. It was Earl Leslie, Mistinguett's official dancer-choreographer, co-author of the show. I had heard rumors of bad feelings on the part of la Miss—it had taken all Monsieur Varna's tact and charm to persuade her to lend us "her" Earl—and Leslie showed signs of strain. I looked at him coldly. How little he knew me! Precisely because he had said I couldn't navigate the steps, I would! Once I was safely on the forest floor, I was pursued by a stageful of dancers. As I desperately tried to ward off the hunters, hopping and flapping, they surrounded me, tore off my wings, stripped me of my plumage and left me writhing on the ground. The dance was a cry for help, a protest against cruelty. "It's beautiful," murmured Pepito, "and very moving."

The atmosphere at the Casino grew tenser daily. The show was sold out for opening night; the demand for seats had been such that the theater could have been filled three times over. Again and again we rehearsed a flamboyant number about the French colonies, which included Algerian drums, Indian bells, tom-toms from Madagascar, coconuts from the Congo, cha-chas from Guadeloupe, a number laid in Martinique during which I distributed sugar cane to the audience, Indochinese gongs, Arab dances, camels and finally my appearance as the Empress of Jazz. It was hard to believe that Monsieur Varna was looking for something *more* spectacular for the second act!

One of the numbers I particularly liked watching in rehearsal involved a lake fairy. The chorus was charmingly dressed as irises, water lilies, dragonflies and nymphs. The fairy herself wore a diamond G-string from Van Cleef and Arpels. Two bodyguards followed her every move! It reminded Monsieur Varna, who loved to laugh and knew hundreds of theater stories, of an actress who owned a fabulous diamond necklace which streamed down to her thighs. Where else? After all, streams return to their source! Without being jealous of the lake fairy's finery, I *did* wonder what kind of special effect Monsieur Varna might have in mind for *me*.

Shortly before opening night, Monsieur Henri called me into his office. "Meet your new partner, Josephine." I couldn't believe my eyes. A sleek, golden-eyed leopard sat calmly on the rug, quietly switching its tail. "We ordered him from Hamburg." I remembered visiting the marvelous Hagenbeck menagerie during our German tour. "What's his name, monsieur?" "Chiquita." I knelt beside the big cat; he didn't stir. "You're not afraid?" "No, monsieur. Animals don't hide their feelings the way people do. That's what I like about them! Look what a beautiful creature he is." I gently stroked the leopard's cheek. Chiquita purred contentedly. "See, he likes me." I slowly reached for Chiquita's leash and gave a little tug. The leopard got to his feet and stretched. "You can take him everyplace with you. It'll be marvelous publicity." There was no doubt about that! I could forget about the lake fairy. She couldn't make it as far as the stage door in her G-string. The minute she left the stage, her diamonds were put away in the safe.

Chiquita turned out to be an excellent trouper. He appeared with me in a number called "Ounawa," which Monsieur Varna considered the high spot of the second half of the show. The plot revolved around a native girl who falls in love with a white man and wants to follow him back to civilization. A charming sequence, but something seemed to be lacking. Our composer, Vincent Scotto, saved the day when he arrived on stage waving a slip of paper excitedly. On the way to the theater he had ducked into an entranceway and scribbled down a tune. Hurrying to the rehearsal piano, he began to sing: "J'ai Deux Amours . . ." Monsieur Varna beamed. "Marvelous!" Leaning over the piano, I joined in: "Two loves have I: my country and Paris . . ." Monsieur Varna was right. The song was perfect. It expressed my feelings completely. Yet . . . I felt a sudden lump in my throat. I would never be able to sing it.

"Of course you will," Pepito insisted as we headed home in our Delage. (He had arranged a profitable advertising scheme in which I stated: "The secret of my hair style is Bakerfix [a hair oil marketed under my name], I buy my shoes at Perugia, I enjoy music from around the world on my Bitus portable radio and of course I drive a Delage.") "Listen, Josephine, if you really believe what you're singing, if the words truly come from your heart, you won't have any trouble with your throat." He was right. I laid my head on his shoulder. "The song should really go: 'Three loves have I: my country, Paris and Pepito.' "

A striking poster had been designed to promote the show. I appeared all over Paris emerging from a cloud of green feathers, nude except for ropes of pearls reaching below my loins, bracelets twisting from wrist to shoulders, sparkling shoe buckles and dangling earrings. Chiquita, seated on his haunches, a bow around his supple neck, was offering me an enormous bunch of flowers. In spite of its charm and humor, the poster was, of course, exaggerated. Chiquita was not one to offer posies, although I had supplied him with a collar to match each of my outfits.

Dress rehearsal was a disaster. One of the chorus girls sprained an ankle, a costume in the "Electricity" number short-circuited, Chiquita, unnerved by the general tension, chewed a hole in a dancer's trousers and the wind machine broke down. I had taken the precaution of stowing my good-luck penny and entire stock of rabbits' feet in my dressing table drawer. It looked as though I would need them.

September 26, 1930. Opening night. I tried to relax, but I knew that the fashionable audience was packed with journalists armed for the kill.

The "savage" would receive no quarter. Pens sharp as arrows were poised to strike at Josephine and the Casino's new management. I recognized Mistinguett in one of the boxes!

When the crowd broke into wild applause, I was so moved that I walked to the front of the stage, placed my hand on my pounding heart and murmured, "Thank you, thank you so much, ladies and gentlemen." Monsieur Varna pounced on me in the wings. "Stop that, Josephine. None of this 'Thank you, ladies and gents!' You're not a street singer. You're the star of the Casino. Just nod from time to time like a queen." And he pushed me back onto the stage. After the curtain was lowered, the clapping continued. I turned to find the cast acclaiming me.

A few days later I woke up in my Louis Seize bedroom (the press insisted that I slept in Marie Antoinette's bed) and discovered Pepito covering me with newspapers. "You've done it, *cherie!* If Paris is bustling, it's you who put it on its toes. Listen to the reviews: 'She sings in French, dances, acts and lights up the stage with her exuberance and rhythm' . . . 'sensitive and sincere' . . . 'a smashing success' . . . 'a true artist.' " "Pepito, uncork the champagne."

During the following weeks Pepito busied himself making a scrapbook of the clippings that poured in from all over France and abroad. I was now being exposed to a new kind of criticism, that of the sharp-tongued music reviewers. My records had appeared on the market and were selling like hotcakes. Pepito assured me that the critics would eat out of my hand, just like Chiquita, and as usual he was right. "Josephine, we've won the prize for the best record of the year," he announced triumphantly one evening. I couldn't help smiling. Pepito always said "we." "We're" going to sing at the charity ball; "we" certainly caused a stir at the art show; "we" have a marvelous new song. Still, I was thrilled at his news. Imagine me, Josephine, at the top of the charts! Pepito was already negotiating next year's tour and Monsieur Varna was thinking ahead to 1932!

"Are you happy, Josephine?" Pepito frequently asked me. Of course I was. Our house was full of friends, animals and friends of friends who seemed to adore the ebony Venus. My dressing room was crowded with celebrities: Marcel Pagnol; Erich Maria Remarque, who said I brought "a whiff of jungle air and an elemental strength and beauty to the tired showplace of Western Civilization"; Le Corbusier, who was moved to tears by my performance; Luigi Pirandello, who wanted to write a play for me. I was also introduced to a Mr. Einstein, but had no idea who he was.

Chiquita and I went everywhere. "Here comes the panther and her leopard," the crowds would shout as flash bulbs popped. There were endless fittings—how I hated being trapped inside that latticework of pins; interviews during which I mouthed stock phrases unless the press answered their questions themselves, thereby simplifying matters for everyone; constant singing and dancing lessons. "You're at the top," Mr. Varna had said. And I didn't intend to forget it. But life is a series of summits and behind each crest looms another peak to be scaled. . . .

There were two Josephines now—the Josephine of Le Vésinet and the Josephine of the Casino de Paris. The latter posed at Monsieur Poiret's in fancy clothes and inaugurated the *Josephine Show,* an inspiration of Pepito's. He had collected portraits and caricatures of me made by a dozen or more well-known artists and hung them like a string of paper dolls of every shape and size, dancing, arms trailing on the ground, rump aloft, pinheaded, balloon-faced with an enormous grin; loins feathered, eyes crossed, breasts jutting. . . . The Josephine of the Casino rode horseback in the Bois de Boulogne, drove a roadster, took flying lessons.

The Josephine of Le Vésinet fed her ducks and rabbits, caressed her cats, exercised her dogs and napped with Chiquita. The Josephine of the Casino appeared at countless functions and gave endless autographs. ("Pepito, can't you find a photograph that doesn't show me *nude?*" "But this is the one they *like, cherie.*") The Josephine of Le Vésinet wore Peter Pan collars.

"Are you happy, Josephine?" "Of course, Pepito." At Beau Chêne my animals surrounded me with love. I drew strength and peace from their affection. It was a good life.

"Noble!"

"Josephine!"

I couldn't believe my eyes. Here was the author of *Shuffle Along,* the show that had given me my start, backstage at the Casino. How strange show business is! We become globe-trotters, touring the four corners of the world. Noble Sissle and his orchestra had been in London when I was in Budapest, in Paris when I was in Germany, in Monte Carlo when I was in South America and in England when I opened at the Casino. "Listen to this," he said. "One evening at Ciro's, the Duke of Windsor sat in for my drummer. He wasn't bad, either. He'd make a very respectable substitute."

"What's Eubie up to, Noble?" "He's doing a marvelous musical on Broadway called *Singin' the Blues*." "You're not working together?" "That's how it goes, Josephine. Eubie wanted to get back to the States on account of his family." "But you made such a wonderful team. You put Negro shows on the map." "I know. . . . By the way, do you remember our producer, Lyle? He's dying of TB. So I may go back with Eubie after all. We're thinking of doing a new version of *Shuffle Along*. Interested?" I shook my head. "I don't think so, Noble." "I know you're the toast of Paris these days."

That wasn't my reason for refusing, of course. How could I make Noble understand that I felt I could be more useful in the white man's world? At the sight of Pepito, Noble raised his eyebrows. "I get it," he said dryly. *"L'amour, toujours l'amour!"* Stepping backward to let Pepito into the dressing room, he landed on Chiquita's tail. Noble started at the leopard's snarl of pain. Then he laughed. "That's right. Eubie told me you're crazy about animals and always have them around. But he only mentioned monkeys and rabbits." "That was back at the Folies. Those rabbit droppings really bothered the cast."

With his usual finesse, Pepito offered around champagne. "I'm sorry you missed me at the Ambassadeurs," Noble remarked. "Thanks to Cole Porter's fantastic music, I was able to get all the unemployed black musicians in Paris together. Including Sidney Bechet. Have you seen him?" "No, not recently." "We had a marvelous audience," Noble continued. "Pola Negri, Elsa Maxwell, Heifetz, Baroness Rothschild . . ." "The same crowd that came to see *me* at the Casino!" Pepito toasted our respective futures. Noble was preparing to present *Central Park Hotel* and Pepito and I would soon be leaving on tour. I sensed how badly Noble wanted to put on another all-Negro show and knew he'd do anything to get me to return to the States with him.

Seeing Noble made me think. I was well aware of his dedication to our people, of the good he had done for colored people and colored theater. But didn't being a *black* star in a *white* show prove something too? Wouldn't it give me more power with which to fight for the cause?

Admittedly, when my dresser hurried in with my coolie hat and feathers for the Tonkinese number and remarked that there were several rhinestones missing from the White Bird's ankle bracelet, it made me wonder . . . Pepito sat twisting his glass. His champagne was untouched. "I wonder why someone like you who defends people of color so loudly hasn't married one," he reflected when we were alone. Dear Pepito. His jealousy was endless. "Because things just haven't turned out that way, *cheri.* It's the person I care about, not the color."

This time Pepito had arranged for me to tour as part of a show based on "numbers from the Casino de Paris Revue." Needless to say, I missed the Casino stage.

As the tour progressed, Pepito began checking the gifts and flowers I received. He had noticed that in every city we visited a note would arrive from Count———, tucked into a bunch of red roses. "It's not possible that you've never met him," Pepito snapped. "It's true, *cheri,*" I protested. Although the bouquet arrived punctually in my dressing room at every performance along with a card expressing the Count's "heartfelt admiration," my suitor himself had never appeared backstage. France, Belgium, England: always the same message in the same flamboyant hand. Pepito was so upset by now that he lay in wait for my admirer in the watchman's loge. But the flowers always arrived by messenger. From time to time in a restaurant or hotel I noticed a young blond man observing me, but when I tried to catch his eye he shifted his gaze to his plate or newspaper. At first I thought it might be my imagination, but I quickly realized that in every city the youth's face and physique were the same. Could Pepito be having me followed? I was afraid to ask. The young man even appeared in stores where I was shopping.

When we finally returned to Paris, the youth disappeared. Then one morning there was a call from a woman who insisted she must speak to me personally. In trembling, frightening, convincing tones, she told me that her son, Count ———, had been rushed to a rest home and it was essential that I join her there at once.

The Countess, a woman in her forties, had a ravaged face which brightened the moment she saw me. "You came! You came!" She quickly explained that I had become an obsession with her son, a delicate, unstable boy. It had been necessary to hospitalize the Count because he refused to eat. When I entered the young man's room it was like walking into a nightmare: this was indeed my elusive suitor, but he was an emaciated, dull-eyed shadow of himself. Stretched out on his bed, he was listlessly playing cards with a deck composed of my photographs—pictures taken from every angle and in all stages of dress and lack of it. His mother spoke to him as if he were an ailing baby. "See, she's here. She's come specially to see you." The youth looked at me distractedly, then suddenly, as if a veil had lifted, tears rolled down his cheeks. I left the room, overcome with emotion. "You've cured him," his mother whispered. The nurse agreed that I had somehow returned him to his senses. Perhaps.

I have always wondered how the scandal sheet that published the story titled "Josephine Drives a Young Man Mad with Love" got its information. Pity and prudence had made me keep the incident to myself. I hadn't even told Pepito, who made a terrible scene when he found out. Thinking I intended to go back and see the young Count in the clinic, he slapped me with all his strength and locked me in my room.

It wasn't the first time Pepito had imprisoned me. He sometimes closed me up in order to make me work. Not that I was lazy! That was one thing I'd never be. There was no job I wouldn't do. I'll never forget our head gardener's face the morning he found me, dressed in one of his smocks, arranging the earth around our little Temple of Love. He had undoubtedly thought I was reclining in a cloud of chiffon on "Marie Antoinette's" bed. I needed to be constantly in motion, driving my roadster, flying my plane, running through the fields with my dogs. It was my way of expressing joy at being alive. What was the point of standing behind a piano practicing scales? So Pepito locked me in my room. We discussed my future by the hour. Of course, I had to keep developing. "Otherwise you'll disappear like the rest," Pepito assured me. "Think of all the names that *used* to be in lights. The public is like a man. We're happy to stick with one woman as long as she keeps changing!" "Is that why you stay with me?" "Of course." "How do you like me best? In my bananas, feathered, or wearing the gardener's clothes?" Pepito smiled. We could never stay angry for long.

I knew perfectly well that Pepito had abandoned everything for me: his family, his job, his reputation—all for love. But he was too proud and intelligent to allow his passion for me to become a defeat. It had to end in triumph. I must reach the top. "Are we doing this for you or for me?" I'd ask. "We're the same, *cherie.*" At times it almost seemed as if his life depended on my success. He drove himself tirelessly, planning, plotting, manipulating, insisting. . . . He even set up a publishing operation to print my songs. So of course I had to continue my singing and keep improving.

I'll never forget the day he shouted, "I've got it! This will *really* surprise them!" "What, Pepito?" "Seeing you toe-dance." "But, Pepito, I'll never be able to hop around on my toes." "You can do anything you want to, Josephine," he said in that voice I could never resist. I wondered what Serge Lifar would say; we had had a wonderful time together on the beach in Venice during my Italian tour. Venice . . . Serge told me that Diaghilev, who had died there, used to take him to Venice to show him what true beauty was. "You ought to visit museums, Josephine. There's so much to learn." "Pepito and I *do* go." "Going isn't enough. You have to learn how to see. Dancing is sculpture in motion and the finest sculpture is dance."

I loved to hear Serge speak. He was more entertaining than all the pigeons in St. Mark's Square. I'd like to have been Picasso in order to sketch him. . . . Actually, he knew Picasso, as well as those who had made me the "ebony Venus" and named him the "bronze Apollo." Paris had welcomed him from the East two years before I arrived from the West. There on the sun-drenched sand, intoxicated with the sheer joy of motion, we danced. What a curious pas de deux—the star dancer of the Paris Opéra and a colored entertainer swaying together in bathing suits on the Lido beach.

Toe-dancing . . . Henri Varna thought it would be an amusing addition to my next show. "You won't forget the thirteen-letter title, Monsieur Henri?" "How about *La Joie de Paris,* Josephine?" Madame Vromska, a Russian ballerina, imprisoned my feet in toe shoes. It wasn't too difficult to balance on the stiff cardboard tips, especially with one hand on the bar, but assuming the classical positions was a real challenge. "Turn out your toes, Miss Baker. Further, further." The ballet master who had been called in to help me prepare my new number seemed to think I had promise. I took home my toe shoes in order to practice around the house. Day after day I teetered from one piece of furniture to the next. "Your dresser top is just the right height for a bar," said Pepito firmly. And he locked my bedroom door.

Jo Bouillon: I spent the summer of 1933 at the Ostend Casino with my dance band. It was quite a shock to my family. My two brothers and I had won first prizes in violin at the Paris Conservatory and my father taught at the Montpellier music school. Yet after completing my military service I had got involved with a small dance orchestra at Montpellier's Capitole Theater. Like so many young people, I was wild about jazz. To my father's dismay, I decided to make a career in show business. Baton in one hand, violin in the other, I was gradually making a name for myself —all the way to Ostend. There, as in all casinos, the aim was to lure the customers onto the dance floor or into the theater by way of the gaming tables. Josephine Baker was featured in the stage show and during one of our breaks I decided to watch her performance.

I had never seen the legendary Josephine, but like everyone else I knew about her furs, her snakeskin-lined car, her jewels, her leopard on its leash, her continual travels. Still, when Josephine walked onto the stage I gasped. Photographs had prepared me for her sparkle and beauty at age twenty-seven, but seen in the flesh she radiated an astonishing magnetism. The way she advanced toward the audience, the lines of her wonderfully supple body, the tilt of her head on its slender neck, the grace of her shoulders, the harmony of her torso, the perfection of her legs, produced an overwhelming impression of balance and beauty. African goddess . . . or Egyptian queen? I asked myself. The divine Josephine greeted us common mortals with a friendly smile, happy to be among us, bubbling with genuine joy. My musician's ear was captivated by the subtleties of her voice, an unusual cooing, uninhibited coloratura as naturally musical as a bird trill. Her combination of know-how and spontaneity was dazzling.

During the course of her performance, Josephine changed costume seven times, as at ease in a gleaming sheath dress as in a loincloth. At one point, facing away from the public, wearing a gold bolero which completely bared her back, this woman with the most magnificent legs of any orchestra leader in the world directed her singers and musicians in a number called "The Soul of Jazz"—which is exactly what it was. Passionate and uninhibited, Josephine *became* the music.

After the show I went backstage and knocked at Josephine's dressing room door. She was wearing a comfortable wrapper, not at all like the conventional "star." I was amazed to see that she was fairly short. Onstage her tremendous presence gave her added height.

I explained that I directed the casino orchestra and asked for a signed photograph. She selected a picture from the pile heaped next to her pots of makeup. "How kind of you," she said. "What's your name?" "Jo Bouillon." "Jo?" "As in Joseph." "We share the same name." She smilingly handed me a photo. It was my turn to smile. She had made a spelling error: "To Jo Boullion with best regards."

And that's the way we met.

Six months later, by sheer coincidence, my orchestra and I were hired to do a stint at the Casino de Paris. Henri Varna liked my work and I quickly became the Casino's permanent conductor. Josephine was making a film, *Zouzou*, at the time as well as performing in the Offenbach operetta *La Créole* Was there anything she wouldn't try? The second time we met was at the Casino. She and Pepito had attended a performance, after which they invited me to join them in the theater's bar. "Mademoiselle Baker and I like your orchestra enormously. You're a fine conductor. Would you be interested in going on tour with us?" "We'll spell your name right on the posters," Josephine added with a smile.

I was extremely flattered to be offered a job as Josephine's accompanist, but I had worked long and hard to build up my orchestra and wanted to conquer Paris. The Casino was a marvelous starting point. I regretfully declined Pepito's offer. Josephine wished me goodbye, gathered her white fox fur around her shoulders, swept across the room on Pepito's arm and climbed into her gleaming Delage, which stood at the curb surrounded by curious onlookers. As Pepito drove off, she saluted me with her gloved hand.

Little did I know that it would be ten years before we met again . . . this time to be married.

Josephine: I've always liked Jean Gabin. He speaks so naturally that it's hard to tell if he's acting or not. When he growled, "With a body like yours, you've got no worries," I wasn't sure whether he was speaking one of Monsieur Willemetz's lines addressed to Zouzou or trying to encourage his co-star, Josephine.

Pepito had created *Zouzou* especially for me. It was a simple, credible role which perfectly fit my idea of the cinema: to make you believe what you saw. Zouzou was a little Creole laundress who longed for her island home and lavished her love on her puppy and pet bird. I'll never forget the scene where I set the bird free. I had hoped to rehearse it again and again, giving a new bird its liberty with every take, but the original bird wouldn't budge from its perch. He liked it where he was. The director was furious; in the film world, every minute has its price. Zouzou finally ends up on the music hall stage and becomes a star. But success doesn't bring her romance. . . . Gabin, who played the part of a sailor who loved me like a brother, was so convincing that he was picked up in the street by a real live quartermaster who thought he had jumped ship! We were filming in Toulon, a busy port swarming with French sailors with their red-pompomed hats. The day of our departure, the sailors gave me a memorial beret for good luck. "You can never have too many good-luck charms," I told Gabin. "With all your fetishes, it's easy to see you're from Africa," he replied.

Pepito had devised an unusual scheme to promote *Zouzou*. We had met the producer, Arys Nissotti, in Tunis during our 1928 tour. Then he was running a casino; now he was making films. Arys agreed to Pepito's idea, and a publicity piece in newspaper form called *Le Journal de Zouzou* soon appeared. The journal aroused quite a stir. "It has one serious omission," a nightclub performer joked. "In the twenty-eight columns devoted to Josephine, not one mentions her glorious derrière." He was right. Instead I was being compared to Réjane and Sarah Bernhardt. Wasn't Pepito overdoing it?

"Why can't the story end differently?" I complained one evening. "Couldn't I marry Gabin? . . . Or would the public object because of my color?" Pepito smiled his sly little smile. "Zouzou is a star. She lives for her work. Like you."

There were times when I wondered whether being a star was enough. I would gladly have married Pepito if he had agreed to my having a baby. But it was always: "Your career comes first right now, Josephine. There'll be time for the rest later."

CHAPTER 8

New York Revisited

WHENEVER I WAS INTRODUCED to a playwright in Paris or Deauville, I asked, "With all your African colonies, why are there so few Negro actors on the French stage?" After a startled silence, my listener would smile and admit that it *was* curious. . . . But no one offered me a part. After my film experience, I was anxious to perform before a flesh-and-blood public, to hear their laughter and provoke an occasional tear. I was possessed by the need to make an audience react. After a year and a half on the road, I wanted to conquer Paris.

Zouzou's scriptwriter, Albert Willemetz, director of the Bouffes-Parisiens Theater, shared my ambition. One day he dropped a bombshell. "I've got just the part for you, Josephine. Offenbach's *La Créole.*" I had never heard of Offenbach, but when I learned that the story involved a West Indian girl, I knew that the role was perfect. Still, despite Pepito's and Albert's enthusiasm, I had reservations. "What if Monsieur Offenbach doesn't think I'm right for the part?" I asked cautiously. Laughter. The author had been dead for over fifty years! What a pity. I prefer my playwrights living so that we can discuss the role together. "Isn't the music lovely?" Monsieur Willemetz exclaimed after we had listened to the score. Silence. "Admit it, Josephine. It's beautiful," Pepito insisted.

"Maybe you think so, but I'll never be able to sing it. It hardly has any beat." Albert raised his eyebrows. "Don't worry," Pepito said hastily. "I know she can handle the part. She'll need some more songs, though." "I'll borrow a few from another Offenbach operetta. And I plan to modernize the script," Albert explained. Maybe it was just as well that Offenbach was dead. "Not at all," said Albert. "He would have adored you."

With these encouraging words, I was hurried off to take voice lessons with Madame Paraviccini, Yvonne Printemps's teacher.

Once again it was goodbye to Le Vésinet and my menagerie. Life now centered around my first legitimate theater, the Bouffes-Parisiens, near the Opéra. At last I would play to a family audience, without my feathers and spangles. Albert explained that Offenbach had created the Bouffes-Parisiens troupe himself and rehearsed *La Créole* on this very stage. "You mean you're assuming his role?" "Not really. By the time the show was actually produced, he was no longer involved in it. In fact, things got so bad for him that he inscribed one of his portraits: 'To my only friend, Jacques Offenbach.' " What a tragic story. Was such loneliness possible? Perched on the stairs that led to the stage, I reflected that there had been times in America when I could have written a similar message, if I had *had* a portrait or photograph. Today I was probably the most photographed woman in Europe; my portrait had been painted innumerable times; I was a celebrity. . . . But what about tomorrow? I often prayed to God to protect me from solitude, to arrange things so that, in St. John's recording of Jesus' beautiful words: "All that the Father giveth me shall come to me."

"On stage, Josephine." My heart sank. I'd never be able to memorize my part. Never.

"Of course you will." Who could mistake Sacha Guitry's unforgettable voice? He had told Albert that giving me the part of Offenbach's Creole girl was a stroke of genius. "Of course you can do it, mademoiselle. You have the makings of a fine comedienne because you're completely natural."

Sacha attended several rehearsals. He, more than anyone, helped me to understand the performer's craft: act on stage the way you do in real life; keep the theater constantly in mind when you're *not* performing; and forget about the critics.

The reviewers were already sharpening their pens. How amusing to have chosen *me* for the part. I was obviously too light. Clearly too dark. Offenbach would have turned over in his grave. I had no formal musical training. (It was true that my voice was unschooled, but I had a good ear and had finally learned to read music.) "Just ignore them, Josephine," Pepito and Albert said calmly. "The important thing is the show."

Luckily some of the critics believed both in me and in my abilities. As opening night approached I was interviewed with increasing frequency. "It's not that I dislike music hall," I explained, "but an artist can't afford to get stale. I intend to be a Creole just like the *other* Josephine, Napoleon's wife."

In spite of Sacha's encouragement, I had trouble with my lines. There were three acts to memorize, plus a new prologue laid in Jamaica. . . . I loved my first entrance, during which I broke every dish on the stage. Had that been Pepito's idea? I wondered. He had seen me smash enough crockery at Beau Chêne in response to his jealous scenes. The last of his outbursts had involved Jacques Pills, then appearing at the Bouffes in an operetta called *Toi, C'est Moi*. I thought the show was charming, but it had been poorly received by the public. Jacques dropped in to my dressing room one evening to tell me that his troupe felt that Willemetz and the rest of the crew were concentrating so hard on *La Créole* that they were neglecting the current show. As we were talking, Pepito rushed in, eyes ablaze. How could such an intelligent man be so foolish? "What's he got that I haven't," Pepito asked sulkily when we were alone. "Nothing, *cheri*. And you've got a monocle besides."

The tension between the two troupes upset me greatly. After conferring with Albert, Pepito and I composed a letter to "Dear Mr. Willemetz," which was released to the press the next day. "In light of the tremendous success of *Toi, C'est Moi*, I, a mere newcomer to the stage, am reluctant to jeopardize its run. May I therefore suggest that if you can find another theater worthy of Offenbach's beautiful score." Shortly thereafter I received the following telegram: CAST OF TOI, C'EST MOI DEEPLY TOUCHED BY THEIR FRIEND JOSEPHINE BAKER'S THOUGHTFUL AND FRIENDLY GESTURE.

How strange the theater is. From that day on, *Toi, C'est Moi* was a hit.

A substitute theater was easily found. The Marigny, off the Champs-Élysées, was delighted to welcome *La Créole*, since it was here that

Offenbach had launched his troupe in 1855. "In 1855, Albert, my family's legs were in chains, and look how I kick mine up now! How quickly times change."

Moving from the intimate Bouffes to the elegant Marigny meant a more lavish production. Among the changes was the addition of a delightful group of children to the corps de ballet. But my heart ached during the tryouts as the young dancers were separated into groups, then chosen or rejected in tears while their tight-lipped mothers looked on.

At dress rehearsal, the director cringed when he saw my pale makeup. "You look like a clown, Josephine." "Creoles are light-skinned," I said firmly. "*You* may think so, but as far as the public and I are concerned, they're black."

December 15, 1934, was opening night. I was relieved to see friends in the audience, including Simone Simon, Jean-Pierre Aumont and Guitry's clan of beauties, among them the wonderfully witty Arletty. Head high, I walked onto the stage, where my plates, trays and vases waited like lambs at the slaughter. . . .

"Many in the audience had come to sneer or be bored. But that's not the way it turned out," one critic noted. Another remarked: "Josephine has so many strings to her bow that it looks like a harp." Not all the reviews were that favorable, but the Marigny's director happily exclaimed, "The show will run for a year." "Maybe," said Pepito dryly.

I knew what he was thinking. Pepito didn't like to rest on his laurels. He preferred to look for new challenges.

During the Christmas holidays, the comedian Eddie Cantor came to see the show. After complimenting me on my performance, he added, "You ought to come back to the States." I was angry to discover that Eddie had already discussed this possibility with Pepito behind my back. "She's conquered South America and most of Europe," he had said. "Now it's time for her to tackle New York." He was undoubtedly right, but suppose I got stranded there? I loved Paris with a passion it would have been hard to explain.

On Christmas Eve, Beau Chêne was crowded with friends. The lamplight picked out the statues of Diana, Venus and Ceres glowing softly on the lawn. The house was gaily decorated. A carpet of cotton wool surrounded the glittering tree. There were gifts for everyone—actors, musicians, dancers, even the various dogs that pawed at my white gown. The conversation turned to recent Broadway hits. ("Josephine, you should go to America. They'd be wild about you.") As the phonograph played the score from *Zouzou*, we danced and laughed until something made me look up. There was Pepito gyrating à la Josephine, my bananas hitched to his jacket. "Stop that, Pepito," I snapped. "Those are work tools, not toys."

The winter of 1935 was bitter cold. As I shivered in my dressing room, sipping hot toddies, the press debated the proper color of La Créole's skin. Let them fight it out with their encyclopedias. All I cared about was that the theater was filled nightly. My dressing room had become a haven for the young members of the ballet troupe, who called me Madame Fifi. Every Sunday I served them tea during intermission. I was particularly fond of two tiny dancers, Simone and Suzanne, whom I invited to Beau Chêne, hoping to put some color in their cheeks. They had a wonderful time with the animals and we all enjoyed their visit except Chiquita. My leopard missed our nightly trips to the theater. When the hour arrived at which he had formerly leaped into the Delage beside me and motored through the goggling crowd to the Casino door, he sulked. Chiquita was no longer a leopard. He had become a ham actor.

February 16 marked my debut on the stage of the Opéra in a benefit performance for the French Navy. I couldn't believe it was me performing in that magnificent red and gold theater. It reminded me of the palaces I had dreamed of as a child. Even more exciting to me than appearing before the President of the Republic and his Minister of the Navy was the thought that earlier that evening, for the first time, my performance of *La Créole* had been transmitted by radio to England. How incredible to think that my voice had crossed the Channel! I adored the radio and always kept a set nearby. It was my window to the world. I had little time for reading and limited myself to detective stories, which were like a game. Books were not for me. They taught me nothing about life. Life was meant to be breathed and touched and smelled. Books tried to package experience. I like my living fresh.

Sacha Guitry had recently married and with his flair for the dramatic had turned the occasion into a theatrical event. Even his fiancée had been convinced that the luncheon he had planned at the Ritz was a belated birthday party. Albert, who had been drafted from among the guests as an impromptu witness, described the event in detail, including Sacha's remark: "I'm fifty and my bride is twenty-five. It's only natural that she should be my better half." Pepito and I burst out laughing, but Pepito's expression quickly changed. I knew what he was thinking. . . . No, I wouldn't marry him. It wasn't because of the unpleasant gossip that always got back to me: "He's using you, Josephine. He's put all your property in his name" (actually, we'd bought everything jointly). I ignored that kind of talk because in show business any man who managed a woman's affairs was accused of being a pimp. No, what bothered me was his constant jealousy, the way he checked my every move. Still, he was undeniably the finest manager in Paris.

When my engagement at the Marigny ended, Pepito decided it was time for me to make a film again. Not another story of backstage life or a dramatic comedy like *Zouzou,* but something new. He settled on a light romance called *Princess Tam-Tam,* the story of an Arab urchin who is transformed into a social butterfly by a French nobleman.

The on-location sequences were filmed in Tunisia. My first scene took place in the street, where I was being questioned by the police. Public curiosity was such that a cordon of real police was needed to hold back the crowd. Between takes the mob shouted to me in a dialect I couldn't understand. Their voices grew angrier and angrier. When I finally asked my interpreter the reason for their rage, I was told that they assumed I was a *real* Arab and couldn't understand why I didn't answer them. I had obviously been well cast!

At one point in the script Princess Tam-Tam appears in a series of exquisite gowns. But our producer, Arys Nissotti, drew the line at a filmy black creation: "That one won't do, Josephine," he snapped. "I'm planning to sell this film in the provinces and abroad! You look *almost* naked, which is even worse than *being* naked!" "Josephine dressed isn't Josephine," one of the stagehands shouted. We all began laughing. I love to laugh, and Pepito and I had been doing it less and less. Nissotti had his way and the gown was lined with silver lamé.

One of the things I particularly enjoyed about filming *Princess Tam-*

Tam was the chance it gave me to introduce the conga to France. Not that the conga had anything to do with Tunisia; it was a dance enjoyed by the slaves after their work was done. We were all convinced that it would be the rage in Paris that winter. What better way to keep warm?

Pepito had done it again. I couldn't believe my ears when he announced that he had signed me up with the *Ziegfeld Follies*. Little did I know how things would turn out. I often wonder what might have happened if Flo Ziegfeld had still been alive.

Things started going wrong the moment we arrived in New York. Since Pepito and I weren't married, we had to book separate hotel rooms, thanks to one of those puritanical American laws of that time which encouraged hypocrisy rather than promoting sainthood. Pepito was free to join me when he liked, but our inevitable separations increased his jealousy and ill humor.

I too grew disenchanted, but for different reasons. Ever since Ziegfeld's death in 1932, his wife, Billie Burke, had been in charge of the *Follies* productions. Our glittering show was faithful to Ziegfeld's "glorification of the American girl." Vincente Minnelli had provided gorgeous sets and costumes (including an Asian version of my banana waistband, which substituted tusks for fruit); George Balanchine had created the ballets; Robert Alton was in charge of the modern-dance numbers; and Ira Gershwin and Vernon Duke had composed the words and music. One of their songs was the exquisite "What Is There to Say" . . . but it wasn't I who sang it. It was performed by the star of the show, Fannie Brice.

Fanny already had more than twenty-five years of show business under her belt. She had started out in burlesque in Brooklyn and debuted with the *Follies* in 1910. A veteran of half a dozen *Follies* shows, she was an immensely appealing figure and had become even more endearing when news of her tragic love affair with the gambler Nicky Arnstein hit the press. She was now married to the famous producer Billy Rose, which further increased her prestige in show business circles. How could I possibly compete? All I had to offer was the slogan "The girl who put Harlem on the map of Europe." I was nothing but a body to be exhibited in various stages of undress. The cast also included an ex-boxer who had abandoned the ring for the stage, Bob Hope, and two gifted, nimble dancers, the Nicolas Brothers. If I had only had more of a part! Compared to *my* Champs-Élysées Theater and *my* Marigny, the *Follies* was a factory that cranked out products for Hollywood. Ed Wynn had started here and Eddie Cantor and Paul Whiteman. . . .

I could tell from the start that I'd never make it. There was no room to be myself; I had been overglamorized, hopelessly type-cast. When the first reviews appeared, one look at Pepito's face was enough to confirm my fears. "Well?" "You rated a few polite words here and there. Fannie Brice got raves as usual." I, who had to be first!

I blamed Pepito for not negotiating a better contract. But after all, this wasn't Europe, where he knew the ropes. In Paris he was unbeatable; New York was something else. We had a violent scene, so violent that Pepito, at his wit's end, packed his bags and took the next plane to France. He had never walked out on me before, but perhaps it was for the best. I had already left him once, fed up with his suspicions. It was during my appearance in *La Créole*. We were giving a party at Beau Chêne and the house was full of friends—*his* friends, more precisely, since he ran our social life the same way he chose my dresses and songs. Suddenly I had had enough of his domination. While our guests danced and chattered, I fled across the lawn, leaped into the car and drove off into the night. I had nothing with me but the cocktail dress on my back, but what did it matter? It had been the same in St. Louis when I was thirteen. Naturally Pepito cornered me at the theater. . . . But this time an ocean lay between us. I was glad that *he* had been the one to go.

Jo Bouillon: Josephine left no further written account of this period of her life. Nor would she talk about it. This was typical of her wish to suppress anything that wasn't a personal victory. The past to her had no value except as a stepping stone in her fight for success. Josephine suffered two crushing defeats in her lifetime. The first occurred in 1936, the period during which she was struggling toward stardom. Her failure to conquer New York in the *Follies* prevented her from achieving her dream of world renown and barred her from a future in Hollywood. Her second setback was the loss of Les Milandes in 1968, which shattered her hopes of fighting racism through the example of a "world village." She quickly recovered from the first of these reverses, but the second almost killed her. In the thirty-two years between the two events, her personality would be molded and tempered by the harsh realities of World War II.

But we are getting ahead of our story.

In 1935 Josephine left Paris rich, adored, famous throughout Europe. But in New York, in spite of the publicity that preceded her arrival, she was received as an uppity colored girl. Thanks to press clippings carefully gathered by Pepito and filed away in folders by Josephine, we can reconstruct what occurred.

The out-of-town tryouts began on November 21, 1935, at the Boston Opera House. Opening night in New York was on Christmas Eve. In early January there was a special press performance, for which Pepito apparently felt it prudent to hire a claque to applaud each of Josephine's numbers. She appeared four times: once in a scene at the Longchamps race track swathed in a sumptuous sari and singing "Maharanee"; next poured into a remarkable silver sheath which weighed seventeen pounds; then as a West Indian girl doing the conga with a minimum of clothing and a maximum of verve; and finally in her bananas. Unfortunately for Josephine, puritanism reigned in the United States during the mid-thirties, and Vincente Minnelli, then twenty-eight, catered to the spirit of the times in his *Follies* production. As one newspaperman put it: "Nudity and high-stepping are no longer favorite themes," but had the kindness to add "except for the appearance of Josephine Baker." Another reviewer limited his critique to the following sentence: "Some people like Josephine Baker. I don't." Others were offended to hear a French accent on the lips of a girl from Harlem: "I couldn't understand a word she sang," sniffed the critic from the *National,* continuing that "it's interesting to see fifty million Frenchmen turn into publicity agents." The *New York Post* spoke of her "dwarf-like voice eclipsed in the cavernous Winter Garden." Although recordings prove that in 1936 Josephine sang in high-pitched silvery tones, which mellowed to bronze after the war, it is probably true that her exotic, cooing voice was doomed to extinction in that vast setting. The most charitable review she received was written by Ira Wolfert in the *American.* Wolfert expressed his disappointment at her "curious voice, which sounded like a cracked bell with a padded clapper," but added: "Still I like it. I'm very fond of Chinese music." The final word was uttered by the ferocious Walter Winchell, with whom Josephine was to lock horns in later years. In the *Daily Mirror* he denounced Pepito's claque and concluded that in spite of it, "la Baker was trounced by the critics the following day. Reviewers are not fooled by noise."

Josephine's way of handling such criticism was to ignore it. She suddenly forgot that she knew how to read. On February 8, in accordance with Pepito's usual policy, she opened her cabaret Chez Joséphine at the Mirage on East Fifty-fourth Street. The critics did an about-face, finding Josephine "more at home" in a cabaret setting "than on the *Follies* stage." As usual, she presided over the show, chatted with the guests and smilingly passed out paper streamers and balloons in spite of the bitterness she must have felt. She never mentioned her outrage except to Pepito; he bore the brunt of her disappointment and the gossip columns spoke of "outbursts against the Italian count." Josephine's setback with the *Follies* was Pepito's downfall because it poisoned his personal life. For years he had been Josephine's man. With her uncanny instinct for self-preservation, she undoubtedly would have found another champion had he not come along, but he had played the role of Pygmalion to perfection. First he helped her develop from a music hall dancer into a rounded artist, then with his flair for publicity he launched her. But he was unable to maneuver in the New York jungle, which refused to acknowledge Josephine as a prophet in her own country. Ironically, she had come full circle. The Plantation, where she had appeared in 1925, was on the ground floor of the Winter Garden building.

Pepito had made a mistake. And it was one mistake too many. The passion that had united him and Josephine ten years before had cooled with time. Josephine craved fire and recoiled from ashes. She mentioned the word "domination." It was clear that she no longer needed Pepito. She had accepted his overbearing, almost brutal, tactics at twenty; at thirty she rejected them. Josephine was a life force, and living means growth and change. Pepito had lost. Josephine hated losers. She needed to win . . . always. The day Pepito left her in New York, she vowed never to see him again.

Arys Nissotti: I was extremely fond of Abatino. I knew him first as a ruthless, highly intelligent businessman, but we later became friends. Our relationship continued to deepen to the point that Josephine, with her usual enthusiasm for anything involving motherhood, asked to witness the birth of my child. She and Pepito were an extraordinary couple. He lived for her alone; her interests were broader.

Pepito returned from America a broken man. "We parted on good terms," he informed the press, adding that Josephine had been very well received in New York. I was shocked by his appearance but attributed it to heartbreak. Instead of returning to Le Vésinet, Abatino moved into a hotel room on the Champs-Élysées. I persuaded him to see my doctor because he complained of constant stomach pains. Immediately after the consultation I received a call from my physician. "Your friend is dying of cancer. He has only a few weeks left." I couldn't believe my ears. Pepito must not be told. He entered the hospital thinking he was suffering from hepatitis. His main concern was Josephine to the last. He had had the good and bad fortune to be enslaved by her charm. She was his greatest strength and severest weakness.

My impetuous, elegant, vivacious friend wasted away before my eyes. I think he guessed his true condition near the end, because he asked me to take care of Josephine for as long as I lived. Then he went into a coma.

Abatino left Josephine Beau Chêne, their Paris home, his gold-piece and stamp collections and all the savings he had put aside, insisting with that sardonic smile of his that Josephine had no sense of money. Which was true. His remains were interred in a crypt in Neuilly. After the war Josephine and her husband, Jo Bouillon, had them shipped to Les Milandes. My friend's final resting place was a tiny cemetery at Fayrac on the banks of the Dordogne, hundreds of miles from the tomb of his beloved.

CHAPTER 9

---◦∞◦---

Wedding Bells

A KNOCK ON MY DRESSING ROOM DOOR. "Who is it?" "Paul Derval."
"Monsieur Derval!" "Josephine!" Monsieur Paul was accompanied by
Maurice Hermite, whom he introduced as the author of the forthcoming
Folies revue.

I crossed my fingers behind my back. "What brings you to America,
monsieur?" "I came to see what was happening in New York and perhaps
pick up some acts." "Were you at the show tonight?" Monsieur Derval
nodded. "They didn't give you much of a break, did they?" I could tell
he had something on his mind. "Are you planning to stay in the States,
Josephine?" he finally asked. "I have two loves, as you know, monsieur.
I've sung about them often enough!" A pause. Then he spoke the words
I'd been waiting to hear and I let my fingers relax. "How would you like
to be in my new show?" I replied by flinging my arms around his neck.

Monsieur Paul explained that he was planning an exceptionally lavish
production for autumn, since 1937 was the year of the Exposition and
Paris would be crowded with tourists. "I've already drawn up a preliminary
contract," he added, extracting a piece of paper from his pocket. I would
receive a percentage of the profits and a handsome monthly advance.
Trying to hide my excitement, I said I'd be happy to discuss the details
with him after my cabaret show.

For the next few nights, Monsieur Derval, Maurice Hermite and I sat around a table at Chez Joséphine discussing the new revue. It would have a thirteen-letter title, of course: *En Super Folies.* "Varna gave you a leopard. I'm going to surround you with tigers!" Monsieur Paul announced. "Show me the contract again, monsieur," I said firmly. The agreement stated that the show would open no later than the first week of October 1936, that I was to be the star, that no other act or performer would receive equal billing, that I had a say in the design of the poster, and that no matter how the revue was received I would keep my monthly advance of 42,500 francs. It was hoped that *En Super Folies* would continue throughout the duration of the Exposition.

"Sign here, Josephine." "Just a minute, monsieur." He looked at me with surprise. Screwing up my courage, I continued: "The reason I'm returning to Paris is because of the Exposition. But that's months from now. I'd like you to add a clause stating that if for any reason you decide to terminate *En Super Folies* and stage a new show during the Exposition, my contract will apply to that show too." There! I hoped I hadn't overlooked anything else that Pepito would have considered. Monsieur Derval smiled. "That's fine with me, Josephine."

Goodbye, New York.

Backstage life at the Folies was as busy as ever. The new production was being readied with the same efficiency I had observed in New York, with one striking difference: Monsieur Derval's kindness. "Josephine, I want to be sure you have everything you need to make you happy in the show." This included a scene featuring jungle beasts, another with a child, which gave me the opportunity to pour out my emotions, and an appearance as a threadbare ice cream vendor pushing a multicolored cart, my rags contrasting sharply with the extravagance of my other costumes.

"You're on, Josephine." My favorite scene was the one in which, gowned in clinging silver lamé, I was borne onto the stage in a feather-trimmed litter which rested on the back of an enormous jade elephant. I had specified that the beast's trunk point aloft since Maurice Chevalier had a collection of elephants with raised trunks and insisted that dangling ones brought bad luck. My mount was surrounded by ten rearing tigers, clawing the air. Although made of pasteboard, they had a wonderfully lifelike appearance. Somewhat less startling but equally effective was a number laid in the Arctic, complete with glaciers, northern lights, a midnight sun, Eskimo dogs and bare-breasted maidens with reindeer headdresses. Swathed in a cloak made of twenty white fox skins, I sang to the chief of the expedition in his icebound schooner:

> Sail with me on a snow-white ship
> To undiscovered seas. . . .

"The key to success is simple," Monsieur Derval liked to say. "Make people laugh and dream." Then he would softly add: "The way Josephine does . . ."

En Super Folies received an enthusiastic welcome. As the weeks passed, I gradually readjusted to French life, but Beau Chêne without Pepito was an empty shell. Nothing seemed to matter anymore; in fact, the only place I felt alive was on stage. Much to everyone's surprise, I withdrew from social life except for the company of a few close friends. One evening the Folies' stage manager handed me an envelope. I recognized the spirited handwriting immediately. "Dear Josephine: In exchange for the garden's worth of flowers you sent me, accept my affectionate thoughts and heart-felt wishes on this ancient sheet of paper which I've treasured for so long that it's yellowed with age. This kind of sentimental writing paper is designed for gentle hearts, children and poets. Which is why I address it to you along with a kiss. Your long-time friend, Colette." The sheet was exquisitely edged with a deep, intricately worked border of lacy paper. In one corner stood a vivid bouquet of embossed flowers. I would keep Colette's note all my life. I love letters. Unlike the telephone, they serve to bind hearts together. What is left when you hang up the phone? Colette cautioned me not to remain alone. She was right as usual. Even thieves seemed to realize that she could do no wrong. While she was sunbathing on the Promenade des Anglais one day, her handbag, containing three thousand francs, was stolen, but two days later it came back with the bills untouched. "I couldn't keep money that belongs to the author of *Cheri.* Your admiring purse-snatcher." What appreciation! When my emerald ring disappeared, it was for good.

After the show had been running for about a month, we were forced to rewrite a sketch which alluded to the Minister of the Interior, Roger Salengro; the subject of vicious public attack, he had killed himself. It was difficult for me to understand the hatred that ran through French political life. It seemed as violent as the racist feeling in America. Since I knew nothing about politics, I limited my friends to show business people. It was in their midst that I welcomed in 1937, the year of the Exposition and, I hoped in my heart of hearts, the year of Josephine Baker.

Despite my expectations, 1937 got off to a poor start. A rash of strikes made it look as though the Exposition would never get under way. I grew restless with the approach of spring and began riding Tomato, a spirited young mare, in the Bois de Boulogne. Afterward I enjoyed stopping off at the Pavillon Dauphine for tea. Dressed in riding clothes and free of makeup, I managed to pass unnoticed.

One day I was discovered in my quiet corner. "Look, there's Josephine." A group of friends, or more precisely acquaintances, descended on me from a nearby table. With them was an extremely handsome young man, whose piercing eyes never left my face. We had already met casually at various social functions, but my "friends" introduced us again. "Josephine, this is Jean Lion."

Jean telephoned the next day. Could he call on me? Sorry, I was busy. I had no desire to return to the social whirl. The only invitations I accepted were those requesting my participation at charitable functions. I had been too close to poverty in my youth not to want to fight it with all my heart and soul. No one has enough time or money to stamp out human misery for good, to care for all the orphans, needy students, disaster victims, war widows, invalids. Rumor had it that I did this kind of work for publicity's sake; let people say what they liked. . . . At a benefit here, an affair I was sponsoring there, I would run into Jean Lion. It turned out that we belonged to the same riding club, that his leisure hours could be adjusted to mine in just the same way his horse adapted its gait to Tomato's rhythm.

Jean Lion was a rich industrialist. Paris was full of women who followed him with their eyes, but his gaze was for me alone. How could I help being flattered? He was a gentle, discreet companion. Colette would be pleased to learn that I was no longer alone. . . .

Shortly after my return to Paris I opened a Chez Joséphine cabaret off the Champs-Élysées. I hoped it would be a popular meeting place. One of my first American guests was Marc Connelly, author of the wonderful folk fantasy *Green Pastures*. Marc looked like my idea of God. Jean dropped by almost nightly. Bouquets of flowers soon gave way to bracelets and necklaces. "And when will we see the ring?" asked Monsieur Paul slyly. He apparently felt it was time that I settled down—especially after a recent escapade when I had taken a few days off for a much-needed rest. My understudy had been delighted to see me go, but when I telephoned Monsieur Derval from the roadside I could tell he was furious. Business had dropped off. I assured him I already felt stronger and would be back in two days; I would meet him before the performance in our usual restaurant. Unfortunately I was detained and didn't arrive at the theater until five minutes before show time. A frantic Monsieur Paul was about to announce to a full house, alerted of my return by the press and radio, that I wouldn't be appearing that night. "Where in God's name *is* she?" shouted the stage manager. "Getting into her costume, monsieur," explained Alice, my dresser. "But she performs in the *nude!*" the manager exclaimed.

The Exposition was finally inaugurated on May 24. On June 3 I celebrated my birthday at Le Vésinet. It was an intimate gathering, inspiring Jean to write me the following letter: *"Cherie:* I'm not going to speak of love here because you know how I feel about you. But I do want to express my happiness at having been with you today along with dear friends and some of my family, who I know would be happy to become part of yours. . . . I hope for many more birthdays together. All of them perhaps? From your Jean, with all his love."

The marriage of the Duke of Windsor and Wallis Simpson was celebrated the same day. One of the journalists who was with us at Beau Chêne asked pointedly if I—the queen of the music hall—would be willing to give up *my* crown for love? "I haven't convinced her yet," replied Jean. "But I'm still trying."

Jean's mother was a warm, charming woman with whom I got along beautifully. Was it because Jean was Jewish that there seemed to be no family opposition to his marrying a Negro? "Mixing blood produces fine children," the Lions insisted. They had no objections to dancers, either. Jean dreamed of giving me social position and family life. I began dreaming too. . . . At thirty-one, I felt I had given my youth to the public in return for money and fame. Weren't we even? Hadn't I earned the right to sink out of sight, especially into the kind of life that Jean was offering? Madame Lion . . . Scores of Parisiennes dreamed of engraving that name on their visiting cards!

As time passed, Jean, unlike Pepito, made me feel that my life as a woman was at least as important as my artistic career. It disturbed him to see me living at Beau Chêne haunted by memories of another man. He decided to take me away for a few precious days. The pretext was a benefit appearance in Limoges, but our real aim was sightseeing. In our wanderings a photograph of a fairy tale castle in a shopwindow caught my eye. "That's the Dordogne," Jean explained. "It's not far from here." Distances meant nothing to Jean and before I knew it we were on our way. The Dordogne was magnificent, with its hills, its rock-strewn terrain, its ever-changing river. "God did his work well here," I exclaimed. Jean smiled. I sensed that he was pleased and reassured by my love of the out of doors.

I delighted in exploring the narrow winding paths which held new discoveries at every turn, in admiring the unspoiled countryside and an occasional château that seemed carved from the rock itself. The crumbling castles with their dungeons and towers were like stage sets. "We're a long way from the theater," Jean murmured ironically, yet the way I discovered Les Milandes was like something in a scenario. What made me follow that twisting cow path to a humble farm whose green pastures spilled to the very gates of "my" château?

We rummaged through every inch of the handsome, abandoned, unlivable structure, from tower to cellar. An immense table for the entire family would be perfect in the huge kitchen. . . . How the children would love running up and down the vast stairways. . . . I would put easy chairs by the fireplace so we could snuggle close to the flames. "*You* curled up at the fireside?" exclaimed Jean delightedly. "And I'll hang a long row of saucepans in the kitchen where they'll reflect the setting sun," I continued. I hated to leave my dream house, but I knew I had found a place I would live in someday. We walked back up the winding path to the car. When we reached the nearby town of Sarlat I asked Jean to stop. "I want to telegraph Limoges that I'm going to rent Les Milandes." "I think the name is Les *Mirandes*, Josephine." "I like Milandes better. I have trouble pronouncing French *r*'s."

I had decided to rent the château without consulting Jean, whom the world considered to be the new man in my life. Still, he seemed delighted.

Back in Paris, the revue, the Exposition and my cabaret were all thriving. One evening Marlene Dietrich told us that in Germany civil servants were obliged to marry and have children. "We're neither German nor civil servants," said Jean, laughing, "but Josephine and I would be delighted to do the same. In fact, as soon as the Expo is over, I'm going to whisk you off to the altar, *cherie.*" The Exposition closed its doors on November 26 and on the thirtieth in a rural municipal building I said "I do."

I said yes because Jean's charm made it hard to resist him; I said yes because I wanted to exchange the artificial life of a star for that of a wife and mother. I mustn't let the real things in life pass me by. I said "I do" in a ceremony that was deliberately simple and far from the public eye.

I listened to the words of the marriage ceremony as if it were all a dream. "Jean Lion, twenty-seven, born in Paris, dealer in raw materials, living at Crèvecoeur-le-Grand, son of Maurice Lion, a livestock trader, and of Ernestine Levy, unemployed; and Josephine Baker, born in St. Louis, Missouri, United States of America, performing artist, daughter of Arthur Baker, unemployed, and of Carrie Martin MacDonald, unemployed . . . I now pronounce you man and wife in the presence of Georges Lion, industrialist, and Paul Derval, director of the Folies-Bergère."

"How kind of you to serve as a witness for Madame Jean Lion when it means losing Josephine Baker," I teased. Monsieur Paul smiled.

"There'll always be a Josephine," he replied.

On December 4, 1937, I received my French passport. Madame Jean Lion, born Baker . . . I was proud to be a French citizen.

Although my official address was now Rue de la Trémoille, off the Champs-Élysées, I was too attached to Beau Chêne to give it up. But things in Le Vésinet had changed. Chiquita no longer was there to greet me with a purr. His golden eyes were closed forever. I had been told he had died of tuberculosis, but I knew the real cause of death was a broken heart. Banned from the stage, forbidden to accompany me on my travels, and replaced in my heart by another kind of beast, a man, he had pined away. I missed him terribly.

Yet I was very happy with Jean. Life takes away with one hand and gives with the other. Jean helped me to forget Le Vésinet. We visited London, Mégève. . . . At last it was decided: I would abandon the stage. But first I must say my farewells. With Jean at my side, I embarked on my "goodbye tour." Tunis, Oran, Nice . . . Wherever we landed there were flowers and photographers waiting at the airport and the next day a story would appear in the local press, stating: "Josephine Baker and her husband, Jean Lion, are in town. The newlyweds report that they will return to Le Vésinet in three months' time, after which Josephine will retire from the stage. 'I want to become a housewife and have at least six children,' the star informed us." At every performance I sang "J'ai Deux Amours" and "Thanks for the Memory," with special feeling.

Jean had managed to schedule a business trip to coincide with my tour. He had contacts throughout North Africa and the South of France. After each show it was the same: "Hurry and take off your makeup, *cherie*. I have to be at the factory early tomorrow and I still have reports to finish." His obligations were such that I finally had to finish the tour alone. During an engagement in Limoges I made a quick side trip to "my" Milandes. "Can you see what a wonderful place this will be for our children, Alice?" "Yes, madame. But I wouldn't make plans until the baby is born if I were you."

I followed my usual itinerary: Basel, Zurich, Warsaw, Berlin, London. Every Sunday Jean was waiting at Le Bourget airport when I stepped off the plane laden with little dresses, shoes and toys. . . . "Are you *sure*, Josephine?" "Yes, *cheri.*" I couldn't wait until my daughter was born, although in fact I *wasn't* sure. Through it all I remained the scandalous Baker. In Glasgow I was forbidden to do my Algerian Nights number, during which I shed my red cloak and danced naked. . . . My heavy schedule prevented me from giving the starting signal for the Tour de France racers in Le Vésinet that year, but Jean, or "Mr. Baker," as the press sarcastically called him, took my place. In spite of the miles between us, we were so close! I knitted everywhere now—in airplanes, backstage, even on the beach in Cannes, where Jean and I met. He had forced me to give up using my private plane to save time. "Absolutely not, Josephine. No piloting. It's too dangerous." "But I have my license." I had recently passed my test in my dual-control biplane. "I know, *cherie*, but Madame Jean Lion will *not* man the controls." I could tell from the tone of his voice that he meant what he said.

By now everyone had noticed my knitting. I could see that Albert

Willemetz was worried. He had hoped that I would star in a musical comedy in the fall with Michel Simon. "I can understand that you've had your fill of music hall and cabaret, Josephine," he admitted, "but you can't give up the stage. I'm sure that Jean won't object. It's a very *dressy* play." "Send me the script, Albert." I could feel Jean's eyes on me and knew that he was thinking it would be impossible to raise a baby and perform nightly. "Being Madame Jean Lion isn't enough for you, is it? You have to be Josephine Baker too." He was right. But why *not* be both? Other actresses had children.

Besides, playing the part of the elegant Madame Lion at business dinners in order to further Jean's work was acting too! And no one objected to that. My real role was on the stage. I was convinced of it.

One day I felt a twinge of pain in my stomach . . . then suddenly I was in agony. The doctor was hurriedly sent for. There was nothing he could do.

I lost my baby.

I lost the only thing that could have bound Jean and me together. Alice had been right. It's bad luck to furnish a nursery too soon. "Can I have another child, Doctor?" "Of course, if you're careful." I knew what he was thinking. I had a dancer's body, long and narrow, with little place for a baby to grow. I burst into tears.

Mama Lion did her best to comfort me. Together we folded the little bibs and booties and locked them away in the closet. She did everything possible to set things right. But I knew that Jean and I were through. André's musical comedy had been postponed for a year. I couldn't remain in Paris. I wanted to flee, like a forest animal that hides in the depths of the forest to nurse his grief.

Rome, Stockholm . . . They named a rose for me. Josephine. A flower . . . flushed and delicate as my baby would have been. I smiled for the photographers. Madrid, Berlin . . . It was January 1939. The judge who proclaimed our divorce two years later said: "They were two strangers who never really met."

CHAPTER 10

———◦∞◦———

The Phony War

Felix Marouani (impresario): Josephine showed the world the radiant face of a star. She kept the pain of her failure in New York, Abatino's death, the disappointment of losing her baby and the collapse of her marriage carefully locked in her heart.

I first met Josephine at a business luncheon at Maxim's in September 1936. I was prepared to be dazzled, if not overwhelmed, and was delighted by her simplicity and the quiet elegance of her white suit. She had an almost childlike quality, playful and grave by turn, and a schoolgirlish way of wrinkling her forehead when she spoke, as if she were deep in her books. Josephine was to open at the Folies in two weeks and asked my opinion of the contract she had discussed with Paul Derval in New York. Only thirteen days until dress rehearsal and she still hadn't signed!

Josephine made up her mind about people on the spot. She and I were to become such good friends that I asked her to be the godmother of my first child. In no time she had engaged me to handle all her contracts and after her separation from Jean Lion, requested that I negotiate her South American tours. She sailed for Rio in March 1939. By the time she returned that July, I had booked her for the Casino de Paris in September. Josephine loved South America and profited from her voyage to stock up on music unknown in France—sambas, macumbas. Her forthcoming revue would have a Brazilian theme.

I'll never forget Josephine's arrival at the Gare de Lyon. She stepped off the boat train surrounded by enough orchids to carpet the station platform, followed by porters carrying cratefuls of coffee beans and armloads of fluttering, bright-colored macaws and cockatoos in cages. Ever since her breakup with Lion, the press had been predicting marriage with a succession of suitors: the latest of these supposed fiancés was Jean Meunier, of the well-known chocolate-manufacturing family. This time it looked as though the rumors might be true. Josephine was extremely anxious to start a family.

Her hopes were short-lived. On September 3, 1939, France declared war.

As a Tunisian, I did not have to enlist, but I decided to join the Special Services. My older brother Daniel, also an impresario as well as manager of the Cannes Casino, chose to enter an intelligence unit. One of his co-workers was a young officer, Jacques Abtey, who was looking for volunteer undercover agents. Daniel suggested Josephine. He knew her well, having frequently handled her bookings on the Côte d'Azur, and felt he could vouch for her courage, sense of intuition, honesty and affection for France. He was not mistaken. The first time Josephine met with Captain Abtey in Le Vésinet, she assured him: "France made me what I am. I am prepared to give her my life."

Josephine's private war had begun. Like everyone else's, it was a "phony" war at first, sluggish to the point of stagnation, with the various participants entrenched behind their respective lines. "It's just like the two sides of the footlights at the theater," Josephine remarked. It was business as usual in spite of the hostilities, and Daniel and I had convinced Henri Varna to reopen the Casino de Paris. The aim of the show had changed, of course; what was to have been a bouncy salute to Brazil had become a vehicle for bolstering the morale of the civilian population as well as French and English soldiers on leave. The revue, entitled *Paris-London*, was really two concert performances, one by Maurice Chevalier, the other by Josephine.

The two stars had worked together some years before in a light-hearted publicity stunt: the christening of the first baby elephant to be born in France, little August of the Circus Amar. Except for one thing, their

heart sank at the sight of those exiles, broken body and soul by defeat. There were old people and innocent children to tend, physical and spiritual wounds to heal. "Look. It's Josephine." And perhaps they would smile. Whenever I saw a young man in the group I fell silent. There might well be a Nazi spy hidden in that stricken, homeless crowd.

With the sudden invasion of France, the front line quickly collapsed. We were still performing at the Casino de Paris in May, but in a matter of days the hall was deserted. The enemy was at the gates. Monsieur Varna gathered us together. After embracing, we went our separate ways. We too were exiles now. My "boss," Captain Abtey, headed for the Loire Valley.

I left Paris by car, taking along what I could: a refugee Belgian couple, my faithful aide Paulette and those of my animals I couldn't leave behind. Destination: my château in the Dordogne.

Les Milandes, deep in the French countryside, seemed like the end of the world. I had spent only a matter of days there between engagements in the last few years, furnishing it bit by bit in the knowledge that I would return one day to stay. I never guessed it would be as a refugee. How peaceful it was in this beautiful setting. It was hard to believe that elsewhere people were fighting, suffering, dying. The vast château with its secret nooks and crannies made an ideal hiding place. And hide we did, concealing a navy officer, an air force captain, a Pole, my Belgian friends. . . . The Dordogne was worlds away from Paris, but not so remote that we couldn't pick up London . . . and General de Gaulle's call to arms.

We were deeply moved by the General's voice uttering words we had despaired of hearing, phrases that touched our innermost beings. His ringing tones reflected his indomitable spirit, the spirit of France herself, which I knew would never die. From that moment on everything seemed possible.

I wasn't particularly surprised one afternoon of that summer—which would have been beautiful if it hadn't been 1940—to see a dashing, fair-haired gentleman pull up in front of the château. He no longer called himself Mr. Fox, as he had in Paris. Sporting an American accent and a passport to match, Jacques Abtey was now Mr. Sanders, a citizen of a neutral nation. His aim: to reach London. "That sounds like a fine idea, Mr. Sanders. I'm going with you."

Things weren't that simple, however. While we tried to find a way to cross the Channel, life at Les Milandes was lived from day to day, always with one ear glued to London. One morning Mr. Sanders learned that the Intelligence Service was being reorganized. Headquarters had been transferred to Marseilles under the leadership of "Monsieur Perrier," in reality Colonel Paillole, now "manager" of a "rural development" concern. "Monsieur Perrier" employed "engineers" in Limoges, Clermont-Ferrand, Lyons and Toulouse. Through one of those rural planners, "Monsieur Daubray," in reality Captain Hofflize, we established contact with the Marseilles "office." Prying ears would have been surprised to learn how interested "rural developers" were in Mademoiselle Josephine Baker's projected singing engagement in Portugal!

I enjoyed Captain Abtey tremendously. He was a born actor. After Mr. Sanders, he became Jacques-François Hébert, a music hall performer from Marseilles, complete with mustache and spectacles. His mild manner and quiet ways made him the ideal secretary for Mademoiselle Baker.

Colonel Paillole: I wasn't very enthusiastic the first time Captain Abtey spoke to me about Josephine. Our department mistrusted would-be Mata Haris. But Abtey vouched for her personally. I was afraid that she was one of those shallow show business personalities who would shatter like glass if exposed to danger. Abtey assured me that Josephine was made of steel. Since there was nothing but routine information involved, I decided to try her out. We desperately required volunteers who were motivated by sheer patriotism.

It quickly became apparent that Josephine filled the bill magnificently. In October 1940, after France's collapse and the reorganization of our department, I badly needed to reestablish ties with British intelligence. Abtey was the ideal person to undertake this dangerous mission since he had trustworthy friends in the Intelligence Service. It was essential to get him to Portugal, where he would contact Bill Dundersdale of the I.S. through the British embassy, without being recognized by the Germans.

Josephine was delighted to serve as his cover, an assignment that had its risks. "Hébert" would transmit the information we had received on German military activity in western France to our contacts in Portugal. Abtey recorded much of this vital material in invisible ink on Josephine's sheet music. It can fairly be said that the destiny of our Allies and consequently of the Free French was written in part on the pages of "Two Loves Have I."

During the time the three of us spent together in Marseilles, I was struck by Josephine's optimism. "The United States is going to enter the war and we're sure to win." Her faith never faltered, not even when the rest of us despaired of the immensity of the task ahead. A confirmed Gaullist, she bolstered everyone's morale.

I watched the two of them set off together, Josephine admirably self-possessed in the face of possible danger, Abtey intending to complete his mission no matter what the cost. It would probably be some time before we met again. Under the pretext of embarking on a South American tour, Josephine and her "secretary" planned to join General de Gaulle in England.

London decided otherwise, however. Josephine and Abtey were more useful in France. Josephine was the first to return. All had gone smoothly, she assured me. At border checkpoints and social functions throughout cosmopolitan Lisbon, Monsieur Hébert had passed unobserved in the wake of the dazzling Josephine.

Frédéric Rey (Josephine's dancing partner): I ran into Josephine in Marseilles. We fell into each other's arms. "Where are you staying, Fred?" "In a bordello." Josephine burst out laughing. "Why not? It's the one place they'll never look for me. I've got to get out of the country, Josephine." To my surprise, she said she might be able to help me. But I would have to be patient. Before making a move, she had to establish a cover. "Why don't you do a revival of *La Créole?* There's no show at the opera house at the moment." The opera . . . Her eyes began to shine. Josephine singing Offenbach in Marseilles! "What a marvelous idea, Fred." But only two weeks remained until Christmas and the task seemed impossible. "You don't know Josephine. She can do anything," I assured the Opéra's management. They felt it was worth any risk to have Josephine's name on the program. She immediately set to work with her incredible energy. I helped her find the costumes and she recreated the sets from memories of the Paris performance six years earlier. Nothing seemed to interest her except *La Créole*. . . . She pulled the wool over the most suspicious eyes. That Christmas Eve, surely the coldest France had ever known, the curtain rose on that radiant bundle of warmth, la Baker. . . .

In the meantime Captain Abtey had reappeared. It was feared that the Germans were planning to take over the Vichy government, and he had been ordered to leave with Josephine for North Africa, where they could be more useful. "We'll take you with us, Fred." Before she could depart, however, she would have to find a way to break her contract with the Marseilles Opéra. Perhaps a medical certificate would do the trick. It shouldn't be too difficult to obtain, because Josephine had been coughing during most of that dreadful winter. After examining her and taking a group of x-rays, the doctor pronounced, "You've got to take some time off, madame." The very words she had hoped to hear! "Whatever you say, Doctor. But I'll need your help to cancel my remaining performances." "I want you to stop work immediately. You have shadows on both lungs." He must have wondered why Josephine took the news so well. "Isn't nature wonderful!" she exclaimed.

The Opéra's directors seemed quite understanding and Josephine prepared to depart at once with her little band for a warmer climate. But she couldn't leave France without her pets. "I can't understand abandoning animals. They would never do it to us!" From the Dordogne to Marseilles, a friend escorted some of her menagerie, including two monkeys and a Great Dane. Josephine would go to North Africa by plane to conserve her strength. I was elected to follow with the "babies" by ship. We would be forced to separate temporarily, and in wartime who knew what that might mean? "The fighting will end soon," Josephine insisted. "The Americans will be joining in any minute. They've got to. You'll see for yourself!" And she shook her fist in the air. It was January 15, 1941. . . .

CHAPTER 11

Time of Trial

WE SET UP HEADQUARTERS in the Hotel Aletti in Algiers. Fred had had a memorable crossing with the animals. Bonzo, the Great Dane, had begun the trip by being seasick and later had been struck on the head by a piece of luggage. Luckily nothing had fallen on the monkeys, or we would all have been wearing black.

No sooner had we arrived on North African soil than "Monsieur Hébert" prepared to leave for Casablanca to pick up our Portuguese visas. During our previous trip to Lisbon, it had been decided that I would perform in the Portuguese capital again. "Monsieur Perrier" had alerted his contact in Casa and we anticipated no difficulty in obtaining the necessary papers at the Portuguese consulate there.

Imagine my surprise when a policeman appeared at the Aletti one morning. Could he please have a word with Mademoiselle Baker? Had he come to inquire about Fred or "Monsieur Hébert"? I asked myself nervously. The person at issue turned out to be me! The management of the Marseilles Opéra had filed suit for breach of contract. I would have to pay 400,000 francs in damages before I could enter Morocco. Clearly my medical certificate had failed to do its job. Captain Abtey was furious. Before leaving for Casa he referred the matter to "Monsieur Perrier's" man in Algiers. What was behind the Opéra's change of heart? They had originally seemed willing enough to let me leave France. Yet now they had called in the police. Why?

Things got steadily worse. Jacques telephoned me from Casablanca to report that the Portuguese consul was hedging about our visas. "Monsieur Hébert's" insistence on the importance of my singing engagement in Lisbon had fallen on deaf ears. "I'm afraid you're going to have to convince the consul yourself, Josephine." I knew he was trying to tell me that the information to be transmitted to the Intelligence Service was urgent. I had no sooner received my Moroccan visa than my bags were packed.

With Bonzo straining at his leash and the monkeys chattering in their cages, I stepped onto the train for Casablanca. Captain Abtey had suggested that I board out my pets, but I insisted that nothing would look more suspicious than Josephine without her animals! By the end of the trip, however, I was sure that compared to spending twenty-four hours with my menagerie on a crowded North African train, dealing with the Portuguese consul would be simple! I was wrong. . . . I had no trouble obtaining *my* visa from the charming, courteous diplomat, but "Monsieur Hébert's" was categorically refused. Trying to hide my mounting concern, I stressed my efficient "secretary's" importance to the success of my tour. How would I manage the details without him? I asked with girlish helplessness. The consul was apologetic but firm. Until he got permission from the Minister of the Interior to issue a visa, his hands were tied.

Back at the hotel, Captain Abtey and I conferred nervously. "Do you think they may have blown your cover, Jacques?" "I doubt it. But we've got to keep going, no matter what." We decided that I would have to travel to Lisbon alone. Taking my sheet music, of course. Who could have guessed that it was covered with invisible notations about German installations in southwest France?

I sensed Captain Abtey's concern when we said goodbye. It was the first time I had undertaken a mission completely on my own. "God bless you, Josephine. And good luck."

Lisbon was crowded with Europeans of all nationalities and persuasions. Without waiting to unpack my bags, I set out to visit the "friendly" embassies. I was determined to use all my connections to obtain "Monsieur Hébert's" visa. But even the Swiss ambassador seemed curiously vague regarding my "secretary's" status. I would have to be patient, Captain Paillole's contact advised me. Whatever he said! Posters announcing my forthcoming performance were posted all over Lisbon. I forced myself to rehearse. By week's end, I still had made no progress with Jacques's papers. Worse, word had arrived of Rommel's advance in Libya. The pro-Germans were jubilant, the rest of us heartsick. I don't know whether it was the news from Africa or a touch of bronchitis, but I felt feverish every night. I was forced to return to Morocco without Jacques's visa.

I had hoped that the dry air in Marrakech would help heal my lungs. The palatial Mamounia Hotel offered a superb view of the snow-capped Atlas Mountains towering over the rosy village, but staying there cost a fortune. I was delighted when a Moroccan friend offered to lend me a house in the Arab quarter. Europeans shunned the labyrinthine Médina with its twisting streets lined with high walls. At the end of an impasse, behind a bolted door, lay my private world, remote from prying eyes. I'll never forget the cool freshness of that patio, the orange trees grouped around a fountain. My pets loved it there and I would have been happy too had it not been for the war. There was talk of a German move against Morocco. Spain was already teeming with German agents. It might be wise to find out what was happening there. . . . After a few restful days in my secret garden I felt as good as new. Wasn't it only natural for Josephine to want to perform in Spain? Captain Abtey, a frequent visitor to the Médina, warned me to be careful. His visa still had not arrived and once again I would have to travel without my faithful "secretary." "Pray to your lucky star, Josephine." Surely I had one. Anyway, what did I have to risk? This time there wasn't a drop of invisible ink on my scores.

Being Josephine Baker had definite advantages. Seville, Madrid, Barcelona . . . Wherever I went, I was swamped with invitations. I particularly liked attending diplomatic functions, since the embassies and consulates swarmed with talkative people. Back at my hotel, I carefully recorded everything I'd heard. My notes would have been highly compromising had they been discovered, but who would dare search Josephine Baker to the skin? The information remained snugly in place, secured by a safety pin.

Besides, my encounters with customs officials were always extremely relaxed. When they asked *me* for papers, they generally meant autographs.

"Monsieur Hébert" welcomed me back to North Africa three weeks later with a sigh of relief. We had a new information channel, Washington, thanks to the American vice-consul, Mr. Canfield, who had recently arrived in Casablanca. I liked him on the spot. Surely it wouldn't be long before the United States entered the war!

While in Casablanca, I decided to have some x-rays taken. I had heard that the city had excellent doctors.

The gentle climate in Marrakech had done its work well. My lungs were clear. Perhaps the radiologist could give me further good news. "Tell me, Doctor, can you take x-rays that show whether or not I'm able to bear children? I want a baby more than anything else in the world!" The doctor looked at me with amazement. "A child? Don't you know there's a war on, madame?" In this ailing world of ours, how could I want to create life in the midst of death? I explained that thanks to American intervention, the war would soon be over. We would need children to build a new and better world. The doctor shrugged. "I admire your optimism, madame." And he prepared a hypodermic necessary to the x-ray process.

As I waited for his diagnosis, my heart pounded more loudly than it ever had on an opening night. My entire future was at stake. "I'll have the results for you tomorrow, madame. But there's no need to worry. I'm certain there's nothing abnormal. You'll have those children of yours and twenty-five years from now they'll be ready and eager to start a new war, providing this one is over!" "How can you talk like that, Doctor?" I exclaimed, seizing him by the shoulders. "Peace is on the way. I swear it!"

I left Casablanca on a pink cloud.

Back in my cool patio, I dreamed of days to come. Assuming Les Milandes survived the war, the old château would one day ring with children's voices. I wanted at least four. . . . My mind was far away when a sudden pain stabbed at my stomach.

I tossed and turned all night in torment. The following day my friends summoned a doctor and for the next forty-eight hours I lay beneath ice bags whose contents quickly melted on exposure to my fever-racked body and the sweltering June weather. The doctor shook his head. "I'm worried about peritonitis." How was that possible? I'd been in perfect health. My raging infection probably sprang from the injection I had received. The doctor must not have taken the proper precautions. And to think I had begged to be x-rayed! By now the pain was excruciating. Dear God, please let me have children. . . .

The doctor insisted I leave for Casablanca at once and put myself in a surgeon's hands. Jacques was unable to find an ambulance but rented a large car, whose back seat he arranged like a berth. The Arab servants wrapped me in a blanket and carried me half conscious down the twisting path to where the car stood waiting. A 250-mile drive lay ahead. I remember "Monsieur Hébert" cautioning the driver to be careful of bumps . . . then nothing.

It was several days before I emerged from my delirium. An operation had been performed; I faced a long convalescence. The doctor was amazed at my resiliency. "You have amazing vitality, Madame Baker," he exclaimed. I couldn't wait to leave the clinic, but Captain Abtey saw things differently. My sickroom provided a perfect rendezvous spot. What was more natural than for Vice-Consul Canfield to visit his compatriot Josephine Baker? Jacques's enthusiasm was contagious. After all, his plan would both help to pass the time and allow me to aid the cause in some small way. Several of our highly placed Moroccan friends joined in the group at my bedside. There was interesting news to exchange.

Autumn so soon? My hopes for a brief convalescence had been shattered by a serious relapse. But thanks to sulfa drugs and good care, I was on the road to recovery again. Rommel had been repulsed and was said to be gravely ill, but the Germans were advancing on the Russian front. The faces around my bedside were grave. The British aircraft carrier *Ark Royal* had been torpedoed off Gibraltar; the destroyer *Reuben James* had sunk, killing 115 American sailors. What was the United States waiting for? There was no way to avoid war now. . . .

While my life had been in danger, "Monsieur Hébert" had slept on a cot in my room. Now he was back to his comings and goings. He appeared at my bedside one day in a state of excitement that contrasted sharply with his usual outward calm. "What is it, Jacques? Has General de Gaulle arrived in North Africa?" "Not yet, Josephine . . . but the

Japanese have bombed Pearl Harbor." Surely the Americans would be forced to act now! They would come, they would land. . . . I felt as though my heart would burst.

Christmas. Jacques tried to brighten my room and my spirits with a miniature Christmas tree. I had been ill for six months!

The new American vice-consul, Mr. Bartlett, like his predecessor, frequently came "calling." He was likely to find "Monsieur Hébert" at my bedside along with other "concerned" acquaintances. "Monsieur Perrier" had recently arrived in Algiers and a counterespionage effort was under way to combat Nazi infiltration in Morocco.

With the approach of spring, my strength returned and I began taking my first hesitant steps in the clinic's garden. One sunny day I called for a carriage. My first outing . . . from which I returned with a raging fever. Another relapse. Peritonitis accompanied by the threat of septicemia. "Keep fighting, keep fighting," I murmured as I sank into unconsciousness. . . .

"Extremely serious . . ." My doctor's voice reached me through a blur of pain. Weeks passed. While the sulfanilamides slowly did their work, the United States put its vast war machine into gear. Despite Rommel's counteroffensive in Libya and German submarine supremacy in the Atlantic, the die was cast. It was only a matter of time and patience now. . . . When I felt well enough to read, Captain Abtey brought me a book on the Middle Ages which mentioned Les Milandes. The sudden surge of longing I experienced for my château must have been like the nostalgia felt by medieval lords fighting their *own* holy wars in far-flung lands.

I was startled to read an interview with Maurice Chevalier one morning announcing that he had found me "dying and penniless" in the Casablanca hospital. What nonsense! He had asked if he might visit me but I had refused. I had nothing to say to him. Maurice was one of those Frenchmen who believed that the Germans had won the war and that it was time things returned to normal—on German terms. To get revenge for my rebuff, or perhaps simply for attention's sake, he described me in tears, begging him not to leave me!

I picked up my book on the Middle Ages. The Crusaders . . . Those were real men! Maurice didn't merit his last name. He was a great artist but a small human being.

Maurice's fabrications had unexpected consequences. Convinced that my life and welfare were in danger, well-wishers flocked to the hospital with provisions. Finding I wasn't there, they proceeded to the clinic. It was over a year now since I had fallen ill. I *must* return to the stage soon and *prove* I wasn't dead.

But not quite yet. Jacques and one of Paillole's men were at my bedside. American intelligence had just informed them that the debarkation was only hours away.

November 8, 1942. When I heard the shellfire, I pulled an old sweater over my pajamas and rushed barefoot onto my balcony. General Noguès's forces, in the name of the Vichy government, were shooting at American planes. "Get back inside, Josephine. You could be hit by shrapnel!" The air crackled with explosions. "No, Jacques. This is no time to be in bed." The battle of Casablanca had begun.

Captain Abtey planned to report to American headquarters the next day. We devised a daring plan during the night. I would ask for a private ambulance. Jacques and one of his men would dress like orderlies and carry me out of the hospital on a stretcher. . . . But "Monsieur Hébert" finally decided against the idea. "You're simply not strong enough yet." Unfortunately he was right. Jacques left the next morning at dawn, using a Red Cross flag to cross the lines. All I could do was wait and see how the fighting would end. When the suspense became too great, I climbed onto the clinic's roof, to the concern of the nurses. In three days the battle was won and on the fourth, November 11, Allied troops paraded through a free Casablanca.

On December 1, I finally left the clinic for Marrakech. "Monsieur Hébert" would stay in Casablanca to help organize Africa's Free French forces under the sign of the cross of Lorraine. My job was to regain my strength as quickly as possible.

A few days after I moved into the Mamounia, I felt so feverish that I was obliged to call the doctor. "It's nothing serious, is it? I'm probably just overtired from the trip." The doctor shook his head. "I'm sorry, Madame Baker. You've got paratyphoid."

Another Christmas in bed. Jacques joined me for the holidays. We were sitting by our Christmas tree when the news of Darlan's assassination arrived.

The New Year ushered in my nineteenth month of illness. I was beginning to feel like a medicine chest.

I could sense spring in the air. It made me want to join the birds in song. "And that's exactly what I plan to do—for the American troops." My doctor looked horrified. "It's out of the question, madame. It's much too soon. I can't be responsible for what might happen." "You tend to your responsibilities and I'll look out for mine," I retorted. "You're being extremely stubborn, madame." "If de Gaulle hadn't been stubborn, Doctor, you and I would be in concentration camps!"

Toward the end of January, the General arrived in North Africa at last —"deigned to come," sneered his enemies. My admiration for de Gaulle remained unchanged. Who could forget that without his call to arms, France would have been plunged into blackest night? After meeting with Roosevelt, Churchill and his political rival, Giraud, the General returned to London. From now on there would be a representative of the Free French government in Algiers.

Eight days after the historic Casablanca Conference, I returned to the stage. I had been asked to inaugurate a service club for black GIs, the Liberty Club. The city was still buzzing with news of the conference, yet despite the talk of peace, the fighting was intensifying in Tunisia, all of France remained to be rewon and the underground movement was gearing itself for a new thrust. How could I best advance the cause? Suddenly I knew. In order to present a united front to the enemy, we would have to be *true* allies, oblivious of color and origins. Surely I could help by launching the Liberty Club and afterward attending the reception to be given by General Clark, commander of an American division in Casablanca.

It seemed like centuries since I had last sat at my makeup table. I studied my face in the mirror. How thin it was. My legs were like matchsticks. I'd better keep them covered. I could feel perspiration dampening the roots of my hair. I mustn't overdo it tonight. My program would include two American songs—a Negro lullaby to prove I hadn't forgotten my origins and a Gershwin tune to show the poetry of the American soul —then "J'ai Deux Amours" to emphasize that I was French now and that France was a land of liberty. For this very reason she must be returned to her people. That would be enough for one evening. . . . The moment the curtain fell I collapsed on a couch. But except for some minor dizziness I had survived the performance unharmed.

I walked into General Clark's reception at the Grand Hotel Aïfa with "Monsieur Hébert," his associate Zimmer and two highly placed Moroccan friends. It was like entering another world. The dinner jackets, gowns, jewels and decorations reminded me of the glittering parties I had attended before the war. For the first time since the fighting had begun, I did what I do so well: I made an entrance. The entire press corps was there. No one would be able to say I was dead or half dead now!

The next day I returned to Marrakech, determined that my convalescence had come to an end. I was ready to put myself at the disposition of General Eisenhower's friend Colonel Meyers, who handled theatrical entertainment for the Allied armies. The colonel, a highly organized, decisive and cultivated man, had already mapped out an extensive tour under the management of our friend Zimmer. We would, of course, donate our services, but our transportation would be paid for and we would be lodged and fed with the troops. In the meantime, there was more high-level entertaining to attend. I particularly remember a dinner at the American consulate, where Roosevelt and Churchill had stayed two weeks before. The host, Robert Murphy, representing the President in North Africa, placed me at his right. Our table was crowded with five-star generals—Clark, Patton, Anderson. Some of my Moroccan friends decided to have a gala evening of their own before we left on tour. "That sounds wonderful," I said. "But be sure to include the staff of the Liberty Club. We've got to show that blacks and whites are treated equally in the American army . . . or else what's the point of waging war on Hitler?"

Frédéric Rey: Thanks to Captain Abtey's intervention, I was accepted as a volunteer member of the Free French forces in Africa. My mission was to help Josephine realize her dream of using entertainment to unify black and white troops. At the same time she planned to embark on a propaganda campaign for General de Gaulle, helping to establish him as the undisputed leader of the Free French. Thanks to her untiring efforts, she was extremely successful in achieving both these goals.

I arrived at her handsome house in the Arab quarter to find the entire household at their prayers, including Josephine, wearing a djellabah. She was in high spirits. "How wonderful to see you, Fred. Now we can get to work."

I hadn't seen Josephine for some time and was appalled by her gaunt appearance. She insisted there was no need to worry. "I'm made of iron," she assured me. The words of her last letter passed through my head: "Dear friend: A word to say that I'm planning to return to work. There are important things to be done. You and Zimmer and I can help. I'm tired of twiddling my thumbs."

My first job was to get Josephine's wardrobe in shape. Most of her costumes were moth-eaten. I would have to try to salvage what I could and make the alterations necessary to hide her thin arms and legs. I was convinced that Josephine was resuming work too soon, but there was no way to make her change her mind. When Josephine got an idea, she stuck to it! The war effort came first.

I collected all the usable scraps I could find and helped to sew them together. When I wasn't involved in dressmaking, I aided Zimmer with the decorations. We hoped to transform Josephine's Arab mansion into a fairy tale setting for the important party we were planning. "The evening *has* to be a success," Josephine insisted. "I want to show that Arabs, blacks and whites can meet as brothers." We had heard rumors of strife between the Moroccan population and the American troops. This was to be more than a social evening. It was an important milestone in Josephine's fight against racism.

The evening was a triumph. Josephine did more to encourage fraternization that night than had been accomplished in weeks of fighting for a common cause. Among the guests were Colonel Roosevelt, the American President's son; the major in charge of the Liberty Club; the American consul; Arab leaders; and French and English officers.

The first *Josephine Baker Show* was a benefit performance for the French Red Cross held at a movie house in Casablanca. Zimmer and I had filled the theater with greenery and Allied flags. I not only served as Josephine's dancing partner, but helped her change costumes backstage. She would announce a "change of scenery," then in record time, while the orchestra played a number, change costume and reappear as a Brazilian, a Breton villager, an Asian, and finally, dressed in a floating red and blue crepe gown I had made her, would sing "J'ai Deux Amours." "Good heavens, madame, you're dressed in the colors of Paris," an officer gasped. That dress and the song that went with it were to become the high spots of her tour.

Colonel Meyers was so impressed by Josephine's impact on General

Clark's troops that he offered her a contract for the duration of the war. "I'm sorry," she replied, "but as a Free French soldier I can only perform on a volunteer basis." How could she accept "exclusive booking" from the Americans when there were French soldiers fighting in Tunisia?

The first stop on our tour was Oran, a city ringed with camps containing some three hundred thousand men. We gave several shows daily, usually on makeshift stages. Josephine's dressing room was an army tent; "backstage" consisted of a rough curtain behind which I "changed the scenery" as best I could. We discovered some excellent black musicians and our evening performances ended with a round of military anthems. Sometimes the stage was set up in an open field and lit by antiaircraft searchlights.

Our final performance in Oran, attended by several thousand men, was brusquely interrupted by an air alert. As German aircraft bore down on us, Josephine was thrown to the ground by nearby soldiers and the searchlights were extinguished, leaving tracer bullets as the only source of light. I'll never forget Josephine's face as she lay there calmly, eating the ice cream she had been given by a soldier from Texas. "Watch out for your teeth, Josephine!" I shouted. She had told me that the only thing she feared about the war was that it might damage her famous smile. She quickly covered her mouth.

Our next stop was the Algerian village of Mostaganem. This time our stage was the village square. The population, composed largely of Italians, had been subverted by the Germans and was extremely hostile to Americans. Josephine felt that the situation called for a change in tactics. Therefore her "performance" consisted of mingling with the villagers, distributing cigarettes and candy, and putting children into the arms of American soldiers who had joined the crowd. Thanks to her charm and forcefulness, she soon had both civilians and soldiers in the palm of her hand. At the end of April, she was back in Marrakech. Needless to say, she hadn't gained an ounce.

Josephine was soon off again, this time to tour British camps in Libya and Egypt. She left in an English bomber and returned in the heat of mid July as thin as ever but loaded with information, impressions, notes. She had also performed in Beirut and Damascus. In Cairo, she had had a run-in with King Farouk in a fashionable night spot. The king, discovering that she was among the guests, had ordered her to sing. Explaining that she was not there to perform, she had continued dancing with her escort. Our stubborn Josephine!

In spite of her clash with Farouk, Josephine intended to return to Cairo to participate in a huge Franco-Egyptian gala the king was sponsoring. It would be the first Free French gathering in a country which had not yet recognized de Gaulle's government.

"It's crucial that French influence be maintained in the Middle East," Captain Abtey insisted. To this end, Josephine decided we should undertake an official propaganda tour, sponsored by General de Gaulle, the proceeds of which would go the French Resistance movement. Before embarking on the first step of our new adventure, a gala appearance in Algiers, Josephine returned to Marrakech for a week's rest. . . . Zimmer and I were there to welcome her in Algiers as she drew up in a baggage-laden jeep driven by Captain Abtey. She was in battle dress. We had no sooner arrived at the theater than Josephine got to work: "We've *got* to find a good jazz band for the first part of the show." "But where, Josephine?" "By talking to the colored GIs, obviously!" General de Gaulle had announced that he would attend the performance with Madame de Gaulle, which gave the evening special meaning. It would truly be Free French Night.

As we were setting up the stage lights, Josephine exclaimed, "Wouldn't it be marvelous if we had a huge French flag on stage bearing the cross of Lorraine!" There was no such flag, of course. "We'll make one," she cried. "It's easy enough to find red, white and blue material." True enough, but the sewing involved presented grave problems. Given the size of the stage, the cross alone would measure six yards across. We'd never have it ready in time. "Never" did not exist for Josephine. Whatever she started she finished. We hurried the bolts of material to a nearby convent. It didn't take Josephine long to convince the mother superior to "do a job for General de Gaulle."

The show began with a sprightly American jazz number to liven up the audience. During the intermission an aide requested Josephine to join the General in his box. At last she would meet the man to whom she had sworn allegiance in June 1940. The General offered her his seat. . . .

She returned backstage clutching a little cross of Lorraine cast in gold. I had never seen her so moved. It was a gift from the General. Josephine had worn fabulous jewels from her admirers in her lifetime, but this tiny

cross was her greatest treasure. It was typical of Josephine to give her all
on stage whatever the circumstances. But that night she outdid herself,
pouring out her very soul to the tall figure in the governor general's box.
When the huge flag with its imposing cross of Lorraine was unfurled at
evening's end to the strains of the Marseillaise, a wave of emotion swept
over the crowd. That was Josephine's gift to General de Gaulle.

When the show was over, we carefully folded the flag and stored it in
our big Hotchkiss. Piling in after it, we set out behind our lead jeep. The
Josephine Baker Show was on its way. All along our route the flag would
be displayed. As we moved from town to town through the ravaged
countryside, slender, feminine Josephine was replaced by soldier Baker in
battle dress. I studied her determined profile beneath her army helmet as
we bumped down the rutted paths. She was muffled in an army greatcoat
against the night air. . . . The Hotchkiss lost its steering gear along the
road. We had no choice but to join the driver in the jeep. With boyish
enthusiasm, Josephine helped us transfer the baggage. Once we were
under way again, she took out her knitting. . . . The sun was high in the
sky and we were still two hours from Tunis when the jeep's motor gave
up the ghost. While we waited for someone to tow us the rest of the way,
Josephine calmly continued to knit.

Sfax, Cairo, Benghazi, Tobruk . . . The blazing heat of day, the cold
nights, sand fleas, war-torn villages, signs marked with death's heads, the
desert strewn with the twisted remains of tanks, grim reminders of the
bitter fighting . . . In that cruel landscape we took turns keping watch at
night to ward off the scavengers who preyed on corpses and would have
preyed on us as well.

Josephine: Lebanon, Syria . . . One evening in Beirut, I sat turning my
cross of Lorraine in my hand. In a few hours my prize possession would
no longer be mine. The Resistance movement desperately needed more
funds. I was certain that auctioning off the little cross I had received from
the General's own hand would bring a handsome sum—money that could
be used to establish another link in the underground network and perhaps
save lives. It wasn't as though I would lose my cross forever. After all, the
things we truly love stay with us always, locked in our hearts as long as
life remains.

My guess was right. The cross spoke to the spectators' pocketbooks as well as their hearts, bringing in three hundred thousand francs. The entire evening netted the Resistance more than a million. Enough to make us forget our fatigue!

Jerusalem, Tel Aviv, Jaffa, Haifa . . . We ended every show by unfurling our handsome flag. The powdered, pampered Josephine of the past seemed almost like a stranger. More often than not, my face was dust-stained now. Life takes on new meaning when death is ever present, ever near, like a watchdog alerting us with his growling. Yet in spite of all we saw and endured, we continued singing. It's not that war hardens our hearts. Many people remain as feeling as before. But war shapes us, forcing us to look deep within to find tenderness.

Algiers at last. We entered the city with a flourish, Captain Abtey driving one jeep and I behind the wheel of the other.

Jean-Pierre Bloch (supply officer, Ministry of the Interior): Algiers was crowded with people during that period. I ran into my old friend Josephine, suitcase in hand, unable to find lodgings. I offered her one of the beds in my double hotel room. Wearily she accepted.

I retired to let her prepare for the night and when I returned was surprised to find her kneeling at her bedside deep in prayer. From conversations we had had before the war, I knew she was religious. It wasn't that which surprised me. It was the nature of her prayers. When she had concluded, I picked up her prayer book.

"But these are Jewish prayers, Josephine." "Of course. When I married Jean Lion I converted." I was astounded. In 1943 many people were doing all they could to deny that very heritage. Not Josephine. Throughout the fearful years of the Occupation, she had carried her little prayer book, half in Hebrew, half in French. Many had gone to the gas chamber for less. What an extraordinary woman she was!

We remained good friends. After the war I frequently ran into her at the International League Against Racism and Anti-Semitism, for which she was a selfless, dedicated active worker.

Colonel Paillole: Josephine presented me with a pair of shoes made of camel skin on her return to Algiers. Her mission had been highly successful and one that she alone could have accomplished. Thanks to her reputation, energy and conviction, she saved a situation jeopardized by all-out Axis propaganda in Muslim circles. Needless to say, she never asked for a penny.

Josephine: I was strolling through the Mamounia gardens with Colonel Roosevelt in early 1944 when I suddenly doubled over with pain. The doctor could do nothing to relieve me and it quickly became obvious that I would have to be hospitalized. Another operation . . . this time for an intestinal obstruction. From my sickbed, I heard a curious chanting in the street. My impoverished friends from the Médina were praying to Allah to save me. I later heard that they had sacrificed a lamb.

Throughout the critical period that followed my operation I knew that I would survive but was too weak to say so. I believe we die when we choose to —when the struggle becomes such that we abandon the fight and let go. That moment had not come for me. Too much remained to be done.

Algiers, May 31, 1944. Acting Sublieutenant Baker, Josephine, is ordered to present herself: wherever her services are required. Motive: propaganda. Means of transport: all means. Qualified military authorities are requested to facilitate Sublieutenant Baker's movements. [Signed] Air Force General Bouscat, Chief of the Air Force General Staff.

I had been living in General Bouscat's residence for some time. My next mission was to tour Corsica. Our group had been re-formed and my party would include Captain Abtey and Zimmer. We took off from Boufarik airport on June 6, immediately after receiving the thrilling news of the Normandy landings. It was the beginning of the end for the Germans.

Suddenly our joy subsided: a disturbing sound filled the air. Just as the Corsican coast came into sight, one of the engines died. Captain Abtey hurried to consult the pilot. "He says not to worry," Jacques reported. "One engine's all we need." The minutes crept by; we barely avoided a cliff. "Brace yourselves," someone shouted. Zimmer wedged our flag around me as a buffer, then crouched down in his seat. *Josephine, your teeth!* I thought. And I covered my mouth. The plane smashed into the sea. Somehow the engineer shattered a window with an ax and we all crawled onto the wing. As the plane began drifting toward shore, African sharpshooters on the riverbank stripped off their clothes and swam out to meet us. Just in time.

Piggyback, draped in the cross of Lorraine, I arrived on French soil. This time my "entrance" had not been planned.

My luggage was ruined, my costumes were drenched, my wigs were soaked and Sublieutenant Baker herself was utterly waterlogged! But I had not been this happy for four years. Had I not been in uniform, my African heritage would have caused me to kiss the ground.

CHAPTER 12

———— ❦ ————

Jo and Jo

Jo Bouillon: It was the end of October 1944. A newly liberated Paris was delirious with joy. I was recording with my orchestra in a radio studio on the Champs-Élysées. What a pleasure to be able to play our favorite American composers again! We happily launched into a Cole Porter tune.

My euphoric mood was shattered by the sight of our business manager, Roger Legrand, gesturing from the sound booth. Roger and I had met before the war and become associates and close friends. I signaled him to join me and as I continued marking time he whispered, "There's someone outside who says she's a friend of yours. She insists on seeing you!" "Tell her I'm recording." "I did, but she says she won't leave until she's talked to you. I have a feeling she means it." Judging from the sly look on Roger's face, I guessed that my visitor was a secret admirer. I'd been getting a good deal of fan mail ever since I had started my own radio hour. "All right. Show her in. It'll amuse the men." I returned my attention to conducting "I've Got You Under My Skin." "You're playing my song," I suddenly heard. As I turned toward that familiar voice, my baton froze in midair. Standing beside me was the uniformed figure of Sublieutenant Baker of the French Air Force.

"Josephine!"

Five years earlier I would have kissed her hand and she would have greeted me with a "How are you, Monsieur Bouillon?" But given the time, the place, the excitement in the air, we threw ourselves into each other's arms. It was a way of putting the war behind us. Then I stepped back to look at her. She was much thinner than before, but as beautiful as ever, with the same dazzling smile. My musicians couldn't contain themselves. One by one they rose to their feet until all forty were standing and clapping. Beaming with pleasure, Josephine took my arm and said, "I have something I want to discuss with you, Jo. Drop by and see me this evening." "But I'm doing a show at Le Boeuf sur le Toit tonight." "Come when it's finished, then." She scribbled down an address, threw a kiss to my men and hurried off. Something resembling a black-and-white ball bounced along at her heels. "What in the world is that with her?" "A dog . . . I think," replied Roger.

At one o'clock the next morning I arrived at the Rue de Dardanelles near the Bois de Boulogne. The street was pitch black, according to regulations. I groped my way up the stairs, counting off the floors until I arrived at Josephine's landing. An elderly man, or so he appeared in the darkness, answered my ring and ushered me into a room faintly lit by a night light. From the bed a voice asked sleepily, "Is that you, Jo? Come and sit down." I dimly perceived a shapeless form bundled in a military greatcoat, a huge turban and several mufflers. This was how Josephine protected herself from the cold. If only the audiences who had applauded the fragile *Oiseau des Îles* could see her now, huddled in her dark nesting place like a great frowzy owl! She certainly hadn't gone out of her way for me. Josephine quietly presented Monsieur Boudon, who she told me had been looking after her goods and properties since the onset of the war, that war which still was not over and in which she continued to fight.

"General de Lattre de Tassigny has commissioned me to follow the French First Army through the liberated countries. My job is to organize shows. How would you like to come with me, Jo, and do your bit for Free France?"

The little black-and-white bundle of fluff sat up and begged. "Down, Mitraillette." Gathering up her pet, Josephine explained that she had found the puppy in North Africa while waiting for repatriation in a convent which had been converted into a pickup spot for women members of the French Air Force. Since animals were forbidden on liberty ships, she had smuggled Mitraillette out of Mers-el-Kebir under her great-coat.

Josephine didn't seem to expect me to answer her question. She simply assumed my answer was yes. In hushed tones, appropriate to the lateness of the hour, she spoke of the tasks faced by the Liberation, the role of General de Gaulle. The very mention of the General's name made her face light up and her voice fill with passion. Despite the cold, she flung back her coat and seized my arm. "It's thanks to *him* that France is here to take part in the victory . . . a victory that's moving eastward—and we'll be following it. But first we're going to head south and do a series of benefit performances for war victims."

I barely had time to ask, "Who's we?" before she replied, "Me, you and your orchestra." "Just a minute, Josephine. What kind of terms are you offering?" "None. You'll be donating your services. I've never been paid a penny for my army shows." "But, Josephine, my musicians have families to support. What makes you think they'll accept?" "They've got to, for a cause like this." As she spoke on about Gaullism and France, I suddenly realized it was dawn. . . .

I broached the subject the next morning at the studio. How would my men like to go on tour? "Under what conditions?" "Free of charge." I went on to explain why. Stony silence. Then: "But what about my parents? . . . the children?" My musicians had a contract guaranteeing three paid broadcasts a week. How could I reconcile that with Josephine's proposal? "Find a way," she said breezily before leaving for Marseilles. A well-connected friend took me to the Ministry of the Interior and we finally arrived at a solution. We would do our three weekly broadcasts wherever we happened to be. Rehearsal time and fees would be reimbursed in accordance with our original contract. After working out a few remaining details, the men agreed. And that's how Jo Bouillon's orchestra ended up in Marseilles with Josephine Baker.

Josephine's showmanship, stamina and determination to achieve her goals never ceased to amaze me. We gave benefits in Monte Carlo, Nice, Cannes, Toulon, and soon had netted nearly two million francs for war victims. Wrapped in her greatcoat, Sublieutenant Baker was oblivious of her appearance until showtime, when she transformed herself into a miracle of femininity, grace and beauty. I watched this metamorphosis night after night as she emerged from the cocoon of her army uniform, exquisitely made up, immaculately coiffed, ready to give her all: her smile, her vitality, her love of life. Once the curtain fell she was Officer Baker again, brisk, totally unaffected, utterly absorbed in following rules and doing her duty. Two distinct and equally compelling Josephines.

Throughout that bitter snowy winter Josephine performed in her North African costumes. The barracks in which we put on our show were sometimes too small to contain all the troops and Josephine wanted to sing for *everyone*. "Throw up a stage outside," she'd order. "But it's much too cold, madame. The men are hardened to this kind of weather—they're soldiers, after all—but it's not fair to you." "I'm a soldier too," she'd retort, and sing outdoors for an hour at a time. "That seems to have warmed you up, men!" she'd shout amid thunderous applause. Moving from camp to camp, Josephine gave as many as three shows a day. In Mulhouse she was the first French performer to have appeared at the Municipal Theater since 1940. During her triumphant tour her name was linked with that of France itself. Beaming with excitement, she asked, "How could I ever accept payment for this?"

The thing that surprised me most about her was the way she instinctively adapted herself to any situation. Whether she was dealing with the highest military official, the humblest soldier, the most brilliant personality or the most obscure, she was always herself yet never quite the same. I remember her in uniform sitting on the bed of a typhoid victim in a room full of Buchenwald victims too ill to be moved. The camp had been liberated a few days before, revealing its hideous secrets. Tirelessly she sang, talked, comforted, bringing a last spark of light to dimming eyes, helping some to die and others to go on living.

We passed through towns whose ruins were still smoking, where the bloodstains had not yet dried. Josephine never flinched or turned away. She simply set her jaw.

Christmas found us back in Paris, where Josephine introduced me to Captain Abtey, on holiday leave in the French capital. As I listened to them reminisce, I learned something about "Josephine's war"—the six years of courage and common memories she and Abtey shared. But Josephine was not one to live in the past. "Guess who I saw in Les Halles at dawn today," the captain said to me one night. "Josephine, loading her car with meat, vegetables and all sorts of other provisions. 'Since when are you such a big eater?' I teased her. 'Every time I see you you're munching a sandwich.' 'Isn't it wonderful, Jacques,' she replied. 'Thanks to the police department, I was able to get all this without ration tickets. The old and the poor deserve a Christmas too.' " She distributed the packages herself, pointing to the cross of Lorraine on her uniform at every door and murmuring, "The Free French Forces and General de Gaulle haven't forgotten you."

In spite of the holidays, we had work to do. Most evenings ended with the words: "Don't forget that we have a practice session scheduled for tomorrow, Jo."

When I stopped by one morning to pick up Josephine for rehearsal, Monsieur Boudon informed me that the tenants in her building were furious because she had given away a ton of their coal to the poor. "A penny for your thoughts," said Roger later that day. "I was thinking about Josephine," I replied. "She's the only woman I know who reminds me of a waterfall, a bonfire and a nightingale rolled into one."

Josephine's papers still bore her address in Marrakech. This was not surprising, since she had been on the move ever since leaving North Africa, laying down her head wherever night found her. Nothing seemed to faze her.

Between missions we returned to Paris to catch our breath and bask in the joy of springtime and the newly won peace. Josephine was ecstatic. "Things will be different now—you'll see, Jo. We're going to have a fresh new world, free of injustice."

One day she suggested that I call on her in Le Vésinet. I knew that Beau Chêne had suffered at the hands of the Germans and that the Americans had occupied it as well. I was totally unprepared to find the house flooded with light and a party in full swing. Dressed in a clinging white gown that molded her marvelous body, Josephine moved among her guests. The room blazed with uniforms of all kinds, decorations, Allied dignitaries, officers sporting multiple stars. Most impressive of all was the obvious respect and admiration these people had for Josephine. I drew her aside. "Why didn't you tell me you were having a big reception?" "I wanted to surprise you, Jo." Josephine loved to make snap decisions and pull surprises. I sometimes thought she liked to practice her Intelligence Service techniques on her friends! She thrived on intrigue. That night she had floodlit the statues in her garden to make them stand out in the darkness; looking at them, I realized that part of Josephine would always remain in the shadows. Except for an occasional brusque revelation, I knew almost nothing of her early life; as for her war years, other than what I had stumbled on by chance, they too lay locked behind that dazzling smile.

It was also by chance that I learned Josephine had pawned her jewelry to purchase the Christmas packages she had distributed to the poor. I was seriously concerned about her future. Ignorant of what she had done for the First Army during the war, many people grouped her with the has-beens, the outmoded prewar stars. Rumor had it that she was no longer in condition to appear on the stage—in short, that she was through. It was my job to convince her that now that Sublieutenant Baker had been demobilized, it was up to her to tour as Josephine again. To my relief, she agreed.

We would begin in Switzerland. I say "we" because my "family" had adopted Josephine; she was now part of a close-knit group composed of the Bouillon clan, my musicians, the ever-present Roger Legrand, and Suzanne Berthe, the orchestra's faithful secretary.

Suzanne Berthe: Throughout the tour, Josephine applied her makeup early in order to watch Jo and his orchestra start off the show. Every night she was there in the wings, as if his success were hers. Her eyes never left his face, and no one clapped louder than Josephine. Then there was the matter of the posters: Jo had asked that even though the words "Jo Bouillon and His Orchestra" were scheduled to appear below Josephine's name, the letters be equally large. His request was ignored, but Jo was much too polite to make a fuss. Not Josephine! She picked up the telephone and lashed out at the guilty parties like a tigress defending her young.

Only Jo seemed to be blind to the obvious. One day I decided to talk to him. "Guess what, Jo. I think Josephine's in love." "Really? Who with?" "*You*, obviously." He looked at me, thunderstruck. "That's not possible!" Jo was well aware of Josephine's many admirers, particularly Jean Meunier's brother, Claude. Jean was dead, but Claude often called on Josephine, who had remained extremely close to his mother. "And Claude's a millionaire to boot!" "Maybe she prefers orchestra leaders, Jo." The musicians and I watched to see what the effect of my revelation would be. Jo seemed extremely upset and uncertain what to do next. We

Josephine at thirty, in the 1936 Ziegfeld Follies. Already a legend abroad, she wears here a modified version of her famous banana costume. (photo Norman)

Her baby picture at two (private collection)

At eighteen, the "funny girl" in Sissle and Blake's *Chocolate Dandies*, who would do almost anything for laughs (photo X, rights reserved)

Consummate glamour (photo X, rights reserved)

"Look at my lace!" (photo Studio Piaz); *below*, A poster by Zig, with Chiquita, the leopard (collection of the author)

JOSEPHINE BAK

Right, In costume by
Lucien Bertaux; *below*,
As Offenbach's La Créole
(photo Studio Piaz)

Josephine with Chiquita (photo Studio Piaz). She loved animals, not to mention the effect she created strolling through Paris with a jewel-collared leopard on a leash.

A young and vulnerable Josephine at the side of her Italian count, Pepito Abatino, her manager for ten years (private collection)

"Head of a girl," almost certainly Josephine, by Georges Rouault (courtesy Detroit Institute of Arts)

Josephine was a favorite subject for painters and sculptors. Here the photograph (by Harcourt) appears almost to be a statue. (courtesy Saul Goodman)

To dear Saul, With all the best and wishing you a Happy New year at a new hintot à Paris. Josephine Baker

Folie Berger.

JOSEPHINE BAKER

1950

Josephine—classic, beautiful (collection of the author)

STUDY IN CONTRASTS

JOSÉPHINE BAKER

Above (photo Studio Piaz)
Right (Studio Romer)

The marriage of Josephine and Jo Bouillon, Les Milandes, 1947
(photo A. Roque)

The tower of Les Milandes (collection of the author)

An early Christmas at Les Milandes with Jo, Josephine and eight of the Rainbow Tribe (photo Spadem)

Sublieutenant Josephine Baker (collection of the author)

Josephine with her mother, the only person she ever stood in awe of (photo A. Gandner)

Josephine newly awarded the Legion of Honor and other medals, with eight fascinated members of the Tribe (photo Georges Ménager)

An entrance at the Folies Bergère, 1950 (courtesy of Saul Goodman); Monte Carlo, 1974: occasionally those feathers almost got too much even for Josephine. (photo X, collection of the author)

Josephine à *Bobino*, la Baker's last triumph in Paris, 1975. If she was true to form, she said to the audience: "Not bad for sixty-eight, eh?" And indeed she wasn't. She died only a few days after this picture was taken. (photo B. Schneider)

This stylish poster, in black and copper color, was created for the Special Tribute to Josephine Baker, New York, 1976. (courtesy William McCaffery)

could only wait and hope for a happy ending. Jo's enthusiasm and kindness had long since conquered his orchestra's heart and we were all drawn to Josephine's radiant personality. We tried to calculate the chances of an eventual marriage. Josephine, with her catlike quickness, had swiftly recognized an ally and companion in Jo, whereas Jo, absorbed in his work, had noticed nothing. Now suddenly he had discovered that the woman he most admired in the world looked at him with more than professional interest. We watched his desperate battle against his own shyness, a struggle which must have amused Josephine. Finally one day, I was able to say to Roger, "I think there's a wedding coming up."

Jo Bouillon: My brother Gabriel had sent me two tickets to a concert he was giving at the Champs-Élysées Theater. Charles Münch would be conducting. "I'll be bringing along a surprise," I warned him. (After all, *everyone* had the right to a surprise or two.) Josephine seemed tremendously impressed by the music. "What a marvelous musician he is," she gasped, fascinated by Gabriel's bowing technique. "Can you play classical music too?" I explained that we had *four* violinists in our family, including my father. After the concert, we went backstage to find Gabriel, who was surrounded by admirers. The atmosphere was very different from the ambience Josephine created during her performances. The congratulations were sincere but restrained. Josephine seemed quite intimidated. When I told Gabriel he was looking at the future Madame Jo Bouillon, he kissed her hand, then complimented me for bringing such a lovely voice into the family. Josephine stood listening, speechless with emotion.

I could see at first glance why Josephine loved Les Milandes. To begin with, its setting was magnificent, deep in a wonderfully harmonious countryside. "This is the real France, Jo!" Beyond the woods, thick with a variety of trees, fields carpeted the sloping terrain. The Dordogne, bathed in soft light, was civilized and wild by turn. Like Josephine, I thought to myself. Then there was the château itself, its crenelated towers recalling the storybooks of Josephine's childhood. Now that the war was over, it seemed the château's owner was willing to sell. I could tell that Josephine dreamed of having this castle for her own.

"Think what we could do with it, Jo." Yes, but my practical eye noted that Les Milandes had only one bathroom, was unheated, and in spite of the restoration it had undergone in the nineteenth century, was nearly a ruin. Still, I could almost hear the ideas clicking through Josephine's mind as she settled on a plan of attack. "It's so peaceful here, Jo, so calm . . . like a beautiful dream, a paradise on earth. It would make a perfect center for people who wanted to get back to nature. And what a wonderful place for children!"

It was typical of Josephine to want to share the happiness she had discovered with as many people as possible, in the process risking the criticism of those who sit by the chimneyside, venturing nothing.

For the moment, reconstructing Les Milandes remained a lovers' dream. Still, Josephine's drive constantly amazed me. Wasn't it enough to come here between performances or tours and curl up together by the fireplace to watch the dancing flames? Fascinated by the past, Josephine had inquired about the origins of the coat of arms over the fireplace. The leopards represented the de Caumont family, she explained, and the gilded lion was the blazon of the Durforts. "Look, Jo." She pointed to the molded edging of a ground-floor window near the stairwell. The inscription it bore had been carved there in gothic letters in 1489 by the château's first owner, François de Caumont, then filled in with lead: *Les Mirandes de Castelnau.* Most of the de Caumont family had died in the St. Bartholomew's Massacre, Josephine continued. "You mean they were Protestants?" "Yes, Jo. When will men learn that it's God, not religion, that counts?" I sensed the anger behind her words. How deep *was* her commitment? I wondered. In some ways I knew so little about this woman I planned to marry. "With all your talk of peace, you were in the war, Josephine. Do you think you could have killed a German if you'd had to?" "A Nazi, Jo?" she corrected me gently. "Of course." And I believed her. She bent down and stroked Mitraillette, asleep in her lap.

Our main problem was finding the time to get married. In early 1946 Josephine was given a new task, performing in a show sponsored by Allied headquarters in Germany. Berlin's courthouse was almost the only standing structure in that grim, rubble-strewn city. Though part of the building was in fact in ruins, a large reception room miraculously remained intact, and it was here that the four-nation show was given, with each of the Allies contributing a share. Josephine, representing France, sparkled under the antiaircraft projectors that lit the stage. After the performance each of the member nations offered a buffet. Most of us crowded around the exotic table prepared by the Soviets. A radiant Josephine found an acquaintance from Marrakech, Robert Murphy, sipping a glass of vodka.

Marrakech . . . I knew that Josephine had a soft spot for North Africa, where she had spent four crucial years. We had planned an appearance there but Scandinavia and Italy came first.

Upon our arrival in Copenhagen that April, one of Josephine's newspaper friends showed us an article that had appeared in the Danish press in 1942, announcing her death. "We have just been informed by wire from Milan that Josephine Baker has died at thirty-six in a Casablanca hospital." The same newspapers now gave her rave reviews, calling her wardrobe "a symphony of colors," her performance "miraculous," commenting that "General de Gaulle's Lieutenant Baker returns to us intact except for her bananas," and concluding that "She can't be a day over twenty-five."

"Not bad for someone who's expired from tuberculosis, want and all sorts of epidemics," Josephine said with a wink.

From Italy we went to North Africa.

It was there that I learned more about her war work, although modesty prevented Josephine from discussing the missions themselves in detail. "What is the theater compared to what I was doing then?" she asked me. I could sense her disdain for the "artist's life" she had led before the war. She would surely never go back to that. With the return of peace, where could she turn to quench her thirst for the ideal?

I think her fondest memory of Algiers was the moment she received her promotion to sublieutenant from Captain Abtey, now a commander. "I was terribly happy. I felt I had begun to fulfill the terms of my contract with the French nation, a contract I value deeply."

One evening in Casablanca, haunted by memories of her nineteen months of illness there, she again felt a stabbing pain in her stomach. "Oh, no; no more," I heard her gasp. This time it was by airplane, not makeshift ambulance, that she was rushed to the hospital—in Rabat—for emergency surgery.

Once again Josephine fought agonizing pain with her tenacious will to live. And once again she was felled by infection. On July 9 I flew with her to Paris for further treatment. The vicious spiral had begun once

more: intestinal blockage, septicemia. . . . I was beside myself. Josephine
had swept into my life like a whirlwind and I knew that come what might,
she was there for good. I would do anything to save her, as would all of
us who knew, respected and loved her. I prayed that Dr. Thiroloix, our
family physician, could pull her through. How well I remember dashing
through Paris trying to locate a type of serum unavailable in that bitter
postwar period. It was only thanks to a concerted effort by a group of
Josephine's friends that I was finally able to find what I so desperately
needed. But the news remained grim. They would have to operate again.

This time Josephine was on the table for three hours. The surgeon was
unwilling to commit himself about her chances, but said he was banking
on her tremendous vitality. I never left her side. The day finally came
when I sensed that although she was unable to speak, Josephine was now
aware of my presence. Hadn't I felt a slight pressure against my hand? But
her eyes remained closed. At last one evening they opened and in spite
of her extreme weakness she looked up at me and smiled. . . . Once more
Josephine had outwitted death.

On October 6, 1946, her sickroom was crowded with well-wishers. She
had received so many flowers that some of them had been moved to a
nearby sitting room; her bedside table overflowed with telegrams. Colonel
de Boissoudy had just pinned the Medal of the Resistance with rosette
to her hospital gown. Among the distinguished onlookers was Madame
de Boissieu, who had come to express the gratitude of her father, General
de Gaulle.

Josephine: The first time I looked at myself in a hand mirror I was
horrified. I had lost over fifty pounds. Would Jo want to marry a scarecrow
like me?

Winning a man isn't everything. You have to keep him close. And for
five months I had been flat on my back with an open incision in my belly.
Still, the surgeon was extremely optimistic. "You're doing very well,
madame. What takes most people twenty-five days, your body manages
in five."

Jo was dividing his time between the clinic and his orchestra. He had
recently been named director of Le Boeuf sur le Toit, a real feather in
his cap. How patient he was with me. He never showed the slightest trace
of fatigue, even though I knew he was extremely preoccupied with the

newly remodeled cabaret, which would soon be celebrating its opening night. No matter what I asked him, he replied that everything was fine. But I could see right through him: dear Jo, with that silly snub nose of his! He never *did* learn how to lie.

I had no choice but to lay my plans with the help of a few close friends.

Jo Bouillon: One morning, I ran into Maurice Chevalier on the Champs-Élysées. Maurice was the official sponsor of my orchestra. "I'm planning to marry Josephine," I announced. "Oh?" With a shake of his head, he pumped my hand as if he were offering his condolences. It was obviously going to take a lot of doing to get those two together! Before leaving on tour, I had given a cocktail party at radio headquarters. As our orchestra's "godfather," Maurice had of course attended. So had Josephine. The press looked forward to photographing them together. It's true that the room was full of people, but I doubt that was why they never managed to find each other.

I held rehearsal upon rehearsal at the Boeuf. The cabaret's forthcoming opening was very important to us all. It was essential that the Boeuf regain the prestige it had enjoyed before the war, that it again become the nightspot where fashionable people went to be seen and to meet their stylish friends. Yet I had trouble concentrating on my work. Josephine's condition continued to concern me and when I wasn't at her side, holding her hand or giving her her medicine, I was afraid she might have another of her relapses. She had had enough operations. . . . "You mustn't worry so, Jo," she insisted. "Concentrate on your work and let me worry about getting well." Easier said than done. At least for me. I couldn't get Josephine off my mind.

As opening night approached, Josephine asked me if I'd notified the press. "Of course, *cherie*. Anyway, they'll come on their own," I answered evasively. "But you have to realize that a new show by Jo Bouillon, whom everyone knows from his radio program, isn't exactly front-page news, Josephine. What people will come for is to see the new décor. Needless to say, the work's still not completed. Typical! But it should all be finished by opening night." "You could at least have given some interviews, Jo." "But there wasn't time, *cherie*. I told you we won't be ready until the last minute." "How are the men?" "Oh, they're in great shape, thanks."

This wasn't exactly the case. Josephine's illness had affected us all.

True, Dr. Thiroloix was extremely encouraging, but he had warned me that it would be a very long time before she was cured. This worried me tremendously; too many people had buried Josephine already! She faced a long, hard fight to reconquer her public. "So what? She loves a good battle," Roger reassured me. Of course. But would she have the necessary strength? In the meantime, I had a fight of my own to win.

As soon as I got to the cabaret that fateful night, I telephoned the clinic. The news was reassuring. Madame is sleeping. Her pulse is regular. It was almost curtain time. The advance publicity had apparently done its work. The room was growing crowded. We mustn't disappoint our audience.

Suddenly there was a burst of activity at the entranceway, followed by an explosion of flash bulbs. Who had arrived? What celebrity could possibly attract such attention? I moved toward the door and stopped dead, blinking unbelieving eyes. Swathed in a djellabah, her head wrapped in a turban, her face carefully painted, was Josephine!

I must be hallucinating, I thought wildly, wondering if the Scotch I had sampled with the orchestra to buck up our morale had gone to my head. No, this Josephine was real. She proved it by throwing herself into my arms and giving me a resounding kiss, after which she turned to the press and said, "I couldn't have missed my husband-to-be's premiere!" How was it possible? Only that afternoon I had left Josephine in bed, her wound unhealed. "Don't worry, *cheri*," she whispered in my ear. "I'm very tightly bandaged."

She slipped from my embrace into the supportive arms of two orderlies. I leaped to the stage and led the orchestra in a rousing rendition of "J'ai Deux Amours." As the audience burst into applause, Josephine returned quietly to her ambulance and sped back to the clinic behind a motor escort.

It was probably the most wonderful opening night I had ever had. Josephine's unexpected presence, verging on the miraculous, inspired us all. What a woman!

The next day when I walked into her sickroom her eyes were closed. A heap of newspapers lay nearby. They were full of reports about Le Boeuf sur le Toit and Jo Bouillon—thanks to Josephine's surprise appearance. She half opened her eyes and tried to smile in spite of her obvious exhaustion. "I told you the press would want to cover your opening night, Jo!"

At last the day arrived when Josephine was well enough to travel to Les Milandes to convalesce.

Irrepressible Josephine, who had given my show such a wonderful send-off, now seemed tormented by doubts. When I tried to discuss a comeback she replied, "I don't think I'll ever set foot on a stage again, Jo." It was so unlike Josephine to utter a negative word that I gathered her in my arms as if she were an ailing child. I had to convince her that she was wrong. "No, Jo. I mean it. Look at me. I'm not only rusty but I'm thin as a rail. I look"—she paused for a moment to find the right word —"rotten! Besides, a whole new generation of stars has sprung up since the war and they're young, Jo, so young. . . ." Day after day I tried to help her regain her confidence. She seemed as timid as she claimed to have been as a girl. Well, at least that meant she was still her youthful self. How could she possibly think that Josephine Baker was through? "Don't you see, *cheri?* You're in love with me, so you're blind to the truth!" I simply ignored her and began to lay plans and work up ideas for numbers, assuring her that I and "her orchestra" would be right there beside her. Together, how could we lose?

"Besides, Josephine, if you want to buy Les Milandes, you're going to need money." That argument was my ace in the hole and I hoped it would do the trick. For safety's sake, I also called Roger Legrand to the rescue. Could he come to Les Milandes at once? Between us we must rouse Josephine from her depression, so foreign to her nature. My plan worked. The idea of owning Les Milandes, of it being "her" château, gave Josephine new direction. "It's true, Jo. There are so many wonderful things we could accomplish here. . . ."

We were on our way! After giving so much of herself to her public and her chosen land and using the rest to keep from dying, Josephine had rediscovered a reason to live. Being my wife was not enough. She was tormented by the need to be a mother as well. Again and again she questioned the doctors: "Is there any hope of my having a family now that I'm forty and after so much illness?" She saw the château as "perfect for raising children." Les Milandes was her salvation. Buying it became her single goal.

Josephine began to accept the idea of a comeback as a means of financing the château. Why not tour South America, where she had consistently triumphed before the war? I was convinced that a series of shows abroad would be less intimidating than performing in a Paris she no longer really knew. Bit by bit she threw herself into the preparations. She would need a lavish new wardrobe, she insisted. Her North African costumes were completely worn out. "My clothes are my only stage sets, Jo. They have to be as eye-catching as possible."

Roger and I decided to make a scouting trip to South America to feel out the ground. "Hurry back," said Josephine. "I've planned the wedding for May 3, Jo's birthday." She was her energetic self again. I could already see her boarding the plane for Rio. . . . "What could be simpler?" she asked. "I'll sell Beau Chêne and use the money to finance a spectacular tour. Then with the money the tour brings in I'll buy Les Milandes!" She made it all sound so easy.

Our stay in Rio was shorter than anticipated. Josephine had given us introductions to several of her prewar friends, including Carlos Machado, who had directed a revue at the Copacabana Hotel. I found the Brazilian music entrancing, but quickly realized that Brazil was far from entranced by us! Josephine was "getting along," they said. She had lost her public appeal.

I couldn't believe my ears. Josephine's fears had been justified after all. I gradually discovered that the press had been printing whatever they wished about her over the last few years. Reports of her death had given way to stories of illnesses that had robbed her of health and looks and hopelessly aged her. "No Brazilian will back a Josephine Baker show," I was told flatly.

Perhaps we would have better luck in Buenos Aires. We no sooner arrived in the Argentine capital than I set to work tracking down every possible lead. We were treated more tactfully here than in Rio. The conversation would somehow turn to the economic situation, appointments would be quietly broken or end inconclusively, we would finally be sent away. . . .

Nervously I watched May 3 draw nearer and nearer. Not only had I been unable to clinch a deal, but even worse, I was running out of ideas. IMPOSSIBLE RETURN EXPECTED DATE, I tersely wired Josephine. ARE YOU SURE YOU WANT TO GET MARRIED? she cabled back. SURER THAN EVER, I replied. IT DOESN'T LOOK LIKE IT, responded Josephine. I was reluctant to tell her about the difficulties I was facing and refused to go home without a signed contract. It was partly a question of pride: this was my first attempt at handling Josephine's affairs and I wouldn't admit defeat. A final cable from Les Milandes informed me: WEDDING POSTPONED UNTIL JUNE 3, MY BIRTHDAY. WEDDING CAKE READY. I'LL PUT IT ON ICE.

Roger and I continued knocking on impresarios' doors with a vigor that masked our mounting concern. Finally one day at a radio station we met Hugo del Carril, an immensely successful Argentine tango dancer. Hugo was such a popular entertainer that his performances usually ended in near riots. We quickly struck up a friendship and before I knew it I was telling him our woes. Horrified to learn that his compatriots had lost confidence in Josephine, he proposed the following scheme: To avoid the need to change money, he would lend me the pesos necessary to rent a concert hall and we would produce the show ourselves. He even found us a hall: the Politeama Argentino in Corrientes.

"How long a run do you anticipate?" Hugo asked. "About two weeks," I prudently replied. "Two weeks it is!" All that remained was to find backup acts to round out the bill. With Hugo's help I engaged seventeen musicians, four ballerinas, a trio of Mexican dancers, an Afro-Cuban, a slinky ballroom-dancing act and two well-known comics. That should take care of the first part of the show. I counted on Josephine for the rest. Now I must hurry home. It was already the first of June.

We were married on June 3, as planned, in a country wedding. The guests were local villagers, the mass was celebrated at Les Milandes in our own chapel, which Josephine assured me dated from the fifteenth century. Shortly before the ceremony, I realized we had no harmonium. On the curé's advice, I bounced off across the countryside in our big Ford to borrow a reed organ from a neighboring church.

The entire Bouillon clan—except for Gabriel, who was on a world tour —assembled for the occasion. I had never seen Josephine so happy. She acted as though she had known my family always and my mother loved her on first sight. Josephine's special guests were the Scoto family from Italy: father, mother, son and daughter-in-law Christina, Pepito Abatino's sister. The fact that she had no legal relationship to the Scotos didn't bother Josephine. "What counts," she liked to say, "is the family of man," and she was quick to adopt those she cared for. Much to the mystification of our neighbors, she introduced Christina as her sister-in-law and the Scotos as her parents. Josephine sprouted relatives like Jesus multiplying the loaves and the fishes.

For the church service, Josephine changed from the pink dress she had worn at the civil ceremony into a white suit. When my older brother George raised his bow and launched into a Bach aria, I saw a tear glistening on her cheek. But at the chapel door she was all smiles again.

Perhaps it seems surprising that we were married in a Catholic ceremony, but it was not until Josephine's death that I learned through some of her friends of her conversion to Judaism upon marrying Jean Lion. She never mentioned this conversion to me, nor was any written proof of it found. But in Josephine's case, the absence of such documentation was unimportant. She followed her heart. Deeply religious, she saw God everywhere and I remember her entering synagogues, cathedrals and mosques with equal zeal. Oblivious to superficial trappings, she worshipped the God that lay beyond.

The bakers in nearby Sarlat had outdone themselves. The five-foot-high wedding cake somehow survived the trip to Les Milandes intact and was greeted with cries of admiration. For the wedding luncheon in the huge main hall, Josephine slipped into a flowered dress. We could hear the Bouillon children laughing in a nearby room. "Listen to them, Jo," said Josephine. "I wish they could stay forever." Smilingly I intoned:

> Protect me, Lord, protect the ones I love.
> Brothers, parents, friends. Guard from above
> My enemies as well, by wrong defiled.
> Spare us from summers bare of flower-sheen,
> Birdless cages, hives without a queen,
> Homes without a child.

"How lovely, Jo. Who wrote it?" "Victor Hugo." "I'm going to memorize it."

That evening Josephine changed once more, this time into a resplendent gown. Gaily she twirled about the room with each of us in turn: the village prefect, our neighbors, the Bouillon men. "What's wrong, Maryse?" she called to Gabriel's seventeen-year-old daughter. "Why aren't you dancing?" "My feet hurt, Aunt Jo." "That's easy enough to fix. Watch me!" And Josephine sent her slippers flying toward the suit of medieval armor that guarded our stone staircase.

CHAPTER 13

For Les Milandes

Gabriel Bouillon: One day before leaving for my world tour, I received a mysterious phone call from Josephine. Could we meet? She had something to discuss with me. After conferring with her lawyer, she explained, she had decided to give me power of attorney. When I expressed my surprise, she added that since one never knew *what* might happen, since she and Jo would probably be traveling for long periods of time and since she had total confidence in me, it seemed like a sensible idea. I was extremely flattered. "Have you mentioned it to Jo?" I asked. (My brother was in Argentina at the time.) "No," she replied. "It's a surprise."

Some time later, I crossed paths with the newlyweds in Buenos Aires. Josephine's comeback appearance had been a triumph. The two-week engagement at the Politeama had been extended to three months due to popular demand and Josephine had managed to squeeze in a second appearance nightly at the Golden Gate. The stakes had been high but the two Jos had won.

Josephine was radiant. The press raved about her singing and her fabulous wardrobe labeled Dessès, Griffe, Balenciaga, Schiaparelli. . . . Every time she walked onto the stage, the crowd went wild.

We three met again a few months later in Santiago, Chile. Together we attended a reception at the French embassy honoring General de Lattre, who also was on tour, inspecting the French Air Force. Josephine, deeply moved at meeting the chief of the French First Air Force again, sang for us. Once more I was struck by her pure, supple voice. Then Jo and I had the rare pleasure of performing Bach's double violin concerto in D minor. Josephine listened raptly. On the way back to the hotel she asked, "Gaby, how much are you paid for a concert?" At my reply she exclaimed, "But I get ten times that!" Then, with surprising violence, she added, "And all I have to peddle is wind!"

Jo Bouillon: Josephine didn't know how to relax. Friends often asked us to spend a quiet day at their hacienda. Josephine would accept politely, but at the last minute would find a reason to break the engagement. There was always something else she wanted to do or see. "Turn off your motor, Josephine," I'd tease. Impossible. She simply couldn't slow down. "Remember, Jo, we're working to buy Les Milandes. Every performance means a few more building stones, an acre or two!" All she thought about was the château. . . . One day Josephine announced that she was having the garden statuary from Le Vésinet shipped to Les Milandes. Here we were, heading toward Mexico, while Venus and Diana traveled toward the Dordogne. "Les Milandes's owner is going to love you, Josephine!" She gazed at me innocently. "But, *cheri,* it's not his anymore. While you were abroad I gave power of attorney to Gaby. As a surprise. I've written our lawyer to draw up the deed in our joint names." As it turned out, by the time Josephine's instructions reached France, the papers had already gone through in her name alone. But what did it matter? The important thing was to continue earning the money necessary to restore the château and its grounds. Still, I wondered whether Josephine would *ever* tire of surprises! There was something about the look in her eye that told me she had another one in store. What now? She suddenly threw herself into my arms and said in a strangled voice, "I think I'm pregnant, Jo!"

Josephine's joy was contagious. I knew that motherhood was the most important thing in the world to her. So *that* was why she was so anxious to finish renovating Les Milandes! "This time I'm not going to knit, *cheri.* It might bring bad luck." But Josephine couldn't resist deciding where we would put the nursery. I prepared to cancel our forthcoming appearances in Cuba and New York. Josephine mustn't overexert herself. "Are you out of your mind, Jo? A contract's a contract. The baby's just beginning to grow. It's tiny, tiny. Besides, I feel marvelous!" She was obviously telling the truth. It was hard to believe that this radiant future mother was the same woman who a year before had been decorated in her sickbed after a four-month battle with death.

Mexico welcomed Josephine with the same enthusiasm she had enjoyed in Argentina, Chile and Peru. She was wined and dined, cheered by the crowds. Her only quiet moments were spent poring over the plans of Les Milandes I had drawn for her. "Maybe I'll put the children's room here." *"Children?"* I gasped. "Don't tell me you're expecting twins, Josephine." "No, Jo, unfortunately not. But think how sad an only child must feel. Suppose you hadn't had your brothers. Can you imagine a person being raised alone in a château like a lonely, selfish little king?" What was she getting at? I wondered. "I'm not at all sure I'll be able to have more children, *cheri*. God has already waited so long—too long, really—to grant me *this* baby. But I'm sure he must have his reasons. He always does."

Josephine was a fatalist. Although she worked hard for what she believed, underneath she felt that things were preordained. "What are you trying to tell me, Josephine? I don't understand." "I thought we might give our baby a brother or sister, perhaps even both. There are so many needy children in the world. Why not adopt some of them? What do you think, Jo?" I gave her a kiss and said lightly, "Why not, *cherie?* What we can't manufacture, we'll find ready made."

We spent a memorable day on a Mexican ranch with the famous French vocal group Les Petits Chanteurs à la Croix de Bois. A smiling Josephine sang with the fifty or more child performers, but when our hosts staged a bullfight for our pleasure, her mood quickly changed. How could they be so cruel, she asked our friends angrily; how could they torture animals? There was no killing involved, our hosts explained gently. Only cape work. But Josephine refused to listen. Her day was ruined. "I'm leaving, Jo," she muttered, gathering up her things.

That night the pains began. I called a doctor at dawn, but by then Josephine knew that once again her hopes of motherhood had been destroyed, this time probably for good.

I braced myself for her tears. But she remained dry-eyed, aloof in her grief, silent, grave-faced, her hands pressed to her empty womb. The doctor explained that due to Josephine's narrow pelvis, she could hope to carry a child to term only by spending her entire pregnancy in bed. "If she ever conceives again, you've got to convince her to be very careful." Forty-eight hours after her miscarriage, a stoic Josephine was back on the stage again.

A surprise awaited us at our hotel in Havana. "Sorry, we're all booked up," the man at the desk informed us. Josephine was furious. "I *know* it's because of my color," she shouted. It did indeed appear that rather than antagonize their many white American customers, the management preferred to turn Josephine away. Little did they know my wife! Within two hours she had mobilized a group of Cubans, "colored folk like me," and called in a lawyer and a witness to attest to the fact that she had been denied entry into the hotel. Anti-American feeling was running high in Cuba at the time, due to Uncle Sam's stranglehold on Cuban commerce.

Josephine's onstage triumph was increased fourfold by her appeal to nationalist sentiment. Although we had scheduled only a handful of Cuban appearances, we spent over three months there. The immensely popular "Josefina" was invited everywhere; wherever she went she spoke out for the importance of solidarity among people of color. An Association of Friends of Josefina was quickly created, with two intertwined hearts as its symbol and the slogan "J'ai Deux Amours." According to Josephine, the hearts represented the black and white races. She and I were living proof that the two could live in harmony.

"I think the association is really accomplishing something," she announced one evening. "But there's so much more to be done. Do you remember our talk in Mexico, Jo, when I mentioned adopting children? What I'd like to do is choose them from different races—black, yellow, red, white—to prove that all of us are brothers." "That's a fine idea, Josephine," I replied, moved by her obvious conviction. "You'll help me then, Jo?" She picked up the plan of Les Milandes. She had moved the nursery around again. . . .

Bit by bit, the idea of a peaceful, joyous haven began to take form: a kind of world village built around a family of multicolored children.

News of Josephine's statements in Havana concerning her reception there seemed to have preceded us to the United States. Could this be why some of our contracts were never confirmed and our American tour was cut short? We spent Christmas that year at the Sheraton Hotel in Boston.

My gift from Josephine was a music box shaped like a stagecoach, which lit up while playing. "We'll put it in the children's room someday," she murmured.

We had booked a hotel suite for our New York stay under the name Mr. and Mrs. Jo Bouillon. But before our bags were unpacked, we received a call from the manager. He was terribly sorry, but there had been a mistake. The suite was free only until the next day. A variation on what had occurred in Cuba. We guessed that the Southern clientele was outraged at the sight of a black in the lobby. We would have to change hotels.

At the sixty-three hotels we tried, it was the same story. After the first day we were asked politely to leave. "They're not going to get away with this," Josephine snapped. "They'll be sorry!" I'd lost patience too. "Apparently because my wife is black, you're suddenly overbooked. That's just too bad. We reserved our room and we're keeping it!" This time they'd have to drag me out, if they dared to risk a scandal. Instead, when we ordered room service the knives and forks were missing. "Sorry. Due to overcrowding, we're short on cutlery!" Or else the meals never arrived. There apparently was also a shortage of maid service to change the beds.

While we were in New York, Josephine was introduced to the black actor Canada Lee, who had become the toast of New York playing Shakespeare. "New Yorkers accept the idea of our playing parts like Othello or Caliban," he explained. "But I could never perform those roles in the South." "Doesn't Duke Ellington tour the South?" "Yes, but with a *black* orchestra. It would be out of the question for me to play Caliban there with a white troupe." We also met Lena Horne, who appeared in Hollywood productions with white casts. "True enough," she agreed. "But my scenes are always cut when the film is shown in the South. Anyway, I never get anything but bit parts." Talk constantly seemed to turn to the South and the prejudice there. Josephine hoped that conditions had changed since the war. "Go and see for yourself," proposed Jeff Smith, a black journalist.

Josephine decided to follow his advice. She had already planned a trip to Nashville, where she had been invited to speak at a black university. I suggested that she pick up her family on the return voyage. Why leave them here, in "such a stupid country"? Besides, we had an entire château to fill. Josephine was delighted by my idea. But first she had a scheme of her own to look into: she planned to make an incognito tour of the South to determine exactly how prevalent racism was. "I'll travel under an alias," she announced. I laughed. "Just like the good old Intelligence Service days."

It was no laughing matter to Josephine, however. When I talked about going with her, she firmly said no. "You'd ruin everything with your white skin, Jo! I've got to look like an ordinary black girl traveling alone if I want to find out the truth about white attitudes. Don't you agree?"

Whether I agreed or not was totally unimportant, because Josephine had obviously made up her mind. I did venture to say that the trip sounded interesting but dangerous and I'd prefer to see her back in the Dordogne. "But what I'll be doing is *for* Les Milandes, Jo! Our World Village will be much more authentic if we know what types of injustice we're fighting against." That was the way she saw things. I often wonder what would have happened if the baby had lived; whether she would still have taken to the warpath. . . .

Although I couldn't change Josephine's mind, I did at least persuade her to take Jeff along. I accompanied them to the train. Josephine was wearing a simple traveling dress. With her youthful figure and the exuberance she clearly felt at being involved again, she could have been a university student returning to school. She and Jeff waved from the train window. "Hurry back, *cherie!*. Remember, I don't know a word of English." Josephine laughed. "I told you we shouldn't speak only in French. But don't worry. New York is a wonderful place—if you're white."

As I watched the train pull away, it suddenly seemed as if *they* were the newlyweds. I felt more like a widower.

I received a phone call the next morning. "There's a Miss Brown on the wire, Mr. Bouillon." That was Josephine's code name. Everything was fine so far, she reported, except that when they had reached the Mason-Dixon line, the dining car steward had tried to make her move to the "proper" side of the curtain that divided the blacks from the whites. Her next call was from Nashville. "It's going fantastically well, Jo." Josephine had chosen the theme "Racial Equality in France" for her university talks. "I've had four or five hundred students at every speech. The most interesting part is the questions they ask. They're very intelligent and quite advanced in their thinking; still, you wouldn't believe how surprised they were to hear that whites often go to black doctors in Paris!"

Josephine went on to tell me about a highly gifted young black woman student she had met who wanted to pursue her studies but was unable to do so because the advanced courses she needed were available only in all-white universities. She had written to President Truman about her dilemma. Her letter had had an effect of sorts, because Congress had voted that a black university for advanced studies be created—but it still remained to be built.

Two days later Josephine called again. The young woman would be admitted to a white university temporarily, but she had been warned to expect unpleasantness from the student body, who might even refuse to speak to her. "She's incredibly brave, Jo."

I worried constantly for the next few days, since I knew that Josephine was traveling through the countryside under her alias. I could hear the disappointment in her voice the next time she called. "The worst part of all, Jo, is that the colored people are very suspicious of anyone who wants to upset the system. They're terrified of reprisals. The slightest thing can lead to a confrontation and it's always the black who suffers. So they prefer to say and do nothing." I sensed that her efforts had been criticized. She was turning back, she informed me, and would stop off in St. Louis on the way.

The telephone call from St. Louis was unforgettable. Josephine had tracked down her family and after describing each relative to me in turn, put them on the phone. None of them spoke French, of course, and I still hadn't mastered any English. "Don't worry," Josephine shouted into the receiver. "Just *talk*, Jo. I know they'll be able to tell how nice you are from the tone of your voice!" And that was how I first made contact with Josephine's mother and her sister Margaret.

"What did your mother *say*, Josephine?" "That she'll be happy to come to France with us, but not without Margaret." "And what did Margaret say?" "That she's married and can't leave her husband." "Why not take everyone, then? . . . Is there something wrong, Josephine?" "No, *cheri*. I'm simply telling them what a wonderful husband I have."

It felt good to be back in France again. We landed in Cherbourg on February 18, 1948, anxious to start work on Les Milandes. After consulting with our architects, we decided to begin by building a pleasure garden with an outdoor stage on the banks of the Dordogne. At the same time we would renovate the château's interior. "We've got to go full speed

ahead, American style," Josephine insisted. But life in the Dordogne was
a leisurely business, meant to be enjoyed. While we waited for the contractors to settle down to work, our plans grew more elaborate daily. Why not
a hotel? A restaurant? A heliport? "After all, more and more people are
traveling," Josephine argued. "I realize that being off the beaten track is
part of Les Milandes's charm, but we mustn't be *too* inaccessible. And
it seems to me that helicopters are the cars of tomorrow."

I thought Josephine was probably right, but the work and expense
involved in our various projects was enormous. This was no time for us
to linger in the countryside. Josephine packed her bags and embarked on
a series of European appearances by which to finance our elaborate plans.

Throughout our travels, Josephine's mind was on Les Milandes. "We're
going to be so happy with our children, Jo. We'll show the world that
racial hatred is unnatural, an emotion dreamed up by man; that there *is*
such a thing as a universal family; that it's possible for children of different
races to grow up together as brothers," and pulling out a piece of paper,
she began drawing yet another set of plans. "Here's the château, where
our Rainbow Tribe will live: there's the pleasure garden, where people can
sing, because everyone loves singing and there's nothing better for you:
and over here we'll put the stage." "Built specially for you, Josephine."
"That's right, *cheri*. Instead of traveling all over the world, I'll let people
come to me for a change."

As luck would have it, while Josephine dreamed of retiring to Les
Milandes and entertaining her public there, she was being pursued by
impresarios worldwide. Her fees had never been higher. "Shall we say yes
to Milan?" "Of course, *cheri*. It'll pay for the soccer field. And do you
know what I see whenever I think of the London Palladium? A swimming
pool. We've got to make Les Milandes as attractive to the public as
possible. It wouldn't be fair to keep our children and what they represent
to ourselves."

Yes, we were bursting with plans. And the funds were there. All we had
to do was earn them.

Spain, Belgium, Italy . . . It was during our Spanish tour that Josephine
first stumbled on a group of animals for sale and decided to take a supply
of monkeys and birds back to Les Milandes. "Won't it be fun to have an
enormous aviary on our property where our wildlife can move freely?"
Before I knew it, we were sharing our hotel room with four monkeys, two
parrots and fifteen parakeets.

In Brussels, where Josephine had been the star of a Red Cross benefit, a painter who specialized in royal portraits asked her to pose for him. The Belgian Queen Mother Elisabeth looked forward to meeting Josephine in the artist's studio to thank her for contributing to the gala. As with all royal appointments, a precise time was fixed. At the appointed hour, no Josephine. I rushed back to the hotel, where her chauffeured car was waiting at the curb. Had she taken ill? I dashed up the steps and into our room. Josephine, stark naked, was half under the bed. "Do you realize the Queen's waiting, Josephine?" "It's not my fault. Gigolo's eaten my birds of paradise!" Gigolo, who deserved his name, was the greediest of the monkeys. I helped Josephine into her Dior gown, gathered up the few remaining feathers and pinned them in her hair. We arrived very late at the studio, where the Queen sat waiting on a pouf. "You must have thought I'd never get here," said Josephine, settling down on the floor at Her Majesty's side. The Queen was delighted by Josephine's blend of enthusiasm and spontaneity and in no time they were chatting away like old friends.

When we stepped off the train in Rome, a red carpet was stretched through the station. Josephine assumed it was there for her and started along it, with me at her heels. Just as I was beginning to wonder why the crowd looked so astonished, we saw the Italian President advancing toward us. . . . When he and Josephine were face to face, the President, who had come to participate in some sort of public function, cordially shook Josephine's hand and invited her to join him in the station's snack bar for a dish of spaghetti!

We finally returned to Paris, where we were booked at the Club 48, a cabaret off the Champs-Élysées. At four o'clock one morning, we returned to our apartment to find firemen swarming up a huge ladder in front of the building. People were rushing into the street. "Is something burning?" I asked the concierge. "No, monsieur." The firemen had been summoned by my nephew Bob, who was tending our animals until we could take them to Les Milandes. Nestor, Josephine's favorite monkey, had mistaken a plane tree for a baobab in the dawning light. He swung happily from its topmost branches, oblivious of the crowd and the banana Bob was dangling from an upper window at the risk of his life, and safely beyond reach of the lasso my nephew had fashioned from a curtain pull.

Josephine was extremely fond of the Bouillon children. For Maryse's eighteenth birthday, she decided to give my niece a party at the club.

Maryse Bouillon: Aunt Jo bought me a beautiful dress at Dior. I had never been in a nightclub before. What a thrilling initiation! Josephine had invited my favorite stars: Robert Taylor, who happened to be in town, Jean Marais, Jean-Louis Barrault and Madeleine Renaud, Gérard Philippe, Katherine Dunham, draped in a white lace shawl, and Carmen Amaya, wearing a black one.

Aunt Jo admired the two dancers immensely and we had seen them both perform. During her favorite parts of the show, Josephine sat perched on the edge of her seat as if ready to leap across the footlights. "What purity," she sighed, nudging me in the ribs. (Carmen was dancing.) "Isn't it beautiful?" Another nudge. (This time the dancer was Katherine.) My aunt was greatly impressed by the fact that both women drew inspiration from folk sources. She described Carmen as "a tall flame in a small body" and marveled that Katherine "knew everything about Africa and more important, understood it." Katherine did, in fact, have a degree in anthropology. Aunt Jo admired diplomas immensely since she had none of her own, and encouraged my cousins and me to work hard at school. At the same time she warned us that having a diploma folded up in your breast pocket was meaningless unless a kind heart beat beneath it. This was the kind of lesson Aunt Jo liked to teach.

My birthday party ended at dawn. My last memory as I drifted off to sleep was of Josephine and Katherine dancing side by side. Unused to night life, I woke up well into the afternoon, to find Aunt Jo rushing about the apartment. She asked me to help her tidy up and as I moved slowly about in a daze, she slapped me hard. Bursting into tears, I buried my head in my pillows, next to the beautiful gown she had given me. And so I began my nineteenth year.

Soon afterward I made an unsuccessful marriage. With the passage of time came a second marriage and the birth of my third son. It was then that a curious scene occurred at the clinic. I was dozing, with my infant son in his cradle beside me, when Aunt Jo burst into the room, peered down at the baby and announced, "I'm taking him home with me." I assumed she was joking. Not at all. She explained that since neither my husband nor I had a job, she planned to adopt Cyril. "But you can't!" I shouted. "He's mine." Now it was Aunt Jo's turn to get angry. Couldn't I see that the baby would be happier at Les Milandes than cooped up in a city apartment? And as soon as she had assembled her Rainbow Tribe, he would have playmates of every color.

"Absolutely not," I cried. Cyril already *had* two brothers of his own and that was quite enough! Aunt Jo said I was a selfish child who couldn't see farther than the end of her nose. By now we were shouting so loudly that the nuns rushed in, to find Josephine shaking her fist and me clutching my baby. All that was missing was King Solomon! After that ugly encounter I never expected to see my aunt again. But the next day she sent me some lovely baby clothes and soon afterward invited the three boys and me to Les Milandes as if nothing had happened.

Jo Bouillon: On November 3, 1948, I went to Le Havre to meet my wife's family. Off the boat stepped three round-eyed, gaping figures without a word of French. Josephine's widowed mother, Carrie, a large woman whose white hair was tucked under a flowered hat; her half-sister Margaret, heavy-set like their mother; and Margaret's tall, thin husband, Elmo Wallace. Elmo had suffered lung damage in the mines and we hoped the country air would help restore his health. At Les Milandes, they fell into Josephine's arms, exchanging hugs and memories. But Josephine was not one to live in the past. The important thing was to get everyone settled down in the château as quickly as possible.

My parents were already there. After making everyone at home, Josephine returned to studying the plans with our architect. Our first job was to bring in electricity. A special power line was being run in from the main cable half a mile away, which meant open ditches everywhere.

During this period, Josephine and I were working at the Club 48 and could only visit the Dordogne on days when the cabaret was closed. We made certain to take along any friends willing to lend a hand. These "country holidays" were strenuous affairs presided over by Josephine, who was up with the sun. (Fortunately, since there was no electricity, we all went to bed very early.) There was plenty of work for everyone: furniture to move from the cellar to the turrets and back; boxes and trunks to unpack, nails to hammer, carpets to lay, raking, weeding, masonry, painting. And when we thought we were done, Josephine would call, "Who's going to cut back the ivy?" She was obsessed by the vines, which had crept all the way up to the tower windows.

With the new year, the Club 48 became the Club 49. Thanks to Josephine's presence, it attracted a glittering crowd, from the King and

Queen of Belgium, visiting incognito, to Rita Hayworth dancing with Ali Khan. Josephine had never been more beautiful. Famous couturiers fought for the honor of dressing her. Between fittings came recording sessions and rehearsals for radio shows, which Josephine disliked because she missed a live audience; she thought the microphones looked like "legless spiders." Josephine loved television, however, where she knew she was being seen, and appeared in such programs as *Café Continental*, the first major show to be rebroadcast to England, and a gala performance honoring the United Nations. After the latter she took the opportunity to question U.N. delegates of every color about needy youth and adoption laws in their respective countries. "There's no time to lose, Jo," she kept repeating. Every week we hurried to the Dordogne to urge the workers on and lend a helping hand. Dressed in a smock and old trousers, a bandanna on her head, Josephine became a muddy, dust-stained country-woman.

Then into the car and back to Paris, where one memorable evening Josephine slipped into a fabulous gown with a fifteen-foot train to appear as Mary, Queen of Scots, at the Folies-Bergère. The new show marked Josephine's postwar Parisian comeback and she pulled out all the stops, impersonating Joséphine de Beauharnais, dancing half naked as Beauty in *Beauty and the Beast*, and singing Schubert's "Ave Maria," framed against an enormous stained-glass window.

Finally the day we had dreamed of arrived: September 4, 1949. The Folies would have to manage without Josephine for a while. Les Milandes couldn't open without her!

Frédéric Rey: While looking for a housewarming present for Josephine, I discovered a marten in a Paris department store. Knowing her fondness for animals, I decided to buy it. A group of us were going to the Dordogne for the Les Milandes's official inauguration. Josephine had insisted, "Everyone's got to come and help out." We drove all night and arrived to find the château like a madhouse. Josephine had been coping with the press and marshaling her forces since six that morning. I was delighted to hand over the marten to its new mistress, as it had a most distinctive smell. "How nice of you, Fred. It's cunning." Josephine wasted no time in putting me to work. Given my physique, I would be most useful behind the bar. A wraithlike Jo rushed by. He looked ten pounds thinner than when he had left Paris a few days earlier. "I just hope they come," he muttered. "They" were the sightseers, the customers.

People had been talking about Les Milandes for months, the news traveling from Sarlat all the way to London. The press had done its job well. But could we really expect people to travel to a remote corner of the Dordogne? "Of course we can!" said Josephine, striking the table with her fist. "What's this table doing here, anyway? It belongs in the pleasure garden. And be sure there are enough chairs down there." When I went to the kitchen to collect glasses for the bar, I was startled to see a large black woman bustling about the kitchen. "I'd like you to meet Josephine's mother," said Jo.

At eight o'clock that morning the first cars drew up. "Here they come," called a voice from the tower.

They came and came and came . . . on foot, on horseback, by car. We had prepared for fifteen hundred people in the pleasure garden: six thousand appeared, of every age and size. The members of the Bouillon and Baker families were everywhere at once, especially Jo, who supervised a bowling-on-the-green competition, organized card games, blew the starting whistle for the foot races and thought up hundreds of games to amuse the children. The high spot for the grownups, of course, was Josephine, singing to them in the pleasure garden. Tireless Josephine, whom the public had seen earlier wiping bar glasses. I'll never forget that bar. Each time a customer asked for a cocktail, I filled the shaker and waved it over my head with a flourish. "More of the same," Jo called, after the first round. "Don't just stand there, Fred. The clients are waiting." "But I don't have the slightest idea which bottles I used, Jo."

The day ended with a fireworks display at twilight.

The day . . . but not the night. Josephine had planned a late supper under the crystal chandeliers of the château's dining hall for the family, close friends and such local "supporters" as the prefect, the mayor and the village priest. The table shone with her finest dishes. Josephine played the role of chatelaine to perfection. But where was Jo? Word came that he was busy estimating the day's take so he could give us the total. We waited and waited . . . the prefect, the mayor, the village priest. Two long hours passed. At 3 A.M. Jo walked in, thinner than ever. His eyes were dancing. After adding up the tickets, he calculated that we had had ten thousand visitors. "Can you believe it?" cried Josephine. "They managed to get here without a proper road, with no tourist facilities, without a train. It proves that they'll keep on coming. We've *got* to keep going!"

Our receipts totaled a quarter of a million francs.

"You're sure, *cheri?*" Jo might well have been mistaken. He had been on his feet for twenty-seven hours, racing bicycles with the young men, throwing volleyballs, bowling. . . . But his figures were correct. "We'll move ahead with the soccer field as planned," said Josephine. She went on to add that she had bought some neighboring vineyards to convert into a heliport. "How does that strike you, Monsieur le Prefect?" "Excellent idea, madame. Excellent." Josephine, regal in her flowing gown, beamed, then raised her glass to Jo, who hadn't had time to change the dust-stained shirt he'd been wearing since dawn.

Josephine and I returned to Paris and the Folies the next day. "We did it, Fred, we did it!" As we pulled out of the drive, she asked me to stop the car. "There's no room for murderers here. He's decimating my barnyard." And she handed me the marten.

PROGRAMME (suite)

LE CAFÉ CONCERT (The Music-Hall)

Mlle Raphaëlla	Mlle **JOSÉPHINE BAKER**
Le Directeur du Bal Mabille	M. Jean LANDRET
Les Spectatrices	Mlles Jacqueline MARCY, ÉLIANE MÉRYL, Lyne KYRE, Leila FROT, Gisèle COLLINE, Micheline ROINÉ, Huguette RASSAT
Les Spectateurs	MM. NELSON, Pierre JANVIER, GRÉGORY, FERREIRA, Marcel LEBAS, LAMBRUN
Les Jeunes Filles	Les Danseuses des Folies-Bergère

AVE MARIA

A. - **Prison de femmes** (The womens Prison)

Marie Stuart	Mlle **JOSÉPHINE BAKER**
Elisabeth d'Angleterre	Mlle **Lyne de SOUZA**
Le Comte d'Essex	M. Eddy MASSA

A part of the program for the Folies Bergère 1950, featuring Josephine (courtesy Saul Goodman)

CHAPTER 14

Supper at the Stork

Jo Bouillon: "We must go on; we must." That was Josephine's battle cry. She was right, of course. But converting the crumbling château, the pleasure garden and the 120 acres that surrounded them into the setting she dreamed of would be an incredibly costly matter.

Josephine was photographed in local dress, her arms filled with flowers; perched on her huge Diesel-Map tractor; in her spacious aviary surrounded by cockatoos and monkeys; on her outdoor stage; shaking hands; kissing children; washing dishes. . . . The contractors had finally settled down to business and estimates were pouring in. We held a council of war. How could we be everywhere at once, we wondered, earning the money to finance the renovations on the one hand and supervising the work on the other? There was planting, sowing, building and organizing to be done if Les Milandes was to open its gates that summer. At the same time, it was essential to bring in all the funds we could. "Now that you've appeared at the Club 49 and the Folies, there's nothing really lucrative left for you in Paris," I told Josephine. "The most profitable next step would be a year's tour." "I'm ready when you are, Jo." "No, *cherie.* This time you're going alone. I've got to keep an eye on things here."

Josephine's itinerary gradually took shape; first the major French towns, then Belgium, Holland, Switzerland, Italy. Afterward Spain, North Africa, Germany . . . Pierre Spiers, a long-time friend and accomplished musician, would lead the orchestra in my place. The jazz he coaxed from his harp and piano delighted Josephine; he in turn admired my wife's singing voice. Pierre's wife, Marie, Roger Legrand and Josephine's new dresser, Ginette, rounded out the group.

I attended the first performance in Bordeaux to turn over the orchestra to Pierre. It was a shock to see him standing in my place, but marrying Josephine had meant marrying her dream as well. I felt honor bound to do everything I could to make that dream come true. After all, Europe wasn't *that* big. I could join Josephine on the road from time to time, taking along the building plans, which were getting nearer and nearer completion.

That spring was a dark one for me, shadowed by my father's death. He would never see Les Milandes in its finished state. But at least he had witnessed the beginnings of the village we were creating. Bound by contracts that obliged her to perform nightly, Josephine was unable to attend the funeral, but curiously enough, the Bouillon and Baker families were drawn closer together by my father's passing. What could be more different than a clan of middle-class French musicians and a group of penniless blacks from the St. Louis slums? But when I saw Mama Carrie quietly take my mother's hands (they had no spoken words in common), I felt it was a victory for Josephine. We buried my father on a bright April morning next to Pepito Abatino in the little cemetery of Castelnaud-Fayrac.

Soon afterward I joined Josephine in Rome.

She had obtained an audience with Pope Pius XII. For the occasion Josephine was dressed in white from head to toe. The traditional mantilla covered her black hair, pulled back in a severe chignon. We waited our turn in a corridor along which glided cardinals, bishops and guards dressed in crimson and purple robes, billowing habits, cassocks. Only the rustle of soutanes broke the oppressive silence. "It reminds me of the Folies-Bergère," whispered Josephine. She reassumed her meditative air. At last it was our turn. Contrary to my expectations, the pontiff was not seated on the papal throne that dominated the room. Advancing toward us, he raised Josephine, kneeling beside me, to her feet. "My daughter . . ." With great simplicity, he drew her into conversation.

Josephine had left her wit at the door and shed her composure while genuflecting. Nothing remained but her ardor. She spoke passionately of Les Milandes and her plan to adopt children of all colors and religions. A smile brightened the Pope's ascetic face. "My daughter, there is a fundamental opposition between the church and racism. The church by universal definition professes the oneness of mankind." And he gave her his blessing.

I was overcome with admiration for the skill with which Josephine had presented her case. She left the Vatican with what she had come for: a papal benediction for her project. She would be able to allude to this in all her future press conferences, thereby spreading the name of Les Milandes throughout the Christian world.

"Just think," she reflected when we were back in our hotel room. "A little more than twenty years ago in this very country, the press carried stories about the possible excommunication of the 'scandalous Josephine.' Pepito was afraid to introduce me to his family."

I had to return to Les Milandes. Josephine sent me instructions scribbled on bits of paper or boldly marked in blue ink on photographs I had left with her. "We need benches and palm trees here. . . . Plant geraniums along the terraces. . . ." Much remained to be done, but nevertheless our first hotel-restaurant opened its doors that summer. We called it Lou Tornoli—"Please Come Back" in the local dialect. Fortunately Josephine's family was enormously helpful, because finding proper assistance was my most difficult task. . . . In October, Josephine and her troupe left for Mexico and Cuba. Since the tourist season was over, I decided to go with them.

Once again Josephine caused a sensation in Havana, both professionally and because of the amazing affinity she had with people of color. Her manager, Felix Alarcon, reported several offers from the United States. "I'll never go back there," she insisted, remembering her "scouting trip" through the South. "It's too painful. Every time you turn the corner, racism hits you in the face."

One day in December, we received an astonishing telegram from a New York agent, Willard Alexander, offering Josephine a fabulous sum to appear at the Copa City in Miami. "I had no idea he thought so highly of me," she said, laughing. What did I think she should do? I couldn't help considering the equally fabulous bills outstanding for Les Milandes.

A few contracts like Alexander's and our worries about what Josephine consistently referred to as "the seat of world brotherhood" would be over. "What's the Copa City, anyway?" Josephine asked a newsman. He explained that it was the most stylish, elegant place imaginable. "Are Negroes admitted?" she inquired. "Of course not." "Then what's the point of offering me a contract?" and she shrugged.

The next day word arrived that a Mr. Ned Schuyler wanted to speak with us. Well known in show business circles from Hollywood to Miami, Schuyler was an impresario and co-owner of the Copa City. He literally oozed intelligence and charm. It had taken only one of Josephine's performances to conquer him. "It's the best act of its kind I've ever seen," he kept repeating. Schuyler invited us to dinner, ordered champagne and got down to business. "You're exactly what I want for Copa City." He then upped the terms mentioned in Alexander's wire to an even more incredible figure. We were now talking about ten thousand dollars a week! I couldn't believe my ears!

Josephine listened quietly. Then she said softly, "I've been told that people of color are barred from Miami's nightclubs. If that's really the case, you can understand that I couldn't possibly perform there. It's as simple as that." For a moment I was afraid that Ned would strangle on his chicken. I thought that I might choke too. . . . Not that Josephine was wrong. But she was kissing a great deal of badly needed money goodbye.

Ned was not one to be put off easily, however. "It's true that colored people aren't admitted to the Copa, but no one's ever questioned it before. Let me talk to my lawyers and see what we can do. We'll meet again tomorrow." Ned was the kind of businessman whose constant deals required the services of twenty or more lawyers. He was back the next morning to report that his legal advisers were studying the matter. In the meantime he continued to press Josephine. But she refused to budge an inch. "I've had nothing but trouble in the States, Mr. Schuyler. Look how successful I am here in Cuba. Why should I break my neck in a country that dislikes the color of my skin? Jo and I have better things to do, things we're very excited about. We're going to turn Les Milandes into a real World Village which we hope will serve as a model in years to come."

"But all that's going to cost money, Josephine!" "There's always a way to find the funds if you have a good cause. I'm going back to Europe, Mr.

Schuyler. Believe me, it's possible to live without the United States!"
"Think it over, at least. Miami is only twenty-five minutes from here by
plane." "Distance isn't always a question of miles, Mr. Schuyler. People
can be at your fingertips and still be as remote as the North Pole. *You*
ought to know; you belong to a minority too." Ned was Jewish.

The following day Ned was back again. The three of us talked far into
the night. I could see that he and Josephine liked each other, but there
was no room for compromise. "If you can guarantee that my people will
be admitted to my performances on an equal footing with whites, I'll sign
the contract." Two weeks passed. Ned was now joining us for dinner after
the show on a regular basis. "What can I give Josephine that she'd enjoy?"
he asked one evening. "I'm sure she'd love a monkey." The next evening
he appeared with a marmoset, to Josephine's delight. Didn't she agree
that he was a charming person? I asked casually. Then I mentioned the
contract. Looking at things realistically, it seemed like a good idea to sign.
I'd received word from the Dordogne that the builders' estimates were
higher than anticipated.

"The two of you make me sick," snapped Josephine. "How many times
do I have to explain that I won't perform in the States unless . . ." And
she repeated her conditions. "But it's not even worth discussing, Jo. I'll
never have my way. You might just as well book our plane seats for Paris."
In an attempt to stall for time, I spoke privately with Ned the next
evening while Josephine played with the monkey in another room. "What
did she say, Jo?" "She won't give an inch. She's willing to sing anywhere
in the South—provided blacks can attend." Ned scratched his head.
"That really puts me on the spot. I'd like to start off the tour in Miami,
since it's my home town. But the city's divided in half by a canal, which
separates the whites from the blacks. There's a bridge, of course, but the
blacks who work in the white part of town have to be back on their side
of the water by nine at night." "It's as bad as that?" "I'm afraid so, Jo.
There have been attempts to improve the situation, but for the moment
any black crossing the bridge has to show his card to the policeman on
duty." I groaned. "Your home town sounds like Berlin. Under the circumstances I don't think any amount of money would change Josephine's
mind. I know my wife. She doesn't give in." "Tell her that I'll arrange
a tour through the South in places that guarantee equal treatment for
blacks." Josephine entered the room, the monkey clinging to her blouse.

"That sounds fine, Mr. Schuyler. Let's start with Miami." "Please, Josephine, don't ask for Miami," Ned protested. "Why not? It's your home town, isn't it? I should think you'd be proud to have *your* city take a leading role in the fight against racism."

We didn't see Ned again for several days. "I knew it. He's lost interest, just as I expected. We can forget about Mr. Schuyler, Jo. Let's pack up and go." But that very evening he was back. His twenty lawyers had reported that there was no actual legislation banning blacks from nightclubs. It was simply a question of custom. He waved the contract under Josephine's nose. "Look at the final clause: 'It is understood that the public will be admitted without regard to race, color or religion.' " We would open in Miami in two weeks and from there embark on a two-and-a-half-month tour around the United States.

"You're fantastic, Ned! This calls for champagne." As we drank, however, Josephine specified certain further demands. To begin with, she needed an English-speaking secretary. "Done. Anything else?" "I hate taking taxis in the States. I'd like my own car and a driver." Again Ned agreed. Judging by the astonished expressions of the passers-by, she must have been the first black ever to be driven along the streets of Miami by a white chauffeur!

Opening night at the Copa will go down in history. Roger and I spent some hectic moments right before show time removing "whites only" signs in the rest rooms and dressing rooms. Ned had done his work well: the press coverage at the dress rehearsal had been excellent. Still, he looked worried. "Is something the matter?" I inquired. He explained that he had cleared everything with the mayor, and blacks were free to cross the bridge—but that didn't mean they would. Ned had been in contact with the leading families across the canal—there were Rolls-Royces on *both* sides of the water. But in spite of their desire to see Josephine, they planned to stay home.

"They don't dare to come, Jo. They're terrified of trouble. Try to put yourself in their place. Whenever there's a confrontation, they're the ones that suffer. I've done my best to assure them that the mayor means what he's said, but they simply don't believe me. Unless Josephine talks to them in person, I'm afraid that . . ." For the next forty-eight hours, Josephine and her white chauffeur scoured the black quarter, visiting local dignitaries and the ten most prominent families. As always, she was her charming, persuasive self.

They all showed up on opening night! Ned in the meantime had flown in a wide range of black and white celebrities from New York. Walter Winchell sat between Sophie Tucker and Joe Louis. . . . Josephine, microphone in hand, moved gracefully from table to table. "This is the most important moment of my life. It's the first time I've been in my native land in twenty-six years . . . because the other times"—and she made a sweeping gesture as if to brush aside the past—"don't count. Today all that is behind me. I can't express my joy. Here I am in this city where I can perform for my people, where I can shake *your* hands. This is a very significant occasion for us, and by 'us' I mean the *entire human race.*" I saw eyes fill with tears at her words.

The impact of Josephine's victory is difficult to describe. Her appearance that night was like a revolutionary bombshell. The next morning she wired President Truman as follows: "My husband and I wish to thank the American people through you for their wonderful welcome that crystallizes the progress being made toward civil rights for everyone, a cause which I know is as important to you as it is to us." The Copa was obliged to turn people away nightly. Our chauffeur, Lew Barr, was crushed to see us leave. "She's the greatest lady I've ever met," he confided.

Josephine's success was a triumph for Ned Schuyler as well. The clippings he brought us were like nectar to Josephine. Especially after the *Ziegfeld Follies* fiasco! Hy Gardner noted in the *New York Herald Tribune* that she walked like Mae West, sang like Piaf, had a hair style that was part Carmen Miranda and part Empire State Building, and she was dressed by Balmain and Dior, which made her one of the world's ten best-dressed women. Ned also brought us a new contract, superseding the old one. We couldn't believe our eyes. Josephine would spend nine months a year in the United States for a three-year period. The remaining three months she was free to return to France. Needless to say, the final clause remained the same: it was understood that Josephine would perform only in places that admitted both whites and blacks.

"I can't help feeling this is a historic moment," Josephine said emotionally. "I agree," Ned replied. "It looks like certain racial barriers have been eliminated for good, which means real progress for the black cause." Soon thereafter other nightclubs followed the Copa's example. The battle had been won. In our euphoria we thought that meant the war was over too. A triumphant Josephine insisted on spending the summer in France. Rather than risk losing her, Ned decided to accompany us to Les Milandes. Our worries seemed to be over. Josephine's contract guaranteed two hundred thousand dollars yearly.

The results of Josephine's success at the Copa were far-reaching. The NAACP and its president, Lindsay White, decided to stage a Baker Day on May 20, 1951, in Harlem. It was their way of honoring Josephine before she returned to Europe. I had already gone back to France to see how the work was progressing, as we had been absent since October. One day I received a telephone call from Josephine in New York. *"Cheri,* I don't have a thing to wear." She went on to explain that in spite of her stage wardrobe, she had nothing appropriate for Baker Day. She needed a white outfit and a black one. "But why are you telling *me,* Josephine?" "I want you to go to Dior for me. They have my measurements on file. Suzanne will help you choose something suitable." I took the next train for Paris. On arrival at Dior, I hurried to the office of the directress, Suzanne Lulling. "I have a real challenge for you, madame. I'm leaving for the states in forty-eight hours and I've got to take two new outfits for Josephine with me." "I'll put our entire staff to work on it," Suzanne assured me. Two days later I boarded the plane carrying a stunning white suit, a hat designed to frame Josephine's famous chignon, a black ankle-length draped dress made of raw silk and an off-white pleated gown.

Nothing Josephine had told me prepared me for what I found on arrival at Harlem's Hotel Theresa. Baker Day had assumed huge proportions. Thousands of blacks had assembled to honor Josephine. Many of the men were in dress clothes and top hats; some carried posters and banners. There were women in their Sunday best, young girls clutching bouquets, small boys spruced up in coats and ties. A parade, four cars deep, wound its way through a Harlem gone wild with joy. Loudspeakers blared, the crowd cheered. Josephine, accompanied by her faithful Ginette, who was visibly moved, waved from an open car. My wife should have been a chief of state, I reflected.

The procession came to a halt in a square where a platform had been erected. Speaker after speaker stressed Josephine's victories, describing how she had stormed that bastion of segregation Miami; how she had struck a blow for democracy by insisting that the stage crew and musicians at Philadelphia's Earle Theater include blacks during her appearance there; how she had requested black orchestra members at the Chicago Theater; how she had bombarded the National Association of Radio and

Television Broadcasters with demands to rewrite their contract to permit the hiring of blacks in their industry. Her efforts were not confined to the world of the arts. She had asked the same thing of the First National Bank, International Harvester and the Chicago Association of Commerce and Industry. It was thrilling to hear a voice from the podium say: "Josephine Baker's life is a gigantic living monument, constructed of talent and courage; future generations of blacks throughout our land must not forget that if their road is easier it is partly thanks to her."

All of New York's black celebrities were in Harlem that day, mingling with a crowd that included members of the American Legion, the Girl Scouts and Boy Scouts, and representatives of a multitude of athletic and cultural groups. There were brass bands, wreaths of flowers, war whoops, gifts, handshakes by the hundreds, the parade, a huge luncheon, an even bigger cocktail party, a ball. . . . Josephine sailed through it all, stopping only to change clothes. She tirelessly seized every possible occasion to put in a word for the black cause, sandwiching an earnest conversation with Nobel Peace Prize winner Dr. Ralph Bunche between two official receptions, stopping to chat with Bessie Allison Buchanan, wife of the owner of the Golden Gate, where that very evening Josephine stood in front of an integrated orchestra and sang to an audience including Ned Schuyler, French Ambassador Roger Seydoux, Gypsy Rose Lee and Frederic March. She had exchanged her day dress for the low-cut, pleated Dior gown.

I boarded the plane the next morning in high spirits. What a victory for Josephine! It looked as if nothing could stop her. How wrong I was!

The extravagance of Baker Day had raised segregationist hackles. In June I received a letter from Josephine announcing that she had canceled her Atlanta appearance after being turned away by three of the city's hotels. From now on, she would appear only in towns where her black-and-white troupe was welcome everywhere. (Under Georgia law, licenses of hotels accommodating blacks were revocable.) She did plan to sing for the NAACP Atlanta convention, however, Josephine continued. The week-long meeting scheduled for the end of June would be attended by a thousand delegates, most of them Southern blacks, who would be lodged at the university or in private homes. I couldn't help feeling concerned. I knew that Josephine was receiving threatening letters. . . .

Poor Ned. When he and Josephine finally arrived at Les Milandes, I'm convinced she made him walk over every inch of the property. He would barely have time to close his eyes before she was there in the doorway. "Time to get up, lazybones! I've got a million things to show you. Over there's where we're planning to build a deluxe hotel. . . . The African Motel will go here. And I've got to find room to put in a trailer park. . . ." If Ned had planned his month in the Dordogne as vacation time, he obviously didn't know Josephine. Up at dawn, she had a hand in everything, hurrying from the newly restored farmer's cottage inhabited by Margaret and Elmo to the pleasure garden to Lou Tornoli, to check out departed guests' rooms.

Ned was stunned by her activity. And there was more to come. "Next year when Les Milandes is ready, we're planning to adopt our Rainbow Tribe," she informed him. In the meantime she met with local builders, went over their final bids and signed for the work to be done. Thanks to her fabulous American contract, her dreams would come true. We decided to construct a hotel for people of modest means. They could picnic for meals or buy sandwiches, cakes and crêpes. "Margaret will run the pastry shop," Josephine said firmly. "And as for you, Elmo, since you two are childless, you can adopt some youngsters too. In fact, why not call our next hotel L'Arc-en-Ciel? . . . That's French for 'rainbow,' Ned." "She's the most astonishing woman I've ever met," Schuyler gasped, wiping his brow. I had to agree.

All too soon, they were gone. Every two weeks I received money to pay for the work in progress. Then suddenly in October came news of the Stork Club scandal, which would have repercussions throughout the United States. Josephine was appearing at the Roxy Theater at the time. One of our friends, the opera singer Roger Rico, then starring in the Broadway hit *South Pacific*, invited her to a late supper. They decided to go to a stylish, very exclusive club. . . .

Josephine: The Stork Club was always mobbed. And limited to a swank clientele. The doorman unhooked the chain barring the entranceway only for people he knew. One look at me and he clicked it firmly in place. "I have a table reserved," snapped Rico. "Oh, excuse me, sir," gasped the astonished guard. *South Pacific*'s leading man was a regular customer. In we walked, Rico, Mrs. Rico (who was part black, although it didn't show), Bessie Buchanan and I.

I ordered crab salad, steak and a bottle of French wine. The looks that the headwaiter and his assistants were giving me made me suspect that something was going to happen. But in fact the exact opposite occurred. Nothing happened at all . . . nothing, by which I mean that my friends received their orders but mine did not appear. Apparently my crab was still in the water and my steer remained on the hoof. Those customers who were forced to pass by our table pointedly turned away. I was clearly unwelcome. The club's manager, Sherman Billingsley, usually stopped by Rico's table to greet him. Not that night. Worse, I spied Walter Winchell, who had fawned over me in Miami, at a nearby table. This time he looked right through me.

By now Rico was furious, and he insisted that my order be brought at once. The flustered waiter returned from the kitchen with word that "They're all out of crab, sir, and there isn't a single steak left." Mrs. Rico begged me to leave before matters got worse. Bessie Buchanan, however, insisted that I should inform the NAACP of my scandalous treatment at once. I went straight to the telephone, where the attendant told me she was much too busy to dial my number. Too bad; I'd do it myself. I placed a call to NAACP executive secretary Walter White, asking him to call an officer to certify that the Stork Club had refused to serve me. By the time I returned to my table, Winchell had disappeared.

Three years before, when Jo and I had been forced to move from hotel to hotel, Canada Lee had offered to take up the matter with New York's Mayor O'Dwyer. And now it was beginning all over again. A pathetic little steak finally appeared on a platter, but since we had placed our order more than an hour before, Rico asked for the check, his superb voice shaking with anger.

The next day the papers carried reports of the complaint I had filed against the Stork Club. The day after that they buzzed with reports of a phone call to the New York Telephone Company from "an anonymous male" announcing that a bomb had been planted in Billingsley's club. A squad of policemen escorted by radio cars had searched the eight-story building in vain. At seven o'clock the next evening, NAACP members picketed the entrance to the Stork Club for an hour—the length of time I had waited for my miserable dinner. Lindsay White went on to write New York Mayor Impellitteri, protesting the club's policy of discrimination and asking for a right to reply via the American Broadcasting Company. When Walter Winchell was asked on the air what had really happened at the Stork, he had the moral cowardice to reply that he hadn't been there!

It should be pointed out that Billingsley's nightclub was almost Winchell's meal ticket, which helped to explain the columnist's subsequent behavior. That November 1, at the mayor's request, Billingsley, who considered the entire matter a "farce," was asked to clarify his position on civil rights and publicly announce that his establishment welcomed people regardless of race, color or religion. Billingsley replied that although his policy was to serve the world at large, at the same time he had to consider his regular customers first. What hypocrisy!

Ten days after my visit to the Stork, the nightclub refused to admit the son of El Glaoui, pasha of Marrakech. The French embassy protested violently. The plot thickened when there appeared in the press a signed letter to Lindsay White from Billingsley, in which the Stork Club manager said that given the nature of his clientele, he was obliged to turn away persons considered undesirable by the majority of his guests. Billingsley promptly filed a complaint, claiming that the letter bearing his name was a forgery.

Shortly before Christmas, charges were dismissed. This did not prevent me from issuing a writ against Walter Winchell for four hundred thousand dollars in damages. He had ripped me to pieces in his *Daily Mirror* columns. "Don't get involved with Winchell, Josephine," Ned had warned me. "But he was a *witness!*" "You don't understand how things work in New York. The sun rises and sets on that column. If you tell the world that he was at the Stork Club and didn't raise a finger to help you . . ." "But that's what *happened*, Ned." The whole affair disgusted me, but I refused to give in. Instead, with my lawyer Arthur Garfield Hayes at my side, I gave a press conference to set the record straight:

"Walter Winchell accuses me of being 'an enemy of my people' and a 'fascist,' " I began. "Surely he knows that I received the Medal of the Resistance for my intelligence work and was cooperating with the Allies well before the North African landing! Mr. Winchell also suggests that I'm anti-Semitic. I would like to remind him that one of my husbands was Jewish and that I have been asked to speak at the American Jewish Committee's Chicago meeting later this month. He insinuates that I favored Mussolini's invasion of Ethiopia, an accusation so ridiculous that it's unworthy of comment. I *must* respond, however, when Mr. Winchell accuses me of being a Communist. I do not belong to any political party. Walter Winchell states that I have provoked previous incidents. People of color are not obliged to resort to provocation: incidents occur on their own. Walter Winchell writes that everything I do is for the sake of publicity. His kind I can do without! But he *is* correct in thinking that I will continue to act to further my people's interests." My lawyer concluded the conference by adding that it was unfortunate that the real issue was being obscured by personal questions since the matter at hand was the fight for minority rights, a cause which Walter Winchell had been known to defend. . . .

True. But perhaps his meal ticket was more important now.

I clearly had a fight on my hands. Although responsible publications like the *New York Times* and *Time* magazine were reporting the facts impartially, there were ugly stories in the tabloids, aimed at discrediting me morally. Apparently I led a scandalous life! The number of threatening letters increased. Thank goodness, such friends as Sugar Ray Robinson were there to support me. "How long is this going to last?" sighed Ned. I understood his concern. The film contract I had signed the week before, which would bring me a quarter of a million dollars, had just been annulled for no apparent reason. How little they knew their Josephine! Instead of frightening me, they were making me dig in my heels! Speaking requests poured in. I accepted whatever I could. I would step up my fight against racism!

Jo Bouillon: In spite of the bleak winter weather, the work at Les Milandes continued. I was knee deep in lumber, concrete and miles of electric wire when a disturbing cable arrived from the States. "Imperative you come. Ned and I need you. Josephine." What could be wrong? I found out the minute I arrived on American soil. Ned's secretary, who had been sent to meet me at the airport, explained that although the tour was going extremely well, Josephine was becoming increasingly involved in her crusade. Ned felt she was carrying things too far. Her beliefs were beginning to compromise the contracts he'd obtained for her. They both felt that I might back up their respective positions.

"Your wife is impossible," Ned insisted. "She spends most of her time flag-waving for the NAACP. That's all she thinks about. She no sooner gets to a city than she's contacting people, offering her services, lecturing, conferring with local authorities, helping however she can. Some of the theater managers who may not share her beliefs but were willing to humor her as long as she drew a big black and white crowd are having second thoughts. Things have changed since Alan Gale of Miami's Celebrity Club said: 'White, black, green, who cares as long as they come!' Besides which, Josephine's received threats and they don't want their places torn up. The next thing you know, we'll have the entire Ku Klux Klan on our backs."

"Ned wants me to make up my mind immediately," Josephine told me. "Either I continue touring as booked, or I go on the road as a spokesman for civil rights. What do you think I should do, Jo?"

We spent most of the next forty-eight hours deep in discussion—minus the time that Josephine disappeared to make a rousing speech to the public. She finished her address at seven o'clock and left for the theater at eight. It seemed to me that we had to face facts. On a return of a minimum two hundred thousand dollars, not counting any additional sums from radio and television sources, we had already undertaken to make equal expenditures for Les Milandes. So far Josephine had received only a tenth of the above sum. Ned was convinced that if she continued her so-called political activity, her contracts would be broken, one after the other. This was already starting to happen. All she received for her speaking engagements was travel expenses.

"But *look*, Ned," Josephine insisted. "You backed me up before. You *knew* I would only sign contracts to appear where colored people are admitted." "True enough, Josephine," Ned agreed wearily. "But that's as far as I went. I never thought things would end up like this. Take the McGee affair, for example. . . ."

Josephine stiffened, then attempted to fill me in. "Listen to this, Jo! McGee died in the electric chair because he was accused without proof of raping a white woman in Mississippi, an extremely racist state. The day of his execution, there was such a mob in front of the jail that it looked like a national holiday. Children were sitting in the trees and everyone wore their Sunday best. Just before pulling the switch, the authorities paraded an empty coffin, symbolizing justice, through the crowd. I was sent photographs to prove it! Members of the victim's family were present in the death chamber, but McGee died alone because *his* people weren't allowed to be there. When I learned that the McGee family didn't have the funds for a burial, I arranged through my lawyer to pay for the funeral. As a result, the witch hunters are calling me a Communist. The intensity of the inhuman feelings at large in the United States today reminds me of a bull that sees red wherever he looks."

Silence. "That's the situation, Jo. There's Ned and the money on one side and what I feel is my duty on the other." "Don't expect me to make up your mind for you, *cherie.* It's up to you to decide. I'll go along with whatever you say." "But what about the money for Les Milandes?" "We'll manage somehow."

Perhaps. But on the Paris-bound plane I asked myself how. In any event, Josephine hadn't really given me a choice. If I had sided with Ned, I would have lost her . . . and I wasn't prepared to do that. Still, any cut in our funds would be a real blow to our treasury and I had the feeling we were going to be short of money for quite a while. Josephine couldn't possibly earn what she had been promised under the terms of Ned's contract anyplace else in the world. It could take some time to make up the difference. But come what might, we would continue working to make Les Milandes as attractive as possible. What concerned me the most at the moment was Josephine's insistence on continuing her fight against racism in an America that was clearly in an ugly mood. "We'll let you know what we decide to do, Jo," Ned had promised me. I could guess. Two days later a telegram arrived from Schuyler. Josephine would try to stay on with him, at the same time pursuing her cause. . . . It didn't take long for Ned's predictions to come true. Within two months all Josephine's remaining contracts had been annulled.

Josephine kept me informed about the way her bitter battle was progressing with letters like the following:

St. Louis, February 4, 1952

My dearest Jo:

It feels very strange to be here in my own home town, where they've just staged a Baker Day. Did I tell you what led up to the celebration? Last December my lawyer in Chicago, Aaron Payne, arranged an interview for me with Howard Weeks, the editor of a Negro publication called *The Saint Louis Argus.* Weeks belongs to a citizens' committee which has been formed because of some very unpleasant things that have happened in the local schools. One particularly horrible incident was the murder of a fifteen-year-old boy, David Broods, a student at the Wheatley School, last November 26. I obviously couldn't refuse to join the committee, but I did set down two conditions: the first was that I wanted no reimbursement of any kind for my participation, but should I bring in any funds they were to be distributed to the local poor; the second was that I could use the occasion to speak out about the urgent need to improve the quality of life in St. Louis. This caused Mayor Joseph Darst to proclaim Sunday, February 3, as Josephine Baker Day in honor of a citizen of St. Louis and an extremely valuable American. They even gave me a scroll stamped with a seal. When I think of my origins it brings tears to my eyes. But enough sentimentality! (Tell Mama all the same . . . and I'll send you the scroll.) The ceremony took place last night, topping off a round of celebrations and receptions at the Kiel Auditorium Convention Hall. It was as successful as had been anticipated. There was a good deal of talk about my twelve trunks and $250,000 wardrobe (a slight exaggeration!), but even more about my anti-racist position. I heard shouts of "Hitler doesn't frighten us—neither does the Stork Club" and "We're right behind you, Jo—keep fighting."

Another letter, this one undated, read as follows:

Jo dearest:

I'm writing this from Florida, where I've come to look into a matter close to my heart. I spent this morning visiting local banks to request that people of color be given jobs as accountants and cashiers in order to earn a decent living. The reply was that blacks aren't "ready" for that kind of work—that all they're good for is sweeping and dishwashing. Then I went to the Medical Association to demand that Negro doctors be hired by white hospitals; this time I was told that "people of color should stick with their kind." Finally I went to the funeral homes, thinking that in the face of death, perhaps . . . "Don't you suppose we're all alike in the end?" I asked. "Then how can some cemeteries be barred to blacks?" Listen to their answer, Jo. "Because that's the way it is!" I was even more upset to discover that blacks are beginning to discriminate against each other. The virus seems to be in the bread we eat, the very air we breathe. I can sense the doors slamming closed even between racial brothers. Fear is a terrible thing, Jo. Fortunately some people open up to me, offer me their hands, but more often than not it's to show me unhappiness I couldn't have

imagined. When I think of the peaceful Dordogne, of my beloved France
. . . I'm so glad that Mama, Margaret and Elmo have left this inhuman
country. And I hear that Richard will be joining you soon. I hope to be
there to welcome my brother to France, but I'm not at all sure. I miss
you all terribly and can't wait to see what's been done at Les Milandes.
How are the geraniums? And the animals? Will the pool be ready by
summer? You know how I hate the water, but I'll still be the first one in.
Noblesse oblige, as they say. I haven't forgotten that I'm the chatelaine.

Richard's arrival from Missouri was followed by Josephine's from California. She had found substantial support among Hollywood actors but a
good deal of reticence on the part of producers, to the point that when
it came to filming certain scenes involving blacks, they preferred to avoid
trouble by going to Mexico.

Josephine was no sooner back than she became a farm woman again.
She found everyone busy doing his job. Maryse ran the souvenir shop;
Margaret managed the pastry shop with Elmo's help; Richard, who had
left a shipping concern behind in Missouri, manned the gas pumps.
Josephine toured the property by pony cart. She was charmed by the
graceful outline of the J-shaped pool, honoring "Jo and Jo"; she inspected
the calves in the barnyard. . . .

The summer went by in a flash and before we knew it, Josephine was
heading for South America.

In Rio, Josephine made the following declaration, which touched many
hearts: "It makes me so happy to see these bright faces, all of which bear
witness to their ancestry, whether they be white, black, yellow or red. I
am deeply moved to find my loftiest ideals and dreams embodied here in
Brazil. I have always believed that different races can live together in
harmony and I am full of admiration for the way the Brazilians have made
this idea a reality, a reality which to my mind is the way of the future.
That's why I regard Brazil as the living symbol of democracy."

At the same time, in the United States, Walter Winchell resumed his
attack, announcing: "Josephine Baker has launched a huge propaganda
tour against the United States."

Springtime brought Josephine back with the swallows. I was extremely
relieved to see her. Things were going from bad to worse on the other side

of the ocean. Josephine's contracts in Europe couldn't hold a candle to Ned Schuyler's, but at least they were firm commitments. Josephine had hardly remained with us long enough for a hug all around, including the dogs, before she was off again by car for Paris. From there she took the next SAS plane to Denmark. During the four-hour flight she slept like a baby, landing dewy as a rose to face press conferences, photographers and rehearsals in three different places, then moved on to give two after-midnight shows without having been to bed for twenty-four hours. Still fresh as a daisy.

When she returned to Paris it was as a star performer at a fashionable charity affair, Le Bal des Petits Lits Blancs. The newspapers called her "the hit of the evening" in spite of the fact that Bing Crosby, Gary Cooper, the Aga Khan and Charlie Chaplin were in the audience and Lily Pons was on the stage. Once again Josephine had taken Paris by storm.

Josephine didn't let her professional success interfere with her work as a militant. She had recently founded two world organizations, one to combat discrimination because of religion, race or color, the other to support the arts, sciences and sports. They had headquarters scattered throughout the world, from Mexico, Cuba and Haiti to South Africa, Scandinavia, Italy, Japan, Los Angeles, Oakland, San Francisco and New York. She spurred on the various association members by mail.

"People can be so unpredictable, Jo," she complained. "As long as I'm on the spot, they do an effective job of fund-raising and getting their organization on its feet. But I no sooner turn my back than they lose momentum. Days at a time go by without their accomplishing anything at all. Why?"

I tried to explain that her incredible energy, her will power and determination, made sparks fly, but that when she moved on she took that momentum with her. "With your power of persuasion you could look people in the eye and tell them to jump out the window and they'd do it, cherie. But when you're no longer there, they go back to their families, offices and petty problems. Their daily lives seem more important than your cause."

She nodded sadly. But I knew she would keep on fighting all the same.

Josephine (late summer, 1953): How strange life is. . . . Each year is different. It seems that only yesterday Paris was calling me its enfant *terrible.* The things I set such store on then seem so frivolous now; even my diamonds. Today I care only about serious matters. There's no country in the world that has integrated its people of color more effectively than France. Look at the value they've placed on President Monnerville, a man of color, on Alexandre Dumas and Colette, both of whom have colored blood in their veins. That's why I feel so at home here. I'm not conducting a personal vendetta against the United States. I simply want to fight supporters of racism wherever they may be.

I recently suffered a terrible loss. It was in 1949 that Jo and I first met Canada Lee. We invited him to lunch in our fleabag hotel—the only one that would have us. But when the waiter brought in our food, we realized that we had no silverware or glasses. We were expected to eat like animals. Canada remarked that since he had become a star he'd lost touch with reality. Our luncheon had opened his eyes, he said, and because of that humiliation he threw himself into the fight heart and soul. He was no longer willing to play the accepted game between blacks and whites which allowed the same side always to win. Gradually Canada's work fell off and he began a rapid decline from the heights of fame into moral and physical misery. Even his friends deserted him. Someone at last had the courage to ask him to appear at a charity function. He no longer had subway fare, so he set off for the theater on foot in a freezing rain, like the pauper he was. His shoes leaked and he had sold his coat long before. Canada caught a chill. Soon he was dead.

Yes, sickness and poverty killed him, but I know it was grief as well. An NAACP investigation proved that Canada was not a Communist, as accused. He was simply a man who believed that human beings have the right to live in love and brotherhood.

I've taken my task so much to heart that it's become all I live for. I've had some wonderful moments during my battle. Neither threats nor loss of work can keep me from continuing to fight for my beliefs. Just the opposite. They serve to convince me that I'm in the right. How can man today commit such atrocities against his brothers? The present tension in the United States is such that the only difference between America and Nazi Germany seems to be that Hitler didn't try to disguise his feelings.

A recent story in *Jet* magazine reported the head of Florida's Ku Klux Klan as saying that he had recruited representatives from ninety-seven groups in thirty-one different states to lead a Confederate army if the

Supreme Court abolished segregation in the South. He even signed a declaration stating that his army was mobilized and ready in Orlando, Florida. . . . Elsewhere a federal court in Sioux City, Iowa, upheld the case of a cemetery which had turned back the funeral procession of Sergeant John Rice, an Indian, because he wasn't white. He was, however, a Korean war hero! . . . Then there were the seven white farm-owners in Alabama who were discovered practicing slavery after one of their black captives died from a beating with a knotted rope. . . . And imagine my horror when Judge Waring of South Carolina's federal court told me in New York that he and his wife had been stoned out of town for defending people of color and Jews.

My grim file of terror and stupidity is, alas, growing weekly. Unfortunately some people of color have switched to the side of the powerful. Adam Clayton Powell, Jr., one of the first blacks to be elected to Congress, whose wife Hazel Scott I consider my friend, declared after my so-called explosive South American conferences that I was presenting figments of my imagination as fact. . . . In Detroit I challenged a group of black clergymen who had returned from a trip to Africa sponsored by white authorities and reported that America was the only country that treats its people of color well! . . . I have argued the same issue with Edith Sampson, the distinguished black lawyer and U.N. delegate, who has made similar statements, and with the highly respected black journalist George Schuyler. If only statesmen had hearts as sincere as their words! Perón was the first person I approached who dared officially to accept the honorary presidency of an association against racial and religious discrimination. I next went to Chile, where President Ibáñez received me and pledged in turn to fight for man's rights regardless of color. But on my return to Cuba last February, I learned that my contract had been annulled, and an American newspaper in Havana wrote that I would be buried there! The year before, a coup d'état had returned Batista to power.

During my stay in Havana, its two largest hotels refused to take me in; worse, when I arrived, contract in hand, at the radio station where I was to perform, a pair of policemen barred the door. I remained in front of the building from three that afternoon until ten at night in protest. Next a theater manager who had formerly welcomed my appearances at his large movie house, and had become my friend, regretfully informed me that he couldn't hold to our agreement. If he did, he would never show another film; he had been warned that he would be boycotted.

A small neighborhood movie house finally took me in. The manager received continual threats, but nevertheless the theater was filled with protesting citizens. I decided to demand an audience with the President of the Republic, a fellow person of color, and request his moral support in the crusade against racial and religious discrimination. He referred me to his minister of information, with whom I had a pleasant conversation . . . but that very evening, as I left the stage, I was arrested by four armed plainclothesmen. They could put away their guns, I assured them. My only weapon was my heart. I was taken to military headquarters, where to my surprise I saw two photographs in the entranceway, an immense one of President Eisenhower and a smaller one of President Batista. My escorts led me into a back room, where I found all my belongings, including my papers, spread out on a table. The authorities had obviously ransacked my room during my absence. A statement lay waiting for my signature, stating that I admitted to being paid by Moscow and indulging in subversive activities. Needless to say, I emphatically refused to sign.

News of my arrest quickly spread through the city. Groups of angry citizens gathered; the French ambassador protested. In the meantime I was taken to a hall filled with photographs of "Wanted" persons, killers and other wrongdoers on the run. After I was fingerprinted and photographed, the word "Communist" was marked beneath my picture and I was assigned the number 0000492. One of the plainclothesmen whispered that my arrest had been political. I didn't doubt it. I was front-page news the next day both in Cuba and in the United States. The day after that, a brief paragraph appeared in the papers reporting that my arrest had been an error; that I had been denounced and it was all an unfortunate mistake. But I'm convinced that at that very moment my photograph was on its way to Washington. . . .

I had the opportunity to be in London during the coronation ceremonies. Every day I went to Hyde Park to hear men of color discussing the situation in South Africa, that land of eleven million inhabitants whose two million whites oppress their non-white brothers so cruelly. I also attended the opening of Parliament and listened in fascination to a debate on the South African question that lasted from two in the afternoon until midnight. The whites who spoke out for the freedom of South Africa's blacks were magnificent. It's true that this was only a small warning for countries practicing discrimination, but the colored are beginning to unite. There are more than a hundred million in Africa. Once these colored people, who cover three quarters of the globe, band together, couldn't it bring about the extinction of the white race? It seems inevitable to me. With ever-increasing improvements in transportation, people will mingle more quickly and easily until racial purity gradually disappears. But I'd like to see this happen through love, not hate.

And now I am back in France, where freedom of thought is paramount. I am very tired after four years of fighting, but a few days of rest in this soothing haven will heal my soul. More than ever I'm convinced that I can realize my dream because I believe in the dignity of man. Jo and I plan to adopt four children: red, yellow, white and black. Four little children raised in the country, in my beautiful Dordogne. They will serve as an example of true democracy and be living proof that if people are left in peace, nature takes care of the rest.

Jo Bouillon: Josephine appeared at a rally for the International League Against Racism and Anti-Semitism in Paris on December 28, 1953.

Then it was back to the Dordogne. Josephine's way of relaxing was to see, learn and understand everything possible. This led to exhausting days if the project at hand was complex. One evening I appeared for dinner in my peasant boots, to find the table laid with unusual care. The candelabra blazed with light, making flames dance in our finest crystal. At the head of the main staircase stood a radiant Josephine in evening dress, her hair piled high. I always tried to anticipate Josephine's "surprises," but she had fooled me again. "If only you'd warned me, *cherie,* I would have put on my dinner jacket." "There's still time, Jo."

I dressed with care, wondering what Josephine had up her sleeve. We dined quietly together, but I found her unusually vivacious, totally charming. My weariness vanished and I tried to forget the fact that I had sworn to get to bed early in order to pick up some hogs in a nearby town the next day. Josephine put on a record; we danced. It had been ages since we'd had an evening like this. Then came the champagne. "What are we drinking to?" I asked. "Us?" "We *three.* . . . Jo, is it all right with you if I bring the first of the Bouillon children back with me?"

So that was it. Josephine was in the process of organizing a tour through Japan for the spring. The first performances would be benefits for war orphans. I replied that it was perfectly fine with me, but she didn't have to play the vamp to get my consent. She burst into laughter. "Oh, this . . ." pointing to her clinging gown. "I just wanted to see if I could still fit into it. But anyway, Jo, how could any dress be too beautiful when we're celebrating our first child?"

And that's how I learned that my first son would be Oriental.

———— ·❦· ————

CHAPTER 15

The Rainbow Tribe

DURING THE ENTIRE TRIP I thought of nothing else. How would I recognize him? How would I know that he was "the one," *my* baby? Would he love me? Would he love *us?* I could feel my heart thumping.

Everything was in readiness at Les Milandes: little beds, little chairs (I was thinking ahead!), little dressers, an array of small dishes, a stock of baby things acquired during my tours.

It was the first time I had ever set foot in Tokyo, but I felt I knew Japan, thanks to a remarkable woman, Miki Sawada, wife of a former ambassador in Paris. Miki had put me in contact with other Japanese in Paris, New York and London, who had given me insight into their astonishing civilization. Then of course there was my painter friend Foujita, who had asked me to pose for him back in the days when I sat with Chiquita on the outdoor terrace of the Coupole.

What would my baby be called? Would his first name be as graceful as Foujita's: Tsougouharu, "Inheritor of Peace"? Alas, the Japanese I met were inheritors of war. A group of citizens who had lived through Hiroshima gave me an unforgettably grim picture of a child framed against a ghost town that appeared to have been flattened by a gigantic steam roller. The peace movement had assumed an importance here unmatched elsewhere in the world because there were still Japanese dying daily of radiation poisoning. The survivors, most of whom felt a mysterious inner contamination, were dedicated to preventing such tragedy from recurring.

I lectured in Osaka and Tokyo, explaining that I had been sent there by the French branch of the International League Against Racism and Anti-Semitism to found a similar association in Japan. Presided over by Mrs. Sawada, it would devote itself to combating social, racial and religious discrimination. "I believe I have a mission on earth: aiding people to join together in friendship and understand each other before it's too late," I told my listeners. "Terrible mistakes have been made. I see events on the horizon even graver than the disasters of 1939–1940. The good are going to suffer for the evil. When mankind casts off its restraints there are no limits to the atrocities it can commit. I'm afraid of what may be done in the name of vengeance. There's nothing worse than revenge that springs from hate."

I went on to express my surprise at the ability of the Japanese to adopt modern ways while preserving their ancient customs. I was often asked, I continued, why, since I was so proud of my African heritage, I spoke a different language than my forefathers and wore Western dress. I could only reply that I would like to learn an African tongue but had had neither the time nor the opportunity; besides, I could make myself understood anywhere in the world in French and English. As for clothes, my people had no choice. When my great-grandparents were brought to America as slaves, they had lost their names, their language, their personality and their pride and had been forced to dress to suit their masters.

I was struck by the vitality, intelligence and cultivation of the Japanese people, their capacity to look ahead, their reflectiveness, their bond with the past and its ritual. Every path in Japan, no matter how winding, leads toward God. Getting there is simply a question of tenacity, patience and time.

Miki Sawada, so knowledgeable about our civilization, opened my eyes to her own, ever present even when invisible, like a Japanese landscape painting exquisitely veiled in mist. Most important, she welcomed me to the Elizabeth Sanders Home, an orphanage she had created. She had been the first person besides Jo I had told of my dream for a World Village and my intention to adopt children of different races. Miki was delighted that my first son would be Oriental. I had given many benefit performances for the home and was deeply moved by its efforts on behalf of young victims of chance, which can be so brutally blind in wartime.

The home was situated in a Tokyo suburb. I was no sooner inside than I was surrounded by children with straight black hair and dancing, slanted eyes. How could I possibly choose? What method would be less blind than the force that had dictated their births? "Stay as long as you like," Miki insisted. Hours passed. I laughed and played with one child after another. They all welcomed my embraces, particularly one little boy, who barely left my side. He was as supple as a little fish, backing away, returning, hopping on one foot, hugging and kissing me, lisping stories in a language I couldn't understand. How old could he be? Eighteen months, perhaps? His voice was like the peeping of birds.

Which one would it be? I wanted to take them all. The agile boy was back at my side, trying to pull himself into my lap, clinging to me with all his strength. I gathered him into my arms. "You've chosen, then?" asked Miki. "You won't regret it. He's a sweet, loving child."

She told me all she could about him. He was Korean. His father had probably been American; his mother, undoubtedly ashamed and penniless, had abandoned him. He had been found beneath an open umbrella that sheltered him from the elements. A note was pinned to his clothing, giving his birth date, which corresponded to our July 7, 1952, and his country of origin. Around his neck hung a small red bag containing a tiny plaque engraved with the precepts of Buddhism: "I will abstain from killing any living thing; I will take nothing that is not given me; I will abstain from all forms of sexual deviation; I will not lie; I will abstain from harmful drink."

The child nestled against me. "You'll baptize him a Catholic, I suppose," said one of the nurses. "Why? He was born a Buddhist and I don't see any difference between the precepts you just translated for me and the Ten Commandments. I believe in one God, which means He is for everyone. My son will keep wearing his red bag. . . . What do you call him?" "Akio. It means 'autumn'; that's when we found him."

I picked up Akio and prepared to leave. As we walked toward the gate, I noticed a grave-faced baby sitting by a tree. He was tiny, much smaller than Akio, and his solemn eyes gazed at me intently. "His father was probably a member of the American occupation force too. He loves it here in the garden and cries when we take him inside." "Where is his little red bag?" "He doesn't have one. He's Shinto, the religion with eight million gods. Their gods are everywhere: in nature, among the believers; even the beloved dead are deified." "How old is he?" "He was born on July 15, 1953." "What's his name?" "Teruya. That means 'light.' "

I studied the baby's serious face. There was something extremely touching about him and I heard myself say, "I'll take him too." Miki burst out laughing. "But what will your husband say if you come home with a *litter?*" "He'll be delighted." Or so I hoped! There was no point in trying to alert Jo by mail. I preferred to surprise him. . . .

When I arrived at the Souillac train station, Jo was on the platform. With the conductor's help, I stepped off the train, a child in each arm. I handed Jo first Akio, then Teruya. He looked at me with bewilderment. "Which one is it, *cherie?*" "Both," I replied, and walked away, leaving him to collect himself. He hurried up behind me. "You were right to order a double helping, Josephine. This way we'll be twice as happy."

Jo Bouillon: After nine years together, I was beginning to know my wife. Still, her astonishing courage, which her critics called heedlessness, never ceased to amaze me. Josephine had embarked on a difficult path. Rather than settling for the pampered life of a self-indulgent star, she had chosen to focus her energies on the fight against racism, just as she had given her all for her adopted country during the war. How could I blame her for bringing two children back to Les Milandes rather than one? Especially after she explained with her usual sensitivity what life held in store for many "occupation babies"—*konketsujii,* as they were called in Japan. Their mixed blood soon made them bigger and quicker than their Japanese brothers, the easily recognizable butts of teasing and even cruelty. Considered by some as "an American problem" and by others as "a Japanese affair," they were innocent victims of a hostile society. Not all of them were lucky enough to be in the home Miki Sawada had created with her own funds in her own dwelling.

Our sons were growing with amazing speed. Josephine, finding the name Teruya difficult in French, had changed it to Janot. Akio's lively, noisy, funny, nimble ways were matched by Janot's thoughtfulness. He would sit cross-legged like his ancestors, lost in some inner dream, while Akio chased chickens through the barnyard.

I was amazed by the speed with which our oldest son had learned to read. Before we knew it he was spelling out labels on cans in our larder. "I'm not surprised," said Josephine. "He was born in the year of the dragon, a sign symbolizing life, motion and fire. Janot, on the other hand, was born in the year of the snake. That makes him prudent, self-sufficient, quick to help others and careful with money."

"Where did you learn all *that*, Josephine?" She shrugged. "You don't think I spent three weeks in Japan twiddling my thumbs." She had even brought back a book about birth dates. As I turned its pages, I was amused to discover that Josephine was born in the year of the horse, known to produce popular, hard-working people able to influence others and tending to talk too much. Children of the horse were also very independent and quick to anger!

Looking up my own sign, I discovered that I was born in the year of the monkey. That made me inventive, resourceful, competent and sensitive. My weak point was an inability to stand up for myself. . . .

I began to think Japanese horoscopes weren't so foolish after all.

Josephine: I kissed my sons and husband and bid my village goodbye. I was off on a lecture tour through Scandinavia, where I intended to find our third son.

My friend "Recky"—the Danish journalist Reckendorf—and a couple named Tornüd, who were deeply involved in social work, had promised to help me. With a pounding heart, I presented my case to the Legal Aid Society. How would I make my choice this time? The nursery, filled with babies, echoed with birdlike chirps. A supervisor followed me down the aisles, saying a few flattering words about each child, but I tried not to listen. I wanted to choose from the heart. They were all so endearing, whether serious or merry, blond or brunette, delicate or plump. I moved from cot to cot, from row to row. What was I looking for? What kind of sign?

My search had brought me to Helsinki because adoptions were relatively easy in Finland. Families overburdened with children could "turn over" an "excess" baby to the state if they could prove that they didn't have the means to raise the infant properly. For a token sum, the government took the child in charge until an adoption could be arranged.

Suddenly a tow-headed, chubby, pink-and-white baby boy kicked back his covers and held out his arms to me. He seemed delighted by his own daring. I leaned over the little blue-eyed Finn, certain that he was the one. "His name is Jari," murmured the superintendent. I sensed that she was on the verge of tears. I soon discovered the cause of her emotion. Come what might, Jari would have been forced to leave the orphanage that very week, because babies were kept there only until the age of two. Then they were transferred to foster homes. "I'm so happy he's going home with you instead, madame."

I left with the chunky baby in my arms. He was a real little heavyweight and almost seemed to take a sly pleasure in making himself as difficult to lift as possible. Jari had been baptized a Protestant and my first gift to him when we got home was a little cross surmounted by a dove, which I hung around his rosy neck. What did the future hold for him? I wondered. He had such an obstinate tilt to his chin! One thing I was sure of, he would never let himself go hungry. He quietly accepted the advances of his slant-eyed brothers and the exclamations of his new-found dark-skinned relatives, Mama Carrie, Margaret and Elmo, at the sight of his flaxen hair. His only concern was getting as much to eat as possible.

"Any regrets, *cheri?*" I asked Jo. "None. I wouldn't have missed this for anything." We were watching our three sons playing on the rug. "After all, why shouldn't they get along?" "Look at the way our cats and dogs, who have been raised together, love each other. Fear is the only true dividing force. Our boys are going to grow up in a climate of love!"

My next round of engagements was in Central America, where I planned to find Jo a copper-skinned little Inca. It was not until I got to Colombia, however, that it looked as though I might be able to augment my Rainbow Family. While I was performing and lecturing in Bogotá, a lawyer friend offered me his help. One evening after the show he told me that the next day we would find my child. I couldn't sleep a wink all night.

Early the next morning we set off by car for one of the city's slums. Ironically the shacks were dotted with color. Flowers somehow flourished in those shantytowns. My friend led me into a squalid dwelling, where I found a black infant who I thought was the handsomest baby imaginable. His sickly mother was unable to tend to him properly. I gathered him up in my arms. What a warm, lovable, smiling, trusting little bundle! As I stepped into the car an ominous murmuring sound rose up around me. "Is there something the matter?" I asked the lawyer. He avoided my eyes. "No; just local superstition." "What kind of superstition?" "Nothing but old wives' tales. Pay no attention, Josephine."

I completely forgot the incident in the joy of having a fourth son. But later that day I noticed a swarm of women circling near the hotel. One look at the hotelkeeper's face told me that something was wrong. Finally a journalist explained; the local population believed that whites cured themselves of the plague by drinking the warm blood of black infants! I couldn't believe my ears. What plague? Bubonic plague, of course. The natives were terrified of it.

I begged the press to inform the people that this was sheer superstition. But superstition is taken very seriously here, they replied, and whites are looked on with great distrust. "But can't they see that I'm black just as they are?" "Yes. But you're going back to a white man's world." So they thought I was an ogress, that was it! I hoped the whole thing would blow over, but just the opposite occurred. The noise grew louder. Murmurs were replaced by cries, then shouts. The hotel owner looked nervously at his windows and my lawyer friend tried to intervene; in vain. Finally, in order to maintain the peace, the authorities refused me permission to take the baby with me. Looking at the infant, whom I already loved like my own, I burst into tears. Then the police took him away. What a brutal example of human stupidity! But could I really blame those frightened people? They believed that what they were doing was right.

That evening, when I returned from the theater, a black woman was waiting in the lobby. She explained that she was desperately poor and already the mother of seven. She bore her eighth child in her arms, wrapped in a tattered shawl. Did I want him? "Why even try?" I asked my lawyer friend. "It will be the same story all over again." "No, Josephine. There's no need to worry this time. *She* brought the child to *you;* you didn't take it. Besides, she comes from a remote part of town." He conferred with our visitor briefly, then set to work convincing me that our prayers were answered. We'd take care of the formalities tomorrow. Our caller was delighted to know that her baby would be well-treated and lack nothing. I looked at the little boy: he had magnificent black eyes. His mother had begun to cry. Was it from joy or sorrow? I passed a second sleepless night.

The next day we made the adoption arrangements for little Luis. I knew Jo would approve of my leaving a handsome sum of money to the needy mother. "It's enough to buy her a house and garden," the lawyer assured me. So much the better! I wanted Luis's family to have a good life too.

The next stop on my lecture tour was Canada. When I arrived in Quebec I discovered a quick way to get Luis to Les Milandes. The French consul's secretary was about to leave for France by boat. She would deliver our son to my sister Margaret in Le Havre.

Jo Bouillon: I was waiting on the platform in Sarlat when the train bringing our fourth son and first Catholic child pulled in. Margaret placed him in my arms with the words: "He's a real handful, Jo." During the car ride to the château, Luis cowered in his seat, his hands over his eyes. "He's like a frightened animal, Margaret. He'll calm down in time." But when we reached the château, Luis rushed under a bed and refused to budge. "Let the children work it out," I insisted. And sure enough, in a few minutes I saw three-year-old Akio dragging our poodle Rosalie over to where his new brother was hiding. Of course! Rosalie was just as black as Luis!

Soon afterward Josephine called me from Paris. She had a surprise for me. I thought I could guess what, or rather *who*. We now had representatives of the white, yellow and black races. It wouldn't surprise me to learn that Josephine had found the Indian she dreamed of in Canada. . . . But when her "redskin" stepped out of the car, he looked more like a paleface to me! Before I could open my mouth, Josephine quickly explained that Jean-Claude was the same age as Jari and Luis, that his extreme thinness was the result of deprivation and that country air was just what he needed. "You should have seen him in the dining car, Jo. He can't get enough to eat." "So you're treating him to a vacation?" "A *vacation?* No, Jo. He's come to stay. This is our fifth son." And she carried him into the kitchen to get "a little something to eat."

That night while the five children lay sleeping in their five little beds, I had a long talk with Josephine. Had she forgotten that we had agreed on *four* children, each of a different race? Perhaps I should have thought twice when she ordered six cots "in case friends spend the night." "Jean-Claude is white like Jari and Catholic like Luis, *cherie,*" I continued. "I thought you'd be bringing us an American Indian." "They're very hard to find, Jo. We'll simply have to be patient!" "But don't you see, if we adopt an Indian now, that will make *six!*" "What's wrong with that?"

I explained to Josephine that our financial situation was precarious. The "gap" created by the two hundred thousand dollars lacking from her 1951 American tour had never been totally filled. Josephine's eyes blazed. Surely one more mouth to feed couldn't matter. . . . Of course not. I simply wanted her to know that we had to be careful. Josephine retorted that developing Les Milandes was a family affair and if everyone lent a hand we couldn't help but succeed. Our property was evolving daily into an important tourist center which would be able to cover its debts. "Once you begin something, you have to keep going! Turning back or trying shortcuts gets you nowhere, Jo."

We were still talking at dawn, the time I usually began work. "I'll come with you, Jo." I did my best to discourage her. She had traveled all the preceding night and needed to rest. "Rest" was a word that annoyed Josephine. In a flash she had slipped on an old pair of pants, knotted her shirttails and wrapped her head in a bandanna. We were off to tour her terrain. Josephine wanted to see everything that had been done during her absence. The fourth bathroom was now installed; all the chimneys (there were twenty-nine!) were working; the ninety-two Persian rugs, brought back from various trips or received as gifts, were in place.

We set off in the carriage. "Do you remember when this was nothing but a farmyard, cherie?" "And look at it now," Josephine exclaimed with almost childlike joy. Gay white-lacquered outdoor furniture brightened the lawn. We passed by the stone fountain standing before Lou Tornoli, embellished with the words "Jo and Jo 1952," then proceeded to the little cottage named Deux Amours, where the two of us had lived until the château was ready. All along the road that led to the château, ruins had been shored up, roofs had been patched, gutters had been repaired. "When I think that this was a dead village with no more than ten inhabitants when we first arrived . . ." Josephine mused. "And now there are seventy inhabitants, all somehow involved with the development of Les Milandes."

Josephine stopped the carriage several times along the way to speak to the villagers. We also paid a visit to Richard at the gas station. Josephine was delighted to hear that her brother was in love with the postmistress. "Another black and white marriage!" she exclaimed. Doubling back past the farmhouse, we greeted Mama Carrie, up at dawn as usual. She came out to meet us carrying her favorite marmoset. Josephine's mother was probably the only person my wife feared, of whom she stood in awe. I had noticed, however, that Josephine had tremendous respect for all old people, especially women. This was undoubtedly due in part to the strength of the matriarchal system and in part to a vague distrust of men. As Josephine had once remarked, "We can never be sure of our fathers, but we all know we came from our mothers' bodies." Although she was still grieved at her incapacity to be a natural mother, her life had been marked by "mamas"—Mama Abatino, Mama Lion, Mama Bouillon. (Alas, my mother had joined my father in his tomb the year before while Josephine was on tour. She would never know our Rainbow Tribe.)

I glanced over at Josephine and her seemingly placid mother. Mama Carrie appeared untouched by her move to a country where she lived as a stranger, unable to speak the language. She passed her days locked in silence, except when she was chattering away with her daughters in her native tongue. Yet she didn't seem unhappy.

Margaret led us through the farmyard. Josephine joyously greeted her animals, carefully examining the stables we had tried to make into models of their kind. She admired the Dutch cows and the Yorkshire pigs, then moved on to the poultry yard to inspect the chicks and baby peacocks. I muttered that I didn't care much for the peacocks, that ever since their arrival we had been plagued with money problems. Josephine shrugged. She liked the birds; we'd keep them! "Besides," she added, "they're the only things around here that remind me of my music hall days."

Elmo was in charge of the animals, from the dogs in the kennel to the six hundred Sussex hens in our chicken house. We were doing our best to make the 150-acre property self-maintaining, but it was a constant and strenuous job, especially since our agricultural activities were matched by an amusement park operation. We provided a wide range of outdoor games: bowling on the green, tennis, volleyball and basketball to attract young visitors. The pleasure garden was also in full swing; loudspeakers filled the air with Josephine's tunes and songs. But we lacked live entertainment and this was a bone of contention between Josephine and me. My wife had ambitious ideas which might have been realized in Paris with its physical and human resources, but would be difficult and above all expensive to achieve in the country. Surely Josephine Baker and Jo Bouillon were enough!

We lived in an atmosphere of joy. Weekends and holidays were devoted to tourists, who arrived by the carload, but the weekdays brought new calm and the delight of enjoying our children in a harmonious natural setting. We loved them more every day. Each was developing his own personality. Akio had a quickness of mind which, combined with the fact that he was the eldest, made him the first to form French sentences. Janot was happy only when surrounded by flowers, which he gazed at by the hour. He wasn't Japanese for nothing. A sweet child, he chose to remain in the background. Jari was a leader: strong, tenacious, firm on his own two feet. Luis, our ex-savage, had blossomed into a responsive, fun-loving child. Jean-Claude no longer threw himself on his food; he had filled out.

We had frequent visitors from Paris, among them Bernard Lecache, head of the International League Against Racism and Anti-Semitism. He admired Josephine deeply and was extremely impressed by the significant work she had done in Japan. Supporters of the League Against Racism she had founded in Tokyo now numbered millions in Asia. Soon after Bernard's departure, Josephine drew me aside. "Jo, our Rainbow Tribe is still not complete." "I know, cherie. We need our little Indian. That will make six." It was impossible for Josephine to hide her thoughts for long: joy, anger, passion burst from her with the exuberance of vegetation in a virgin forest. I could tell that she had something more to say. "Jo . . . don't you agree that any attempt to stamp out racism in the modern world has to cope with the Jewish question?" "Of course. So . . . ?" "So we absolutely must adopt a little Israeli. Which will make number seven!" She turned her face to mine. "How does the idea strike you?" "During the ten years we've lived together, or tried to, you know that we've always thought alike, cherie." Josephine threw her arms around my neck. "I'll go to Israel and look for him."

Josephine was right. A little Israeli was essential to our Rainbow Tribe. Therefore I was astonished to see her return from her trip empty-handed. She explained that although she had used all her influence, she had been unable to obtain permission to take a male child out of the country. "Israel needs every one of its sons, Jo. It's a young, growing country, prey to a thousand dangers. Each child is worth its weight in gold. I could have adopted a son, but only if I had been willing to let him remain in his homeland. I explained to the authorities that in order for our Rainbow Tribe to have true symbolic value, our children must be raised together." We talked for most of that night. When the first cocks began their crowing, our decision was made: we would adopt a Jewish baby in Paris to join our other sons.

Moses (Moïse) was nine months old when he arrived at Les Milandes. Josephine had found him through Legal Aid, living with a proxy mother. He was a dark-skinned baby with a stubborn set to his chin. "He and Jari will make the sparks fly," I remarked. "I suppose you'll be bringing home our Indian next, *cherie.* But I warn you, Josephine—he's the last! You know how I love children, but raising them properly is a serious responsibility." "Very serious," Josephine agreed. "But if you hadn't been up to it, Jo, I would never have married you!"

That was typical of Josephine. When she seemed to be joking she was at her most serious.

While waiting for Josephine's return, I tried to prepare the older children for a little red-skinned brother. The idea seemed to delight them. We were a joyous family and my bouts of bookkeeping were often interrupted by childish laughter, which made up for all our worries. I imagined Josephine, over in America, spending her time between recitals and lectures visiting reservations in search of our seventh and final son. Imagine my surprise when news arrived that November that Josephine had been arrested in Quebec! She needed my help. It would take a five-thousand-dollar bail to free her.

There was a flurry of phone calls between Les Milandes and Paris, Paris and Quebec, Quebec and New York. It was an extremely complicated affair, especially when viewed from thousands of miles away. It seemed that Josephine had been accused of fraud involving the smuggling of furs and jewels out of the country. Her luggage had been seized as she was about to leave for France. There was no point in trying to fight the law. The important thing now was to get her free on bail. We'd see about the rest later. But the financial picture at Les Milandes was such that we didn't have five thousand dollars to spare. Fortunately we were saved by the generosity of friends.

Josephine's first words on her return were: "With everything else that was going on, Jo, I couldn't bring you your little Indian." Later that day, as we watched our six sons playing on the rug, she continued: "I've been thinking things over, *cheri,* and my mind is made up." When Josephine talked that way it always frightened me a little. "I've decided to give up the stage. Now that we have the children, I can't keep traveling all over the world. Our search is almost over. We'll find our little Indian eventually. I want to devote myself to Les Milandes. Do you realize that I've missed out on a large part of Akio's childhood? The nurses have been the ones to enjoy him!" I couldn't help smiling. Josephine resented the nurses tremendously. They were the ones who received hugs and kisses and heard youthful laughter while my wife was busy at work.

We spent Josephine's first evening back at home with our boys. Josephine pointed out that we could have enjoyed a tranquil married life alone. But wasn't it well worth having the children? she continued with sparkling eyes. Look how well they got along. Wasn't that definite proof that different races can live together? Wouldn't the world be a wonderful place if every village were like ours? "I've telephoned Bruno Coquatrix at the Olympia Theater in Paris," she went on. "I've decided to give my farewell performance there. From now on, if people want to see me they'll have to come to the Dordogne. How many visitors did we have last summer, Jo?" "One hundred and forty thousand." "Don't you think that with me in residence we ought to be able to double that figure?"

It seemed so to me. We had all tried so hard to make Les Milandes succeed. The village now even had a Josephine Square, complete with a Virgin with Josephine's face. This quickly became a source of hilarity on the Parisian nightclub circuit, but it was only the sculptor's way of paying Josephine tribute. The Jorama Wax Museum traced Josephine's life from the days when she put on shows for her brother and sisters to a scene portraying her scaling nearby Mount José with her seven children (they had rushed things a bit, but we were convinced that our little Indian would soon be with us). Other events captured in wax included our audience with a surprisingly lifelike Pius XII. Close by, a glass cabinet displayed Josephine's war mementos: the flag of the Twenty-fourth Colonial Infantry Regiment, her air force field jacket, an inscribed photograph of General de Gaulle. . . . Back at Les Milandes, our zoo and winter theater were ready. Our hotels and restaurants were in operation. This was Josephine's true domain. Her dream had become reality. And her decision didn't surprise me. It had taken us five years to arrive at this moment.

The announcement of Josephine's farewell made the splash I had expected. When she arrived in Paris at the end of March, after a final series of recitals in Scandinavia, she reaffirmed that after the Olympia she would live full time at Les Milandes with her Rainbow Family. "I'll be fifty this year. It's time to retire. I want to say goodbye to my public while I still have the physical strength." *"I'll* be delighted to hire you, *cherie.*

You're more beautiful than ever." It was true. I never tired of looking at her. Josephine's final performance was set for April 10, 1956. With the unsparing self-discipline that I knew so well, she relentlessly went into training: nothing but spaghetti! "It's my secret weapon," she insisted. "The best way I know to avoid intestinal upsets." (Given her past history, stomach trouble was her greatest fear.) At the same time, she indefatigably rehearsed her songs and dances.

The evening was unforgettable, a magical moment which proved that Josephine's incredible presence surpassed mere talent. Cocteau described it delightfully: "Paris had ensnared her and without the look in her antelope eye which pleaded 'Free me,' that trap would never have been sprung."

It was no surprise to me that French café society acclaimed her. What *was* extremely moving was to see an anonymous black man, overcome with emotion, sink to his knees before her. "What did he say?" I asked later. " 'Thank you from all of us.' "

"That night," Josephine said later, "I wore my heart on my toes and my soul on my lips. I sang for the Paris that had created me and I wept as I danced. I hope it didn't show."

The evening ended at dawn among friends. The beginning of a truly new day for Josephine and me. And then it was home to Les Milandes. Josephine had invited in the entire village. This would be another kind of celebration. She had piled her old trunks in front of the château, along with the costumes she knew she would never wear again. "Take whatever you want," she insisted. The villagers picked through what had been such an intimate part of her life. The clothes that remained, my Josephine, always thirsty for symbols, set on fire. Then, joining hands with our sons and the village children, she led them through the steps of a farandole.

CHAPTER 16

———— ·•୨⚬୧•· ————

Dream's End

"Where's *Maman?*" asked Akio, who had just turned four.

"Working." Yes, Josephine was on the road again after devoting the early part of the summer to promoting Les Milandes. The atmosphere in the pleasure garden had been exceptionally lively; one of the season's highlights was the appearance of the remarkable child poet Minou Drouet, reciting her verses while accompanying herself on the guitar. She had captivated our sons and Josephine had memorized a poem for them:

> I asked my little finger
> To whisper to me why
> My apple tree
> Strokes fanlike
> At the pink cheek of the sky. . . .

"Wouldn't it be fun to have a little girl of our own?" sighed Josephine. "No, Josephine," I replied sharply. "An Indian boy, yes, but *not* an Indian girl. We've got to think ahead. Our children have no blood relationship. If we add a daughter to our collection of sons, we'll just be asking for trouble!" "I guess you're right, Jo," Josephine reluctantly admitted.

During the summer a group of mannequins was brought to Les Milandes to model the latest fashions. "I want you girls to absolutely *spar-*

kle," ordered Josephine. "Wear your most elaborate gowns and plenty of jewelry." It was a colorful sight to see those exquisite young women in evening dress parading before our tourists in their stout shoes and casual clothes. On days when we had no such "added attractions," Josephine performed alone. "She gives as much of herself to our hordes of visitors' as she did to the celebrities at her Olympia farewell," Maryse remarked. "It's one more example of her refusal to discriminate," I told my niece. "An audience is an audience to Josephine." Our visitors were delighted, after battling summer heat, sudden storms and dusty roads, to enjoy Josephine first as a star, then a half hour later, stripped of her finery, as a barmaid serving them drinks. She had a friendly word for everyone and fussed over the visiting children, who played on the grass with our own. But the best time of all was when the last car had left and we were alone. As the children climbed over our knees, Josephine told stories that always had happy endings. . . .

Josephine's farewell performance had blossomed into a series of goodbye tours. She had been forced to repack what trunks had not been destroyed in the celebration bonfire.

In my wife's absence, I supervised the children. At the same time I spent long hours in my office, conferring with my farm manager and answering our voluminous mail. Josephine's ambitious experiment brought us letters from far and wide, most of them sympathetic but some harshly demanding why it was necessary to have a château in order to raise six children. That was a fair enough question and I could understand the bitterness of housewives who had trouble making ends meet, but I had that problem too! Our World Village couldn't function on idealism alone; it had to survive commercially, a fact which gave me many sleepless nights. I spent weary hours studying columns of figures, receipts and expenditures and checking through piles of bills, both money we owed and money due from our customers. Unfortunately the balance was always unfavorable. Frequent surprises, usually sprung by Josephine, left us with a constant, nagging deficit.

Compared with the bookkeeping, handling the mail was a simple matter. I tried to explain that anyone could take in children, but that the Rainbow Tribe, both a symbol and a model for a better world, could never have become public knowledge without Josephine's personality and fame.

Before her departure, Josephine always prepared several hundred autographed pictures, but we now had a photograph of the entire family as well, which complicated my task. I longed for the day when the children could give me a helping hand. But I would have to be patient. July was a month full of birthdays and candles. On the seventh, a sturdy Akio had snuffed out his four candles with one breath; on the tenth Luis had been three, followed by Janot on the fifteenth. Their brothers had helped them blow out the tiny flames. Jari and Jean-Claude would be three in midwinter and Moses would be two in the fall. No matter how busy I was, I reserved an hour each afternoon for the children. We visited our animals, toured the vegetable garden, romped in the park and checked on the hothouse plants. This was my way of introducing our sons to the world around them and we spent delightful hours together, punctuated by their cries of surprise and wonder. Every member of our animal family had been baptized by Josephine, who could identify them all with uncanny ease. The rest of us had no trouble recognizing the Dutch cows in their marked stalls, but we found it almost impossible to distinguish among the young.

Janot: At the end of our daily walk we carried armloads of flowers into the kitchen, where tea was waiting. After a huge bouquet was arranged, the jam pots were opened and *Papa* buttered our bread. He always managed to be there. We learned at an early age that we were adopted. *Papa* and *Maman* made no attempt to hide it; just the opposite. If we had been only children, our origins might have been difficult to accept, but being one of so many made it hard to feel like an orphan.

Papa tried to clarify our situation one day during our regular tour of the farm. A sow had just given birth to thirteen piglets. Like all sows, she had only twelve teats. The last-born, who was also the weakest, tried in vain to suckle. There was no teat for him. Pushed aside and neglected, he seemed condemned to starvation. Fortunately, our Alsatian bitch had just whelped. She had delivered only three pups, so *Papa* gave her the thirteenth piglet. To our delight, she allowed the rosy newborn to suckle. During our daily rounds, we watched the piglet wriggle, nurse and finally roll up in a sleepy ball with his puppy brothers. As the piglet grew older, he showed no interest in his pig family, but chose to remain with the dogs. *Papa* explained it this way: "It's easy to see what counts: having a baby is simple, but raising one is something else. A real mother is the one who gives love, not life."

We older children never forgot that story and passed it on to our younger brothers. Each one of us had shared that thirteenth piglet's luck.

Luis: It was always exciting when *Maman* came home. Each return was like a party. She had all sorts of wonderful things in her luggage and a heap of packages lay next to her trunks. There were gifts for the entire village, which she distributed at the château: scarves, skirts, dolls, games, toys, trifles. She buried *Papa* in shirts, most of which didn't fit, and smothered us with kisses and questions.

Maman moved through the house like a whirlwind, turning things upside down as she rushed from cellar to attic, moving furniture and completely upsetting our daily routine. Then it was off to the stable, the chicken coop, the monkey house. *Maman* often brought back to the house chicks, baby turkeys and young monkeys that she felt looked neglected. To our delight, they often ended up in our bedrooms and even in the living room. At bedtime we had to be careful not to squash the chicks tucked cozily under our pillows. Each of us had his favorite animals and we had wonderful baptismal ceremonies, following occasionally hair-raising births. When a cow had trouble calving, *Maman* often stayed in the barn for hours, helping the veterinarian. Unfortunately we had funerals too. One end of the garden served as an animal cemetery. Our beloved pets lay under little slabs bearing their names: Tchitchi . . . Zouzou . . . Caramal . . . a monkey, a cat, a faithful dog. "They'll never die if you keep them alive in your hearts," *Maman* insisted. We learned much about life and death from our pets. They taught us philosophy!

Jo Bouillon:

ARRIVING SATURDAY VIA TOULOUSE WITH SURPRISES STOP LOVE AND KISSES TO ALL STOP JOSEPHINE.

Josephine was en route from North Africa. She had been sending me rave reviews from towns that she remembered with bitterness from World War II days. The thought of my wife in Algeria worried me; after all, the tragic situation there was nothing short of war. But that hadn't stopped Josephine. Thank goodness she would soon be safely home. I was waiting in front of the château when she drew up, stepped out of the car, leaned back inside, extracted a pair of bundles and held out . . . two babies! I heard myself shout, "Oh, no!" Josephine looked at me reproachfully.

"No? You can't be serious, Jo. These children are survivors of the Palestro massacre! Do we have any goat's milk?" *"Goat's milk?"* She tapped her foot impatiently. "We do own goats, don't we?" "Yes, but none of them have milk right now." "But the little girl is hungry, Jo." "The little *girl?* Josephine, you *know* what we decided about daughters!" "But I had no choice. The two babies were found together, wrapped in swaddling clothes. They had been hidden under a cactus . . . a bush . . . well, a small tree really. That's how they escaped the massacre. Look at them, Jo. He's a Berber, probably the son of a wet nurse; she undoubtedly is a colonist's daughter. There was no one to give us details. Everyone had been killed. Someone had obviously tried to save the two babies and God had heard their prayer. The infants were brought to Algiers, where Robert Lacoste, the resident minister, was named their godfather. He knew about our Rainbow Tribe and told me the children's story. How could I turn down two babies God himself had saved? Look at the little girl, Jo. She's smiling at you. But we've got to find goat's milk immediately." The baby's smiles were quickly replaced by hunger cries. I hurried off to Souillac for milk.

As surely as Marianne was Catholic, Brahim was Muslim. We celebrated Christmas 1956 under an enormous tree lovingly decorated by the entire household and placed in the middle of the living room near the reed organ. The two youngest children shared the role of baby Jesus; they were tiny compared to their older brothers, who were almost all the same height (Moses seemed to have made it a point of honor to overtake the others). When I watched our smiling, resourceful, impish sons, I said to myself that Josephine was right: preoccupation with skin color is sheer human stupidity.

Soon afterward my native city, Montpellier, decided to honor my father by placing a plaque on the wall of its music school, where *Papa* had begun teaching in 1925 . . . a date that had memories for Josephine as well. She appeared for the speeches, the unveiling of the plaque and the banquet and ball that followed. It was one of the rare times that I danced with my wife. At one point during the evening, someone said, "What a beautiful family you have!" I never did find out whether they were talking about the musical Bouillons or the Rainbow Tribe. That night I even played the violin, a pleasure I rarely enjoyed at Les Milandes. If I ever found a spare moment to lock myself in my room for a practice session, Josephine would quickly appear at the door with an urgent matter that forced me to lay down my bow.

"A few more goodbye performances and I can settle down with my family for good," she said, repacking her bags for Africa. When she returned from the Ivory Coast carrying a black baby, I was beyond surprise. She had been visiting a hospital when the infant's mother died in one of the wards. The father was unknown. "I talked to President Houphouet-Boigny about the child," Josephine informed me. "He said he would act as godfather. The baby's name is Koffi." The blackest of our sons was undoubtedly a fetish worshipper.

"Josephine, do you know those songs with endless numbers of verses? That's what our household is like. But this time you've gone too far. We agreed on four children of different races. We somehow acquired six. Now we're up to *nine.*" "But some people have families of fifteen and the parents don't complain." Again I tried to explain that our Tribe was meant to serve as a model; that we must therefore raise our family in the best possible way. Could Josephine do that in view of her work? Could we do it together? "Les Milandes will take care of us," she replied. "Don't be too sure, Josephine."

I felt obliged to explain our financial picture, which had become catastrophic. In 1952 we had been 27 million francs in debt; in 1953 the figure had risen to 37 million; by 1954 our debts totaled close to 64 million; they neared 83 million in 1956 and now, in 1957, we were over the 83 million mark.

We exchanged some extremely ugly words that night. In spite of my fear that the children might hear us quarreling, I felt obliged to reproach my wife for going her own way in spite of my advice and my power to do business in her name. In 1955 I had suggested that we use the money Les Milandes had netted to pay off debts to our contractors before undertaking further improvements. But Josephine had done just the reverse, asking our suppliers to disregard the money owed to them and begin new construction. She would pay for this, she insisted, through the sale of her apartment building in Paris. I knew from bitter experience that Les Milandes would become a bottomless pit if we weren't extremely careful. It had already swallowed up the Bouillon family home in Vaucresson. Only Maryse and her children had been living there in 1952 when Josephine decided the house was "much too big." "Maryse can move in with us," she asserted before hurrying off to her lawyer.

Today things looked as bad as ever: just as I had feared, the sale of Josephine's Paris property hadn't covered the expenses we had incurred, especially since we had been faced with unexpected costs. "What's your solution, then?" Josephine shouted. "Things can't go on like this," I replied. "We've got to cut back our spending drastically. The figures speak for themselves. If we manage properly, Les Milandes should bring in an annual profit of twelve million francs—but this means living much more modestly and paying off our suppliers." Josephine glared at me. "I sometimes wonder if slapping you would help!" I snapped. "But the Bouillons don't hit women; we're much too middle-class." "I know," she replied. "That's one of the reasons I married you."

Four days later, after I had sent in little Koffi's adoption papers, I received a legal summons from Sarlat that left me dumbstruck; it was a divorce action from my wife!

What had divided us was the need to prove who was boss.

Curiously enough, it was a letter from Japan that brought about a truce. In a note dated October 30, 1957, Miki Sawada wrote to Josephine as follows:

"A few months ago I read about your impending divorce in our local papers. Ever since, everyone who knows about our friendship has been anxiously asking me if the rumor is true. I reply that it's idle gossip. But deep in my heart I've been extremely worried. I know how well your husband looks after the children and how much love he gives them. They trust him completely. Having lost their natural parents, it would be unbearably cruel to be deprived of a mother and father again. Even if you no longer love your husband, your property and château are big enough so that you could remain together without ever having to meet; you could have your freedom without a divorce. Please don't tell me it's too late. Your friend and sister, Miki."

The fact that Josephine informed me of Miki's letter proved that she was having second thoughts—or was she? Either way, the evil had been done. The newspapers had seized on the story. I hoped to manage things so that nothing would change for the children, but I knew how hard this would be. Office chatter, village scandalmongers and backstage gossip would prevent things from ever being the same. I tried to analyze what had gone wrong. I had done my best to help build the family which Josephine planned to use as a standard bearer for an ideal that I understood and respected. Yet here we were, bogged down in life's sordid realities like any other family, A remarkable, strong-minded woman, Josephine couldn't accept being challenged. But after all, I was devoted to our multicolored children too. Day by day each in his own way had strengthened the love that bound us. Perhaps because I knew how alone in the world they were, I was determined not to abandon them.

During the following weeks, talk of divorce seemed to vanish like a bad dream. Christmas time found us peacefully gathered together at Les Milandes, as harmonious as a family with nine children can be! One nurse followed another; Josephine's need to control inevitably drove them away. Only Hélène, who adored the children, remained. The older boys had been taken in hand by Madame Besse, the elementary school teacher at Castelnaud, until the school Josephine hoped to create at Les Milandes was built. If we ever found our "redskin," we would have the number of children necessary for the establishment of a village school. This caused Josephine to remark with a wicked gleam in her eye: "See, Jo, we've *got* to have at least ten!"

Every Sunday the children and I went to mass; Josephine accompanied us whenever she wasn't on tour. "How do you deal with the fact that each of you has a different religion?" a tourist asked one day. Josephine answered this kind of question with great patience. "You're quite right, madame. We all have different faiths." She pointed to the children. "This is our Protestant . . . here's our Buddhist . . . this son is Shinto . . . this one's a fetish worshipper; the rest are Catholic . . . except for our Jewish son, of course." The woman rolled her eyes. "But, madame," Josephine continued politely, "this isn't Paris. There are no Buddhist temples or synagogues. At least our Shinto son has no problem. He worships nature, and all he needs for that is paper frills." "Paper frills?" "Yes, madame. Each time a Shinto thinks lovingly of God, he hangs a paper frill on a tree. That way the trees remain in flower all year long. Isn't that a lovely way to worship, madame? After all, it's men who have given God different names. It's one and the same to our Lord. That's why my children meet with him here in his Catholic dwelling place. . . . In Tokyo or Algiers, madame, we go to a temple or a mosque."

One thing that Josephine insisted on, however, was that each child learn his native tongue. "If they ever want to trace their origins, it would be painful to feel like strangers in their homelands." I agreed. But it seemed like an enormous task. "We'll hire tutors, Jo, and when I'm touring I'll take the children with me whenever possible."

Jari: When I was five I returned to Finland with *Maman.* I had left my homeland at the age of two. My first memory of Helsinki is going into a crowded church. Everyone stared at us. I don't know if it was because of *Maman's* enormous hat or because of her skin. I had quickly noticed that everyone in Finland was extremely fair like me, and they had the same straw-colored hair. After the service *Maman* took me to a house full of blond, pale-skinned people who seemed very glad to see me. I didn't understand most of the conversation, but I heard *Maman* say that since Hitler had called the Nordics the "master race," she had wanted an Aryan son to prove he could live with a black mother. The old man of the family shook his head. "Whatever you say or do, Jari was born a Finn and he'll remain one!" It was soon time for *Maman* to leave for the theater. When she kissed me and left me behind with those fair-haired strangers, I became very frightened. Why had *Maman* abandoned me? Hadn't the old man said that I belonged to his race because of my eyes and skin? But I didn't want to stay here! Bursting into tears, I began to call for *Maman* and make such a fuss that the old man agreed to take me to her. We finally arrived at an entrance that looked strangely familiar, because stage doors are the same all over the world. I had been to the theater with *Maman* before and I knew that behind that door lay a corridor which led to a dressing room. We entered a little room filled with a haunting, bittersweet aroma: a mixture of eau de cologne, foundation cream, flowers, makeup and costumes damp with perspiration. *Maman's* scent, a comforting odor that made me feel at home. I began to cry again and saw tears in the old man's eyes. "I can see that he's really yours," he murmured. I buried my head in *Maman's* lap and hugged her with all my might. She gently stroked my head. "But you *know* that I'd never leave you, *cheri.* It was just for the evening, while I performed." Despite the gruffness of her voice, I sensed her pleasure.

Some time later I questioned *Maman* about that night. No, she didn't honestly know if I still had parents in Finland; institutions there kept that information secret. Who was the old man who had wept with me? "A patriot," she explained, "who wanted to return a little boy to his country. And you *will* go back later, Jari, when and if you want to." I smiled and took her hand. *Maman*'s hands were beautiful; long and fragile. Her dusky skin made them seem even more delicate. For the evening's performance she had lacquered her tapering nails with silver. But I knew how strong those fingers were when it came time to weed, pick up the soup tureen, harness a horse . . . or give a spanking. *"Maman,* I know what a mother is. It's the person you want to be with." I can still feel the hug that she gave me.

Jo Bouillon: Josephine and I had an ironclad rule when it came to the children: never to play favorites. This was made easier by the fact that they were all so different. Koffi, our ebony-skinned newcomer, was the best-natured of all our babies, continually smiling and laughing. God knows I hadn't wanted him, but who could resist that chubby, defenseless body? Numbers seven and eight, our little Algerians, were walking now, Brahim with surprising agility, Marianne with girlish grace. Moses had become pugnacious, critical, quick-tempered; Jean-Claude remained the most timid and retiring of our sons, Jari the best organized. While Janot went his own secret way, Luis was extremely outgoing. Lively, thoughtful Akio continued to fulfill his role as leader.

Our oldest son was with me when domestic friction burst out anew. The summer had been a good one, in the course of which Les Milandes had welcomed three hundred thousand visitors. This spoke well for the future *if* we proceeded with care. One afternoon without warning, Josephine blocked the way as Akio and I were descending the stairs. *"You'll* stay with your father, obviously," she snapped. She had gathered together the staff in the hallway and to their dismay was asking them to choose sides: "Will it be Monsieur or me?" To make matters worse, she insisted, "Everyone on my side stand over there." I tried to make her see how foolish she was being. After all, servants were hard to find. Why didn't we talk things over alone, instead of airing our grievances in front of the staff? Above all, I didn't want the children involved. Shutting ourselves in an upstairs room, Josephine and I had another unpleasant scene. As usual, my wife accused me of telling her what to do and I reproached her for countermanding my orders. It was apparent that we could no longer remain together.

In the hope that some sort of solution would present itself, I moved in with some friends in Souillac. It was our first real separation. But at least I was only a few miles from the children. I could continue seeing them. Surely Josephine would realize how useful I was at Les Milandes and discover that she couldn't run the estate alone. But I should have guessed that although she knew these things, she would never admit it. I returned to Paris. It was obvious that I would have to start a new life.

Hélène: When Madame obliged us to choose sides, we didn't hesitate for a minute. My fiancé, Ercole, and I left for Paris with Monsieur Jo. I was very attached to the children, of course, and admired Madame immensely, but although she was a wonderful woman, she was extremely unpredictable. And the constant bickering couldn't have been good for the youngsters.

Monsieur Jo rented a Paris apartment with enough room to welcome the children. I was kept on to take care of them during their stays. The six older children, then aged from four to six, visited their father in turn for two-week periods. Monsieur and I made a point of praising their mother and explaining that the family separation was due to professional obligations.

Upon his return to the capital, Monsieur Jo had reassembled his orchestra. In spite of a ten-year absence, Paris had not forgotten him. All six of the older children were present at his opening night at the Alhambra music hall. I remember them trying to learn the "stroll," a dance introduced by their father.

A year later Ercole and I found ourselves back in the Dordogne. Happily for the children and Les Milandes, Madame and Monsieur had had a reconciliation.

Jo Bouillon: It was about now that I called Roger Legrand to the rescue. Josephine had always respected him as our business manager and she got along well with his wife, Malena. Perhaps the Legrands' friendly presence and good sense would act as a buffer between my wife and me. Josephine agreed that it was worth trying. Before setting off on tour again, she also admitted that Les Milandes needed an overseer.

Roger and Malena's arrival was like a breath of fresh air.

"How did you get *into* such a mess?" Roger exclaimed after going over the books. I tried my best to explain, at the same time attempting to clarify for myself why our situation was worsening daily. True, our marvelous Josephine had her feet planted squarely on this earth, whose wrongs she struggled to right, but her head was in the clouds and someplace in between, her left hand was busily squandering all that her right hand amassed. Moreover, Les Milandes, as brilliantly conceived by Josephine, was years ahead of its time. It would require an era of leisure, travel and favorable exchange rates to show easy profits. In the meantime it was difficult to staff, and harder to run, especially with Josephine at the helm.

"Why not form a company with you as president and Josephine on the board of directors," Roger suggested. "That would limit her powers." "Josephine won't hear of it. She has a suspicious streak that prevents her from signing papers. I have the right to sign for her, but that isn't much help since we're constantly at cross purposes. For example, she fired our agricultural consultant, who was doing an excellent job, and hired a man who knows nothing about local farming methods; then, because she's against the war in Vietnam, she hired a Vietnamese orchestra, although I had already engaged a different group for the season; not to mention the Spanish ballet she brought in, which can't possibly earn what it's costing us."

"What are your plans for the future, Jo?" "Josephine has enough work abroad to keep her busy, but since we need money so badly she's decided to make a comeback at the Olympia this spring . . . three years after her farewell performance there. It's going to be billed as a rescue operation and Coquatrix plans to back her up with a marvelous show. I just hope the public gets behind her." "They will," said Malena. "Josephine is fantastic." I couldn't help smiling. Fantastic was right—but at what cost?

Margaret: Mama Carrie died suddenly on January 12, 1959. Fortunately she didn't suffer. Jo immediately wired Josephine, who was on her way from Rome to Istanbul. Her distant engagements prevented her from attending the funeral.

Carrie Martin MacDonald, born in Little Rock, Arkansas, on April 4, 1886, was buried in the little cemetery at Castelnaud-Fayrac near Jo's parents and Pepito Abatino. Poor Mama. So far from home . . . yet thanks to Josephine, her last ten years, spent in France, had been the only happy time in her life. Not that we saw much of my sister. She always seemed to be traveling. But the moment she returned, she'd be down at the farmhouse with an armload of gifts. "For Margaret, for Elmo, for Mama," she'd say, distributing scarves and shirts and blouses from around the world—all of them white. "The more the years eclipse us, the more we have to provide our own light," she insisted. Therefore, Mama ended her years dressed in white or an occasional floral print, but this didn't lessen her air of severity.

"Where's Josephine?" Mama asked one day shortly before her death. "In Rome, Mama." "Good. Then she'll be seeing Pope John. She can offer a prayer for us." Mama had grown accustomed to Josephine's adventures, to photographs of her daughter posing with famous people. She simply shrugged and smiled. To think that her little Tumpy was visiting the Pope, chatting with the Queen of England, receiving letters from General de Gaulle! St. Louis seemed very far away.

I was crushed by my mother's death. I had lived with Mama all my life. She had always been strict but fair and Josephine had feared and respected her. Mama was the only person my sister heeded. There was no one to guide her now. As I watched Mama's coffin being lowered into the vault, I wondered what else had died with her. . . . Jo gripped my hand. Was he wondering the same thing? Over a year ago, when Josephine had wanted a divorce, Mama had discouraged her, reminding her of all Jo had done for the children, for all of us. . . .

I had a child now too. A daughter.

She had arrived in Josephine's arms one day in the midst of a train strike. It all began with a telephone call from my sister: "There aren't any trains running beyond Bordeaux, Margaret. Could you please pick me up?" I heard a curious sound in the background. "What's that noise, Josephine?" My sister burst out laughing. "It's your baby crying." I threw my arms around Elmo. We had to hurry, I shouted. Josephine had found us a child! Time and again she had insisted, "You two are going to dry up like prunes without a baby in the house. You've got to have at least *one!*" It wasn't as if I didn't have Josephine's children to tend to, but I must confess that I found my nieces and nephews unbearable. "The trouble is you spoil them, Josephine." "Spoil them? But I'm terribly strict." Strangely enough, it was true. She was even *too* strict when she was overtired. Still, she indulged her children in other ways, giving them gifts, bringing them up in a château, taking them to luxury hotels when she traveled, exposing them to a life that Mama described with a sniff as "unsuitable for children."

Josephine had been delighted when Elmo and I announced that we were ready to adopt a child of our own. But she wanted to make one thing clear; she could guarantee neither color nor sex. We'd have to take what she found for us; whatever the "good Lord sent." And suddenly here I was on the way to Bordeaux, not knowing what lay in store. In my excitement, I had neglected to ask for details.

Our child was a beautiful little girl who appeared to have Hindu blood. Josephine had found her in a Belgian orphanage. We decided to call her Rama.

Jo Bouillon: Les Milandes wouldn't be the same without Mama Carrie, but we had little time for mourning. The Legrands and I were busy trying to erase the château's debts. It sometimes seemed like bailing out a boat with a thimble, but we were determined to do our best. When Josephine left to tour Venezuela I braced myself for another surprise. After all, we had been talking about our "redskin" for years. And my wife was heading for Indian country.

("Sure enough," reports Bruno Coquatrix, who took time off from preparing his new show, *Paris Mes Amours,* to meet Josephine at Orly airport, "she stepped off the plane holding a baby. Within minutes she was proudly pointing out his golden skin, his coal-black eyes and his typically Indian features. 'What are you planning to call him?' I asked with a smile. 'Buffalo Eyes? . . . Black Eagle?' Josephine gave me a withering look. 'His name is Mara.' ")

Josephine couldn't wait to introduce Mara to his new family. She arrived at Les Milandes with an exciting story to tell. It had all begun in Caracas, where word had spread that Josephine wanted an Indian child for her World Village. Many people offered their aid. . . .

Josephine: I was visited by an emissary from a desperately poor tribe. He informed me that he had learned through drumbeats about a woman anxious to adopt an Indian child and offer him a happy life in Europe. His people suffered from dreadful privation, he continued. Therefore the tribal chief had decided to entrust his youngest grandson to safekeeping in a foreign land so that the boy might someday perpetuate his race. . . . Together we set off for his village.

It was a long, hard journey. We first took a plane over a drought-stricken countryside, then traveled by car, and when the road ran out, switched to a jeep. I finished the trip on donkey back. When my guide suddenly appeared to be addressing the heavens, I realized that we were approaching his village and that he was talking to sentries stationed in the trees. There on the shore of the beautiful Caribbean a man and a boy stood waiting. In the distance lay a primitive village furnished mainly with hammocks, used to avoid surprise encounters with fauna on the ground. This was a strange land, plagued in turn by lack of water and torrential rains, infested with vermin and mosquitoes. In Caracas it is said, not without reason, that Venezuelans come down from the coconut trees in Cadillacs. Yet even in this land of stunning contrasts it was hard to believe that twenty-four hours earlier I had been performing before a cosmopolitan audience reeking of oil and perfume. Now I was here on the gleaming sand, the focus of hundreds of eyes peering down from palm trees, conversing with an ancient Indian, his interpreter and a naked little boy, who struggled with all his might when I tried to pick him up. Thanks to the drums, the tribe was prepared for my arrival. Once we had concluded our business, we were served a farewell dinner comprised of scrawny goat and a curious drink with a corn base. I had been told that Indian women chewed the kernels to facilitate the brewing process. For Mara's sake, I did my best to empty my plate and cup. As my new son lay sleeping in my lap, the village men performed a joyous dance. . . .

Mara had a beautiful face. But his belly was badly swollen and his legs looked like matchsticks due to malnutrition. I left him at Les Milandes under the care of Hélène. It was time for me to return to Paris and devote myself full time to rehearsing my new show.

Bruno had pulled out all the stops with *Paris Mes Amours*, assembling the finest composers, dancers and comedians. My first day at the Olympia, he introduced me to the young man who was in charge of sets and costumes. His name was André Levasseur. There was a timid quality about him which I found very appealing. "I'll need a scattering of strategically placed feathers," I explained. "After all, I'm no longer twenty."

When André returned with his sketches I was delighted. "No complaints?" he asked with surprise. He had obviously heard that I was hard to deal with. In daily life, yes, but at the theater I was gentle as a lamb —as long as people knew their business. As usual, I would be descending a staircase, this time in a sweeping cloak, surrounded by my dancing boys dressed in white. A towering umbrella of feathers would sprout from my chignon. We set to work in high spirits, but as the days passed I felt a subtle change, a creeping doubt, fear, hesitation. Was Josephine still Josephine? How could I possibly outdo my triumph of three years before? I sensed the eyes of the gossip columnists raking over me, lingering at my waistline, looking for sags and blemishes. A performer is like a country cousin: when he bids us goodbye we feel overcome with love and memories and shed a sentimental tear. But should he return, we say, "So soon? Are we going to have to sit through those same old stories *again?*" At least I knew I had some fine songs: a Gypsy palm-reader number, Jo's amusing tune "Don't Touch Me Tomatoes," which ended with a cha-cha, a Charleston-samba routine which should bring down the house . . . and a Negro spiritual about a drought-ridden wasteland that made me think of little Mara.

Despite my fears, *Paris Mes Amours* was a smash success. Rave reviews on opening night, May 27, ensured a long and lucrative run. The ushers were forced to add extra chairs at every performance. For the first time in its history, the Olympia planned to keep the same show for nine months. Could our worries be over at last? . . . Jo and I rented a little furnished apartment on the Rue Saint-Roch, not far from the theater, where he could come and visit during the winter months.

During that busy happy summer it really looked as though our luck had changed. I often wonder what would have happened if the tragedy involving Noël hadn't blown our world up in our faces. . . .

Simone Dauthieu: I sold records in the Olympia during the run of *Paris Mes Amours.* Like all of us, I was quickly conquered by Josephine's charm. Her kindness, her energy, her concern for other people, were irresistible; she never forgot to inquire after someone's ailing parent or refused to give an autograph. We all adored her. Every night I went to Josephine's dressing room to tell her how many records I'd sold during intermission. "They're going like hot cakes." "Marvelous," she'd reply. "I'll be able to turn Les Milandes into a 'World University.' " It was common knowledge that the two Jos were having money problems and we hoped they could solve them. Jo was obliged to spend most of his time in the Dordogne, but in November he joined his wife in Paris.

Shortly after Jo's arrival, on one of those bitter nights when it's so tempting to curl up by the fireplace, or judging from our full house, to sit in a crowded theater, a ragman poking through a pile of trash discovered a newborn baby. The infant was rushed to police headquarters, where an ambulance-chasing journalist picked up the story. When I arrived at the theater the next evening, Ginette, Josephine's dresser, told me that she too had read the article in that day's *France Soir*. We agreed not to breathe a word to Josephine. But as fate would have it, Josephine had gone to a cocktail party at the Eiffel Tower late that afternoon. During the reception, a newsman had told her about the abandoned child, adding that if the ragman hadn't appeared when he did, the "package" would have been tossed into the grinding mechanism of a passing garbage truck. Josephine had been thunderstruck. "Where's the baby now?" "At the Bretonneau Hospital." "Come with me." Pulling the startled journalist by the hand, she left the party and hailed a passing taxi. On the way to the hospital she learned that the infant had been found in front of a restaurant called Le Périgord, the name of the region in which Les Milandes was situated. This struck her as an omen. The nurses at the hospital had baptized the baby André, after the saint on whose name day the infant had been found. When Josephine swept into the ward they couldn't believe their eyes. When she left, the baby went with her. There would be time for formalities later.

Josephine had called me from the hospital and I was waiting at the Rue Saint-Roch when she hurried in carrying the infant. The journalist was at her heels, along with several photographers who had got wind of the story and wanted to snap a "family portrait." A dumfounded Jo gave her a furious look, then locked himself in the bedroom. Josephine rushed into the kitchen to prepare a baby bottle, requesting the press to be patient. Jo finally got himself under control and reappeared. "It's like a Christmas present from heaven," Josephine cried. "We'll really have something to celebrate!"

The baby obviously couldn't remain at the Rue Saint-Roch, so Jo took him to Les Milandes, where three nurses looked after the other ten children. "I know Jo's angry," Josephine confided. "But it's not the child's fault he was born. With everything going so well for us, it doesn't seem right to sit back and allow an innocent baby to suffer. You *do* understand, Simone, don't you?" Of course I did, but I understood Jo's feelings too. "I don't like the name André," Josephine continued. "I'm going to call the baby Noël to remind us that he's ours because of a miracle. I'd like you to be his godmother." We decided to postpone the christening until after the holiday rush.

One night in early January after the show, we all piled into the big blue Hotchkiss: Josephine, me, the ragman, whom Josephine had chosen as the baby's godfather, and the ragman's wife. The roads were slick with ice, so it was not until noon the next day that we pulled up at the château, followed by two carloads of journalists. A whirlwind of children rushed out to greet us. *"Maman, Maman,"* they shouted, hugging and kissing Josephine, burrowing into her coat. Josephine was the picture of joy. Moments like this more than made up for all the strains and stresses of her hectic life. Then it was time for the presents; we moved into the house in a welter of paper and string.

Suddenly we heard church bells. Father Tournebise was calling us to worship. One of the nurses handed me Noël, dressed in white lace, and I carefully picked my way down the icy path that led to the chapel. At the gay family luncheon that followed the ceremony, the children were wearing their Sunday best. Jo and Jo seemed closer than ever. But during the afternoon, I heard Father Tournebise murmur, "It looks like you're going to reach twelve." Josephine burst out laughing. "Why not? Jo's always wanted his own soccer team and someone to manage it!" I glanced over at Jo. He was scowling. "He's still furious at me," Josephine whispered. "But things will work out with time."

Ginette Renaudin: The final performance of *Paris Mes Amours* took place on January 17, 1960. With full houses nightly, the show could have continued indefinitely, but Monsieur Coquatrix was bound by previous commitments. He had never dreamed that Josephine would be so well received; besides, Edith Piaf refused to adjust her schedule.

We threw a cast party on closing night. It's always sad to see a show end and this was a particularly gloomy occasion for me. Because of family obligations I was leaving Josephine after nine years of service as her dresser. Josephine did her best to brighten my spirits. "Death is the only *real* dividing force," she insisted. "Who knows how long other separations will last?"

True . . . but nevertheless, I was bidding farewell to a large chunk of my life and a tear plopped into my champagne. Memories washed over me: Josephine shouting, "Contact, Ginette!" as we roared away from the

Grand Hotel on my motor scooter, heading for the Olympia (the theater was only a stone's throw away, but Josephine was often late because she liked to write or talk until the very last minute). Josephine in Stockholm, bareheaded and wearing spike heels, setting off on foot for the theater through the bitter night: "It will do us a world of good, Ginette"; I hoped so, since we didn't have the taxi fare. That day in Mexico—where Josephine was performing three times daily—when she discovered a button missing from one of Jo's shirts. "Idiot!" she shouted as I burst into tears. "If you're that tired, go home to France. I have no time for weaklings!" I stormed off to the hotel, but was back at show time, full of remorse. Josephine had laid out her clothes herself and was busy slipping into her first costume with the help of the concierge. "What in the world was the matter, Ginette?" "Exhaustion, madame." "It's hard to keep going, isn't it?" she said, giving me an unexpected hug. We both burst into tears.

Life with Josephine was either feast or famine. In Mexico we lived in a luxurious rented apartment with separate rooms for the cook, the maid and me. But our New York quarters were spartan: Josephine and I shared a single room, in which she led a monklike existence. At bedtime she said her prayers, her head in her hands, but Josephine actually slept very little. She would soon be out of bed, preparing her lectures, checking through notes, writing letters, reading (she read constantly). Her speaking engagements invariably seemed to take her to the far ends of the city and since she made a point of answering all her audience's questions, it was usually a mad dash to the theater. . . . One day I searched frantically backstage for an iron. "We'll have to buy an iron, madame. I can't find one anywhere." "An iron? Just send the dress to the cleaners." The bill we got back in return made her cry, "You're out of your mind, Ginette!" "But you wouldn't get me an iron, madame." "I've had enough, Ginette. Tomorrow you're leaving for Paris." The next day she handed me an envelope. I opened it, my heart in my throat. It was twenty dollars with which to buy an iron.

Jo Bouillon: It was time that Josephine and I had another serious talk. Things couldn't go on this way. Noël was a sweet little baby, but it had been understood that our tenth child would be our last. Josephine would have to face the fact that our company wouldn't put up with her caprices, no matter how public-spirited her gestures might be. Rather than cause a scene, the Legrands had left for Argentina. Hélène and Ercole had also departed after Mara had been nursed back to health. My attempts to salvage Les Milandes and our marriage had clearly failed and my allies had deserted me. I saw only one solution: to refloat the company. "Over my dead body," snorted Josephine. "I refuse to entrust my cause to merchants." I decided to go back to Paris. "Since we can't seem to agree, I think it's best that I leave, Josephine. I wish you luck from the bottom of my heart." "You're probably right, Jo. We'll tell the children you'll be gone for a while on business."

"One thing I want to make clear, though, Josephine. I refuse to divorce until all the children are of age. I've given them my name and I intend to remain responsible for their welfare."

Noël was barely three months old, so that gave us plenty of time. . . .

Upon my return to Paris I rented a studio apartment in Saint-Germain-des-Prés. It reminded me of my student years, but those days were gone forever. "What will you do?" asked my brother Gabriel. I shrugged. "People are saying that you walked out on Josephine when she most needed you." "I can't keep people from talking. We simply couldn't agree on how to run Les Milandes, so I turned the job over to her. It seemed better than quarreling in front of the children. Don't you agree?" "Yes, Jo, but I only wish I hadn't been on tour at the time. I might have been able to act as a go-between." Perhaps, though I doubted it. Still, one never knew. Gabriel adored Josephine . . . as did the rest of us.

CHAPTER 17

Hard Times

Dominique Perrin: In November 1959 we began preparations for the Thirtieth Gala de l'Union des Artistes, the charity affair I stage yearly for the benefit of needy members of the French Actors Guild. The next show was scheduled for March 4, 1960. Guild president Gérard Philippe had asked Josephine to officiate.

Josephine was deeply moved by this honor. For the first time in the gala's history, a woman would open the show; this would also mark the first appearance of a person of color as president of the glittering evening staged at the Cirque d'Hiver and featuring prominent entertainers performing circus acts, often of daredevil proportions.

A few days after receiving a letter from Philippe in which he commended her "dedication to hard work," "professionalism" and "good will," Josephine was as shocked as the rest of us to learn of the ailing Gérard's death. The beloved young actor personified youth, selflessness and dedication to the kind of world that Josephine dreamed of; his untimely disappearance rocked the theatrical community. Madame la Présidente did her best to keep up the company's morale. "As we say in America, 'The show must go on,'" she insisted. While continuing to star at the Olympia nightly, Josephine devoted much of her incredible vitality to frequent trips to the circus, the gym and the riding ring to supervise rehearsals and encourage the performers' efforts.

In mid February, pressing business demands forced Josephine to leave for the United States. Her first stop was New York, where she would help with the preliminary staging of *Paris Mes Amours*, scheduled to open there in April as *The Fabulous Josephine Baker*. Then, after appearing as an honored guest at an American Jewish Congress meeting in Westchester, she would proceed to Chicago for a two-week booking at the Regal Theater. She planned to fly back to France for the night of March 4.

"I hate to walk out on you like this three weeks before the show, Dominique," she said, sighing. I did my best to reassure her. The preliminary work was done. Michel Simon would take over as ringmaster in her absence. I'd keep her informed on how things were progressing. "I'll stay in touch too, Dominique. Goodbye." And she was gone. True to her word, press clippings bearing scribbled notes in Josephine's handwriting began pouring in. She had been met at Idlewild with flowers and journalists eager to discuss the opening of her New York show on April 15. When one reporter asked, "Would you ever consider returning to the United States for good?" she replied, "Yes . . . *if* I could live here the way I do in France." The press quickly pounced on "Josephine Baker's *if.*"

Other clippings reported on the American Jewish Congress conference, which had honored her anti-racist activities; she had also been praised for her work in behalf of universal brotherhood. A press account of Josephine crowning the queen of the Beaux Arts Ball included the comment: "Judging by her skin and posture, which are said to reveal a woman's age, she appears to be pushing thirty." She wrote about how her long-time supporters the Duke and Duchess of Windsor had once again warmly encouraged her efforts one night when they met at the theater; she reported that she had appeared on television, that her record *The Fabulous . . .*, containing her Olympia numbers, was causing a stir; that she had been given a musical comedy score about gospel singers, entitled *Drums of Glory*, to read. "My head is spinning with ideas," she concluded.

On February 23, I received the following telegram from Chicago: IN TROUBLE STOP ONLY YOU CAN HELP WILL EXPLAIN ON YOUR ARRIVAL PLANE TICKET FOLLOWS MANY THANKS BON VOYAGE LOVE JOSEPHINE. She had reserved a seat for me on an Air France flight two days later. What in the world could be wrong?

A distraught Josephine greeted me at the airport. The impresario William Taub had confiscated her papers, including her French work permit and passport. She would be unable to get back to France for the gala. Taub obviously wanted to cash in on Josephine's excellent Chicago reviews. I didn't know one word of English; hardly the way to tackle the ruthless Taub! But I went to see him all the same and chatted away in my politest French until in an unguarded moment he handed over the documents I had guilelessly asked to "study." That was the last he would see of them! Snapping that I was off to our Washington embassy, I rushed out the door. I've never quite known how I managed it, but arrangements were made for Josephine to fly from Chicago to New York after her last performance. From there she would take a plane for London and pick up an airplane taxi, arriving in Paris in time for the gala. It seemed I had thought of everything.

Everything but bad weather! The airports were snowed in that night. At one o'clock the morning of March 5, the chic Parisian audience was regretfully told that Josephine was snowbound. This spelled disaster for two of the French morning papers. In order to include accounts of the gala in that day's edition, they had been obliged to jump the gun. "Josephine arrived in the nick of time from New York to pronounce the traditional phrase: 'For the thirtieth time our circus show begins,' " enthused the *Figaro*, while *L'Aurore* announced: "It was well after midnight when the projectors lit up. . . . As Jo Bouillon's orchestra played 'J'ai Deux Amours,' Gala President Josephine Baker, back from New York specially for the occasion, stepped regally into the limelight. . . . Radiant in her clinging white gown, she introduced 1960's ringmaster, Michel Simon. . . . Deciding that drawing the lottery numbers required an innocent hand, Josephine Baker and Michel Simon allotted the task to a young chimpanzee."

The show was a huge success. At dawn, as performers and spectators savored onion soup in the lions' cage, a group of us, including Michel and Jo, set off for Orly airport. Josephine stepped off the plane with a fur hat pulled low on her forehead. "I've never seen such snow! But I promise to be on time next year."

In the meantime, Josephine's New York contract had fallen through. Instead she left for Brussels on March 17 for what proved to be a highly successful run of *Paris Mes Amours*. She had asked me to look over her contract, and also wanted advice about Les Milandes, which she was hoping to open for Easter. It was clear that no matter how much she was paid, her earnings would not be enough to get Les Milandes back on its feet. But keeping the operation closed down was no solution, either. I alerted several provincial newspapers where I had contacts, and articles soon appeared announcing the reopening of "The Village of Brotherhood, situated in one of the loveliest regions of France." Imagine enjoying the Lescaux caves, soaring cliffs, dramatic chasms, medieval cities and the hundreds of châteaux that dotted the Dordogne River, all within a twenty-mile radius. . . .

"*You* understand what I'm trying to do, don't you!" Josephine cried delightedly, giving me an excited dig in the ribs. "It's all there for the sharing. Americans will eat it up. Think of all those tourists, Dominique! And they'll come. I'm sure of it. We could even organize helicopter tours. The view would be spectacular!" I accompanied Josephine to Les Milandes between contracts to see the property for myself. The village was extremely well planned, but it reminded me of a stranded Rolls-Royce, useless because there was no gas to run it. The property's carrying costs were enormous. . . . Josephine spent that summer performing in *Paris Mes Amours* at the Olympia.

The following January, Josephine received an offer that struck me as nothing short of miraculous. She and I hurried to Vienna, where we met with Ernst Marischka, director of the popular *Sissi* films, based on the life of Elizabeth of Austria. Marischka wanted to make a film about Josephine and the children. The terms he proposed were excellent and it seemed like a perfect way to save Les Milandes. Josephine would receive several million francs on signing, an advance on the balance, which would be followed by a second advance when shooting began, and the rest when the film was completed. This would pay off her debts in the Dordogne. In addition, she would get a healthy cut of the take. Marischka was convinced that the film would match *Sissi*'s success. I shared in the general euphoria. Champagne flowed that night. . . .

The next morning at dawn I heard a sharp knock on my door. There stood a glum-looking Josephine. "I didn't sleep a wink all night, Dominique. I want you to tell that man that I'm not going to sign." I couldn't believe my ears! "I mean it, Dominque. I simply can't. I won't have my children exploited." Despite her air of conviction, I tried to reason with

Josephine. Didn't she understand that this kind of "exploitation," if that's the way she viewed it, was beneficial? It would enable her to bail out Les Milandes in one fell swoop. She shook her head and pounded her knee with her fist. "No, Dominique. I don't want my children filmed. Their role is to express an ideal, not to perform like trained monkeys!" "But how about when they pose for fruit juice and knitwear advertisements, Josephine? That's exploitation, isn't it?" "It's not at all the same. Those sittings last only as long as it takes to click the shutter. I know what film-making is like. Their lives would be disrupted for months; even longer. They'd never be like other children again."

I was well aware of Josephine's stubbornness, but I could be pigheaded too. "Look, Josephine, your children have *never* been like other people's. Tourists come to Les Milandes to gape at them the way they visit landmarks in the Dordogne. Keeping your dream alive takes money, and this film is one way to get it, not only now but in the future." Josephine shook her head. "Money, money . . . all good works require money. But that doesn't mean accepting it from anyplace. You never know how a film will turn out. None that I've ever appeared in has ended up the way I expected. After all, a director can do whatever he wants. I won't let anyone tamper with my concept of the Rainbow Tribe, Dominique. It's too important. In fact, it touches on what may be the most vital question human beings face: how to deal with each other." Eyes blazing, Josephine launched into one of the themes she dealt with in her lectures. "Listen, Dominique. As you know, I had to come to France to forget my blackness. Color doesn't matter here. But France isn't the world, and I see serious trouble ahead if we don't watch out. I'm used to the words 'filthy black' and 'dirty Jew' . . . but recently, both in America and in Africa, I've begun to hear the phrase 'filthy white'! A new kind of hatred and racism is in the air and it could have terrifying repercussions because the white race has caused enormous suffering. What's essential now is to teach people of color that it's a serious error to believe that all whites are brutes and exploiters; that more than ever, mankind must unite or else the good will suffer for the evil, and chaos and injustice will reign. The children represent a ray of hope in a struggle that may be the cruelest we have ever known. They mustn't be relegated to a film scenario."

I understood her feelings. But what about Les Milandes? How would she preserve her World Village? Josephine shrugged. "God will provide.

Tell Marischka I've changed my mind."

We took the next plane back to Paris.

In that year's Gala de l'Union, Josephine did an elephant act. When she walked into the ring and flung back her cloak, in her inimitable way revealing those matchless legs, she eclipsed the younger, more beautiful women on the program. Jean Cocteau, who graced the box of honor that night, softly remarked, "It's as if the beauty of her heart had rubbed off onto her body. . . ."

Marc Vromet-Buchet: As I saw retirement from my government post approaching, I bought a property in the Dordogne about a mile from Les Milandes. I admired Josephine immensely and became increasingly involved in life at the château. As I watched the situation there deteriorate, I decided the best way to help was to volunteer as Josephine's secretary.

By now she had grave money problems. Many of the local merchants, tired of IOUs, had slammed their doors in her face. On days when there was no performance at the Olympia, we filled the car with foodstuffs bought at cut-rate prices through friends. Paris was bailing out the provinces!

During the revival of *Paris Mes Amours* Josephine stayed at the Grand Hotel . . . in a room reserved for chauffeurs. To hide this fact, she would sweep into the lobby down the main staircase whenever she had an appointment. She disguised her money worries with enormous dignity. In February 1961, on her return to Les Milandes, she told me that she had begun writing a book. The first page read as follows:

My Life as I See It

February 23, 1961. It's 7 A.M. I don't know how or where I'm going. How will I manage? I have only a few thousand francs left. Everything's going wrong. I feel so alone and think of the way Christ was abandoned. But I also realize *how difficult it must be to live with people like me.*

I'm caught up in a web of intrigue. The only important thing is that the children and the staff have enough to eat. My own stomach is in knots. I've been offered the chance to do several gala performances but I'd rather not. I hate leaving the children. It makes them cry. *"Maman,* stay with us," they beg me.

A few days later Josephine was complaining that she didn't have time to turn around, there was so much to do. She must leave at once for Paris to perform in the Gala de l'Union. Then it was back to Les Milandes again and the simple life. The staff now consisted of the Rodriguez family, the father serving as butler, the son-in-law as chauffeur, the daughter as chambermaid. I came to the château every morning to help Josephine with her mail. She had already been up for hours; in fact, she was probably the first in the household to arise. She insisted on taking care of Marianne, with whom she shared a room. The six younger children attended the local elementary school and the older ones were part-time boarders at Belvès.

Since Josephine had few visitors now, the family lived in her office and the kitchen, where a log fire burned. We roasted chestnuts in the ashes. It was an incredibly rustic life and it was hard to believe that this was the dazzling Josephine who maneuvered her way down cabaret staircases wearing towering feathered headdresses. . . . Or that this same Josephine had appeared in Paris on April 26, 1961, in a flight suit. She had heard that French paratroopers were preparing to take over Paris. As one of the original Gaullists, she had hurried to the capital dressed in her version of battle garb . . . but due to lack of funds—or perhaps the Dordogne's climate—her uniform was so moth-eaten that she'd been forced to darken the lining with India ink!

Life with Josephine was one surprise after another. That August 18, Les Milandes, already busy with summer tourists, was swarming with visitors. The crowd included village friends and local gentry. Diplomats' cars flying flags brought admiring cries from the children. There were consuls from Norway, the United States, Spain, Morocco and Italy, as well as several air force officials and two French generals, who arrived by helicopter. Telegrams flooded in from all sides. CONGRATULATIONS AND KISSES, DEAR JOSEPHINE. JEAN COCTEAU. SURPRISED AND DELIGHTED. SURPRISED BECAUSE I ASSUMED THAT THE FRENCH REPUBLIC HAD HONORED YOUR MILITARY WORK LONG AGO. TINO ROSSI. Tino had assumed correctly. Josephine had been promoted four years earlier, but there had not been time for an official ceremony. That August morning, however, Josephine, who disliked turning back, was forced to look more than twenty years into the past and remember her days with the Free French Forces.

She stood before the château in the sun, frozen at attention in her lieutenant's uniform. General Vallin retraced Josephine's life from the onset of World War II to victory day. "But in your case, peace did not mean rest," he continued. "You found a new role to play on the world stage, that of moral educator. It is the sum total of your contributions as an adopted Frenchwoman that France honors through me today." And he then pronounced the traditional phrase: "In the name of the President of the Republic and by virtue of the powers conferred upon me, I pronounce you Chevalier of the Legion of Honor."

The ten oldest children (Noël was still too young) lined the main staircase holding bouquets. They couldn't wait to rush down and kiss their mother, but managed to restrain themselves while Josephine, in a voice thick with emotion, replied: "I am very happy that this ceremony could take place here at Les Milandes because this is where I first heard the General say that all was not lost." Going on to speak of the World Village as a symbol of brotherhood, she added: "Without being chauvinistic, I am proud to be French because this is the only place in the world where I can quietly and surely realize my dream."

The formalities ended in a round of applause. The children swarmed over their mother, who tried to hug them all at once. What a wonderful celebration! Josephine had somehow managed to scrape up the wherewithal for a huge outdoor luncheon, which even the tourists attended, and there were fireworks that evening.

Tomorrow would be time enough to go back to our usual boiled potatoes.

Jari: In January 1962 we all left by car for Stockholm. *Maman* was behind the wheel of our Peugeot 404, which was piled high with baggage. We had packed a basketful of sandwiches and looked forward to a pleasant journey. None of us know to this day what happened on the outskirts of Orléans; we were all dozing at the time. A violent bump woke us up with a start, especially me. There was a nasty gash over my eye. *"Maman's* hurt, *Maman's* hurt," screamed Marianne. *Maman* was slumped over the steering wheel. It had struck her in the chest. "I'm all right. Jari's the one who needs help," she insisted, bandaging me with her handkerchief. A passing doctor recognized *Maman* and took us to the Orléans hospital. "The child's more frightened than hurt," he pronounced, "but I want you to be x-rayed, madame." "It's a waste of time," *Maman* grumbled. "I have a singing engagement in Stockholm tomorrow night." "Out of the question, madame. You have two broken ribs."

After *Maman* had been bandaged as tightly as possible, she telephoned

Noël's godmother, Simone. Would she meet us at the train station in Paris? The car had been damaged, *Maman* explained. She didn't have money enough to buy us all tickets to Stockholm. Simone telegraphed money, telling *Maman* to pay her back when she could. "Never forget how Simone helped us, children, even though she's not wealthy. It's not the rich we can count on these days."

Maman performed in Stockholm in spite of her damaged ribs, then went on to tour Scandinavia until our return to France in early March. It was already springtime at Les Milandes. "A trip like the one we just made teaches you more about life than hours of school," *Maman* remarked. "I ought to know. Still . . . it's time the older children went off to boarding school." The idea clearly upset her, though she tried not to show it. Her happiest moments were the ones we all spent together.

Jo Bouillon: I decided to move from Saint-Germain-des-Prés to a less expensive apartment in Antony, a Paris suburb. Josephine was a frequent visitor and even "surprised" me by turning up complete with luggage for a few days' stay. During our time alone together she seemed more vulnerable than usual. She especially enjoyed watching me cook and it almost seemed like the good old days. Perhaps our separation wasn't final. So many things bound us together. Was it possible we would share our old age after all? On one memorable visit she arrived anxious to discuss two things: de Gaulle and Bizet's opera *L'Arlésienne.* She had written the General a long letter containing her firsthand observations of North Africa, to which he had replied: "I am fully aware of the depth of your loyalty to France, which you convincingly demonstrated during the bitter Resistance years. I thank you most sincerely for this further proof of your allegiance as evidenced by your willingness to share your thoughts on the current situation. Please accept my heartfelt good wishes. Charles de Gaulle." The letter was dated May 15, 1962.

"Do you remember how you used to talk about staging *L'Arlésienne* at Les Milandes, Jo?" "Of course. The heroine is a dedicated mother and the part would be perfect for you. Besides, our country courtyard would make an ideal setting. Think of the advertisements: Josephine Baker stars in *L'Arlésienne* in her own back yard. It should pack in the tourists." "I've been toying with the idea ever since last February as a possible summer program. Do you think it would work?" How typical of Josephine to ask for advice after her mind was made up! Her need for reassurance made it impossible for her to live alone. I repeated that it seemed like a fine idea. She intended to get our highly professional friend Max de Rieux to direct the opera.

"I know you've dreamed of conducting Bizet's score, *cheri*, but we simply don't have the money for an orchestra. Max suggests we use a first-class recording. How do you feel about that?" I sighed. How could any record equal a fine live ensemble? "If there's no other solution," I replied, "there's an excellent recording conducted by Albert Wolf." "That's the one Max chose too. We'll have to dub in our voices, otherwise we'll never be heard. The one thing that worries me, though, is forgetting the words. Suppose my lips move when they shouldn't or my mouth hangs open when my voice is heard singing?" "I *know* you can do it, Josephine." "You really think so?" "Of course." "I haven't forgotten that it was your idea, Jo. I can't get you off my mind!" Dear Josephine. There wasn't a trace of sarcasm in her voice.

Josephine wrote me the details of opening night in a letter dated August 23, 1962, the day after the first performance:

Dearest Jo:

I really think yesterday was the most important day of my life along with my debut in the *Revue Nègre*. I've finally won my laurels as an actress. At least I hope so. The audience actually wept. Max was up the entire night before, fiddling with the lights while I watched, rolled up in a blanket. Two hours' sleep on the courtyard floor was all I needed. At eight the next morning I was at my desk tackling my mail and the bookkeeping. At eleven I went back to the courtyard to rehearse with twenty-five tambourine players sent all the way from Arles. It was a marvelous experience. . . . I barely had time to lunch on a chocolate bar before the tourists arrived. At two o'clock there was a dress rehearsal. Everyone was in costume but me. I hadn't had time to change from my pleated skirt and run-down shoes. A seventy-six-year-old woman had accompanied the tambourinists just to dress me. Adjusting my Provençale coif was more difficult than arranging any feather headdress. "Try to keep calm," my elderly visitor insisted. I explained that with fifty years of show business under my belt, I had mastered the art of self-control! I wish you could have heard the applause when the curtain fell. After the show the audience and the cast, accompanied by cowboys on horseback, paraded through the village by torchlight. There was folk dancing and a cabaret show that lasted until dawn. Now, after three hours' sleep, I'm here at my desk. I think I've been bitten by the theater bug, Jo, which is why I'm not tired. I wanted to write to you at once, since the whole thing was your idea.

Josephine's euphoria was short-lived. Less than a month later, *L'Ar-lésienne* was staged at the Olympia in a rather slipshod production. Much of the charm of the outdoor performance was lost and the acoustics were poor. So were the reviews. A further blow was Max de Rieux's death in a car accident. . . . I never heard Josephine mention acting again.

Marianne: I got very tired of being the only girl in the family. I was always the one who got scalped when we played cowboys and Indians, and someone was constantly pulling my hair. Couldn't I have a little sister? I kept asking *Maman.* She didn't take me seriously at first, not until 1962, the year we went to Italy together. I loved traveling with *Maman;* it was a fairy tale existence. We were invited everywhere. There wasn't time to get bored. When we weren't at the theater, we were busy visiting local charitable organizations, day nurseries and social service agencies. One day in a Milan orphanage, I noticed a tiny baby girl: a beautiful "little sister." Her name was Stellina. I pictured myself cuddling and dressing her like a real-life doll. But as we stood by her crib, a woman arrived and whisked her away. The child's mother had come to claim her. I was heartbroken and continued thinking about Stellina when I was back in France. I even laid aside toys and clothing for her.

That November, *Maman* was invited to Morocco to attend the wedding of one of her royal friends. She took Koffi and Brahim along to be circumcised. It would also be an opportunity to introduce Brahim and me to our homeland. After spending a few weeks in Abidjan with his godfather, President Houphouet-Boigny, Koffi joined us in Casablanca, where *Maman* was greeted with bouquets of flowers. Between lectures, she looked up wartime friends. It was through one such acquaintance that she heard of an orphan girl. The baby had been born in France of a Moroccan mother. "Do you still want a little sister, Marianne?" "Oh, yes, *Maman.*" When she came to us that spring, we named her Stellina, after that first baby girl. I took care of her as though she were mine. Stellina badly needed love. Because of her extremely fragile bones, she was forced to wear high-topped orthopedic shoes. But that didn't make her any less beautiful to me. How I adored her! We were sure that with proper care she would soon be walking normally. Akio, Jari, Luis and Jean-Claude were now away at school in Switzerland: Brahim, Mara, Koffi, Janot, Moses and I were among the forty-three students at the local public school. I regret to say that we were more remarkable for our numbers than for our academic achievement. None of us knew what we wanted to do when we grew up except Janot, who thought he'd be a gardener. What a happy year for me! Not only did Stellina join us . . . but *Papa* returned to the Dordogne.

Jo Bouillon: Josephine burst into my apartment in Antony one day. "You've *got* to come home, Jo." Les Milandes's financial picture was now even more catastrophic than when we had separated in 1960. We had another of our "discussions." Josephine counted on her lucky star to save her property, but it would take more than a heavenly body. She needed a horn of plenty! Unfortunately her many contracts in Scandinavia and the United States were offset by "benefit evenings" and "charity performances in honor of . . ." Money flowed out of Les Milandes as swiftly as it came in, leaving a constant deficit. Josephine was convinced that the public would help her continue her life work. I was less sure. "I'm counting on love and good will to pull me through," she insisted. I reemphasized my conviction that the only realistic way to save the property was to enter into some kind of commercial arrangement. The word "commercial" caused its usual violent reaction and we were off. . . . I realized yet again that Josephine was much too pure and childlike for our times. Yet who could deny that our world would be a wonderful place if she had her way? "Things can be changed, I *know* it, if everyone tries like me!" As usual, we couldn't reach an agreement.

My main reason for returning to Les Milandes was to see the children. At the same time I was faced with an extremely important and difficult decision. The idea of rebuilding my orchestra and attempting to reconquer Paris seemed overwhelming. Roger Legrand had written to me from Buenos Aires with a business proposition involving a French restaurant. The prospects looked encouraging. "You've got to make a new life for yourself, Jo. Argentina isn't the end of the world these days. You can make a quick trip to France and visit the family whenever you like. Malena and I hope you'll come." Before I replied, I wanted to try once more to convert Josephine to my way of thinking. As I watched her tuck my possessions into her car, I said to myself that perhaps this time we would patch things up for good. But I soon realized that her head was still in the clouds. . . . It must have hurt her to learn that I was moving to Buenos Aires. Her first reaction was one of amazement, followed by reproach. "You've lost confidence in me, Jo." "No, Josephine. I still believe in you and your dream, but I can't accept your methods."

Perhaps I will never know for sure exactly what went wrong between us, but one thing seems clear. Josephine was a fighter, constantly trying to perfect herself, to conquer her own nature, sometimes at the risk of great personal sacrifice. Could it possibly have been that very taste for battle that made her risk losing Les Milandes? She wanted to wage and win her war *alone!*

I left for Argentina after arranging for Stellina's adoption papers. She would bear the Bouillon name like the eleven others. My name was the best thing I could offer the children. I asked Josephine to keep me informed of their progress. After all, I was still their father, and in spite of our separation, remained her husband.

How can I ever forget the date of my arrival in Buenos Aires: November 22, 1963, the day of President Kennedy's assassination? Josephine had been in New York since October, appearing at the Shubert, Brocks Atkinson and Henry Miller theaters. Knowing her as I did, I realized how profoundly the death of this leader, whom she had never met but to whom she had written, would affect her. I sent her a telegram. She wired a six-word reply: OUR WORLD IS TOPPLING. AFFECTIONATELY YOURS.

In April 1964 Josephine reopened at the Olympia. An article I came upon in *France Soir* convinced me that she was keeping up her usual breakneck pace. " 'I never stop to rest. Weekends are a waste of time. Mothers must stay on the job.' " The report went on to say that Josephine had no sooner arrived at Orly than she took the night train for the Dordogne, where she was greeted by the children and a television team, who monopolized her until it was time to reboard the train for Paris. After another all-night trip, she attended an 8 A.M. rehearsal at the Olympia, which lasted all that Wednesday. Her show opened Thursday night. After three weeks at the Olympia it was back to New York and excellent reviews on May 21. "I found the warmth of my reception in the United States even more gratifying because during the last thirteen years as a black woman battling racism I've been shunned there. . . . They went wild over my clothes. 'Be sure to wear them next time,' they insisted. No wonder. Those costumes cost me fifty million old francs!"

In spite of Josephine's success, the news from the Dordogne was so alarming that I felt obliged to fly to Paris. Josephine's creditors would wait no longer. What would she do if her furniture was seized? It would be the beginning of the end for Les Milandes. Sick with worry, I racked my brains for a solution. One hope remained: the same alternative we'd had before. Surely we could find a large company interested in putting Josephine back on her feet, paying off her debts, giving her titular control of Les Milandes and keeping the property afloat with new money. I had traveled six thousand miles on the basis of that conviction. But Josephine greeted talk of the money world and merchants with her usual disdain. In fact, she was more adamant than ever. I gradually realized that Les Milandes had become hallowed ground to her and she saw herself as keeper of the flame. She would rather die than compromise. "There are plenty of kind-hearted people in France. *They're* the ones who will save me, not the businessmen." "But, Josephine, *cherie,* if the creditors decide to foreclose, they've got the legal right." "I'll fight the law, then! I'll organize housewives everywhere! You *know* that my dream is my reason for living, Jo. How can you ask me to give in?" I should never have come. It was the same dead-end argument again. Was it possible that in my heart of hearts my conviction wasn't as strong as hers? Still, we lived in a world of money.

I left for Buenos Aires sick at heart. Les Milandes's furniture was scheduled to be auctioned off on June 9. Every June 3 since Josephine and I had met I had sent her birthday flowers. This year I would do the same, with one difference. I ordered thirteen roses and a card reading "Papa and the children." Perhaps it would help.

The list of articles to be auctioned seemed endless, ranging from our bridge table through kitchen appliances, ice chests, pots and pans and even farm tools and tractors. Everything would be sold. It seemed clear that Les Milandes was doomed.

On June 4 I learned that Brigitte Bardot had made a television appeal to save Les Milandes.

"I'll organize housewives everywhere," Josephine had insisted. And so she had, through a voice that was sure to command attention. I couldn't help admiring my wife's special brand of stubbornness. She let nothing stand in her way.

The auction was canceled.

But on July 25 Josephine was rushed to Boucicaut Hospital. She had suffered a heart attack.

Luis: We knew that *Maman* had almost died. She was very weak when she returned to Les Milandes. It was August, the height of the tourist season. We had never seen *Maman* sleep late in the morning before. Aunt Margaret did everything she could to spare her. We were surrounded by kind-hearted people as well as others who seemed displeased that we were still on the property. One day Moses came home in tears. A neighbor had commented to her son that my brother had a Jewish nose. *Maman* assured him that he had nothing to be ashamed of. On another occasion, a passer-by called Jean-Claude and me "Baker scum." And I remember other allusions to our religions and origins. Perhaps they were made in fun, but they hurt all the same.

We probably should have fought for the family honor, but that's a great deal to ask of boys the oldest of whom is twelve. Still, in spite of such occasional unpleasantness, Les Milandes had proved *Maman*'s point: the fact that we lived there in harmony showed the world that racial barriers are man-made. In fact, her experiment had succeeded beyond her wildest expectations. We formed a unit, a clan, a tight little group which grew closer and stronger in the face of the outside world. There were no walls between us; the only barriers we knew were those we threw up to protect *Maman.*

As *Maman* regained her strength, she flung herself into the American electoral campaign. She was a staunch supporter of Robert Kennedy, with whom she corresponded. I remember well because I was the one who found a letter from the senator in our mailbox one morning. She answered it that very day. "What did you say, *Maman?*" " 'Good luck and hold tight.' That way you can't go wrong. Of course, there *are* times when you hold tight but are unlucky, or have the luck but can't cash in on it." She shrugged. Then stabbing at the air like a boxer with her clenched fist, she continued: "The thing to do is ask God for good fortune, then fight for it."

Margaret: During most of October 1964 my sister almost forgot Les Milandes and its daily concerns for those of America. More specifically she was preoccupied with the relationship between the forthcoming election and the racial issue. She summed up her thoughts on the matter in a three-page letter to the executive director of the NAACP, Roy Wilkins:

Johnson's presence is indispensable at the moment since you can pretty well control his behavior, whereas a newcomer who wants to impress the public might not be as good for the country and the future of civil rights. Bobby's role as Senator from New York is equally vital. He is carrying on the fine work begun by his brother. I realize that his youth concerns you, but you mustn't forget that this is a young country and government by our youth can only make us prosper. Remember the hope we felt for the future during John Kennedy's presidency? Remember the feeling of stability and security? Bobby was standing right at his brother's elbow, participating in his decisions. Robert Kennedy's presence is essential today because he is certain to do his best to uphold civil rights legislation as his brother would have wished and as we all desire. We've got to back Johnson and Kennedy to the hilt! It would be disastrous to lose them. . . . Many of my predictions have come true although my "big mouth," as it used to be called, earned me thirteen years of exile during which only a handful of friends dared stick by me. But I've come into my own at last because the sleepers have awakened. . . . My only concerns are our national honor and peace for all people regardless of color.

Josephine continued to drive herself unsparingly and on October 24 had a second heart attack, this time mercifully slight. It nevertheless required three days of hospitalization.

CHAPTER 18

The College of
Brotherhood

Jean-Claude: I was terribly ashamed the day I was expelled from school for leaving the grounds without permission. I hadn't meant any harm. My friend and I had just wanted an evening's fun. What would *Maman* say? She was touring Switzerland at the time and I joined her in Montreux. It was agony waiting there in her dressing room. I knew she had a great deal on her mind and would probably be on edge. She might even slap me. I only hoped no one would notice. . . . As usual, *Maman* didn't arrive at her dressing room until a few minutes before curtain time. When she saw me, her face fell. "Oh . . . Jean-Claude!" she murmured. Then she held out her arms. I threw myself into them, sobbing.

The year 1965 started off poorly. Marianne, Moses, Luis, Akio, Jari and I were scattered about at various boarding schools. The other children had remained at Les Milandes. Our family seemed to be disintegrating. "Don't worry," said *Maman*. "We'll all be together again soon." She was wrapped up in a new idea: a College of Brotherhood. It was becoming increasingly apparent that Les Milandes could not support itself through tourism. But suppose an international learning center were built on our beautiful domain, a University of World Brotherhood? "I got the idea from you children," *Maman* explained. "It's impossible to change the world unless something is done about the educational system. Our university will be dedicated to nondiscrimination, be it racial, religious or social." "But how will the school operate, *Maman?*" "There will be several participating nations. We'll begin by creating a building fund and a board of directors composed of delegates from the various contributing governments." "Which countries will they be, *Maman?*" "The friendly ones. Those where I travel, lecture, sing. Morocco and Italy have already expressed their interest. . . . We can save Les Milandes and help the world at the same time!"

Bit by bit, *Maman*'s ideas began to take concrete form. She consulted a well-known Italian architect, Bruno Fedrigolli, who had designed a modern college in Brescia. *Maman*'s close friend Maguy Chauvin, who had been in on the idea from the start, checked with lawyers about chartering the College of Brotherhood. "What a wonderful idea, *Maman.* Does it mean that we can all go to school together?" "If you study hard from now until you're eighteen. Only scholarship candidates and good students will be admitted. Having the Baker-Bouillon name won't help. There'll be no favoritism! You'd better not sneak out of school again, Jean-Claude."

When Fedrigolli's plans arrived, I assembled my brothers and sisters. "Come and look at the college." *Maman* and Aunt Margaret spread out the drawings. "Isn't it beautiful!" Janot exclaimed. "It looks like a huge bunch of flowers!" Ten paths radiating from a main artery led to ten round constructions shaped like corollas. *Maman* helped us read the inscription: *"Collegio universitario della fraternità universale Fondazione Josephine Baker—Les Milandes—Dordogne—France."* She explained that each of Janot's "flowers" was in fact a two-story house containing a common room, service areas and dormitories. What appeared to be petals were actually beds. Four hundred of them. Two additional "flowers" contained staff housing and administration offices. There were also provisions for an auditorium, terraces and a college square. "Will it all fit into Les Milandes, *Maman?*" "Easily. The château and the surrounding buildings including the restaurants won't be affected in any way. The charter is ready to be sent to intellectuals around the world. They'll name delegates to an initial conference which will determine curricula. The college will focus on economic, social and political matters as well as courses designed to improve human relations: studies examining the correlation between primitive cultures and modern civilization, classes in comparative religion. . . . Students will learn that all creeds like all people are essentially one. And when they have mastered that lesson, they'll go home and preach it to their people. . . ."

The months flew by. Before we knew it, our summer vacation had come to an end, but the cornerstone of our college was yet to be laid. *Maman* explained that it might be some time before the various nations involved reached an agreement, but that wherever she toured she would promote the College of Brotherhood. . . . At Christmas, when the family was reunited, there had been no noticeable progress, although we learned that tragedy had been narrowly averted. Les Milandes had been put up for sale at auction that November and only the desperate efforts of friends and lawyers had saved it.

Immediately after the new year, *Maman* left for Cuba to attend the first Tricontinental Conference. Delegates from Asia, Africa and South America were there representing over two billion people, wrote *Maman*. The high point of her trip occurred on January 15, the last day of the conference, when she went to hear Fidel Castro speak at the Chaplin Theater. "He's a remarkable man," she reported, "and very enthusiastic about the College. In fact, I have wonderful news for you, children. 'Uncle Fidel' has invited us all to spend a month's vacation in Cuba." Our joy at this news was short-lived. *Maman's* letter was immediately followed by a cable. She had been rushed to Paris for emergency surgery to correct an intestinal blockage. . . . *Papa* arrived on the first plane from Argentina and joined the family at her bedside. "How sweet of you all to come," she murmured. "But I'm not dying yet!"

We were thrilled to see *Papa* again, in spite of the reason that brought him. "Do you have to go back?" Akio asked shyly. *Papa* seemed very preoccupied. Les Milandes was threatened with another auction sale. How would we get through the summer? "Can't you stay, *Papa?* Nothing's gone right since you left." "I have my business in Argentina now, son."

Maman recuperated with astonishing speed. Her will to live was amazing. When *Papa* learned that there was nothing laid aside to cover the hospital bills, he paid them himself. Then he was off.

After a brief rest in the country, *Maman* was back on the road. Appearances in Dakar, Abidjan and Madrid apparently netted enough to forestall sale by auction again.

July finally arrived and with it our long-awaited trip to Havana. Fidel Castro set us up in a spacious villa, complete with swimming pool, a stone's throw from the Caribbean. He also provided guides to show us the island's points of interest—in an armored car staffed with bodyguards, just in case! My most vivid memory of our stay is Castro's visit to our villa on the eve of our departure. It was pure Hollywood. We were sitting in the living room when there was a sudden screeching of brakes and the sound of car doors slamming. Before we knew it, Castro, escorted by two guards with machine guns, strode into the room. He was in full regalia; general's uniform, sunglasses, the inevitable cigar stuck in the side of his mouth; he barely had time to remove it before giving *Maman* a bearlike hug. We were wild with excitement as he embraced each member of the Rainbow Tribe in turn, half smothering the younger children in his beard. At the snap of his fingers, presents appeared for everyone. Real little soldiers' uniforms, baseball suits . . . and for *Maman*, the rank of officer in the Cuban Army. Then he was gone, as swiftly as he had come: a brisk salute for Lieutenant Baker, attention, about-face, clattering heels, the bang of a door, car doors crashing, screaming tires, sirens. Silence.

"What a man," gasped *Maman*.

The next day we left for Buenos Aires and a visit with *Papa*.

Jo Bouillon: My restaurant, Le Bistro, is situated in Palermo, the stylish part of town. A French name usually means French cooking, and business was thriving. I couldn't believe my eyes when Josephine and the entire Tribe appeared at the door. I had been waiting so long for this moment! "Here's someone you don't know yet," said Josephine, smiling. It was true. I had adopted Stellina sight unseen. Her gentleness impressed me at once; quite a contrast to Marianne, who had spent her early years scuffling with her brothers.

The children all seemed to be thriving. "As you can see, I live simply but well, Josephine. You can send me the Tribe without worrying." Josephine made her usual inspection, just as at Les Milandes, even lifting the lids off my stewpots and sniffing their contents. She apparently liked what she saw, because she left me so I could enjoy a wonderful vacation alone with the children. It ended all too soon. How empty my house seemed!

Three months later I received an urgent telegram from Josephine. "Need you immediately for trip to Marrakech." We met at Orly. She explained that her Moroccan friends hadn't forgotten her. Luckily, because she desperately needed help. Her case had gone before the court in September. It would take two hundred million francs to save Les Milandes. King Hassan, under pressure from mutual friends, had come up with a possible solution. He was ready to give Josephine a sizable piece of land in Marrakech and the chance to begin again. The offer included a house big enough for the entire family and the possibility of her own restaurant-cabaret. . . . The prospects looked promising. It would take tremendous effort, of course, but work had never frightened Josephine. "Can I count on your help, Jo?" she asked. "Of course." We debated for three long days. At last Josephine said, "I can't bear to leave France, Jo." She *had* to save Les Milandes. The thought of giving up the property and beginning again was unbearable . . . partly because of her love of France, partly because she refused to be driven away. Besides, there was the College of Brotherhood to consider. "It's got to be built in France and nowhere else, Jo. France has a tradition of freedom; it's served as a model for democracy; it supported American independence." I understood, of course; in fact, I shared her feelings. Josephine went on to tour Morocco with the sole intent of rescuing Les Milandes and I returned to the Dordogne.

"*Papa's* coming back!" That time-honored phrase again! But I didn't know for how long. I had to analyze the situation, then I'd decide. "Maybe forever?" Janot breathed in my ear. *Papa* was back and it was time to trim the tree. We had a wonderful family Christmas, but how long would it be before the children were once again exposed to the sight of their mother, distraught and choking back tears, emerging from her office surrounded by creditors asking for money, more money? *Papa* was back and there were plans to make. Les Milandes would reopen at Easter. In the meantime, after the holidays, *Maman* would leave again for Algeria, Lebanon, the Middle East, Asia. . . . "I'll pack my bags and gather up my walking stick," as she liked to say, and off she'd go, knocking at statesmen's doors pleading the cause of Les Milandes and the College of Brotherhood. . . . It was *my* job to keep the home fires burning. After much hesitation ("I don't want to ask for money as if I expected payment for my services to France"), Josephine had requested an audience with General de Gaulle. "But I simply can't talk about sordid money matters, Jo." It was true; the idea repelled her. She didn't like money, nor did money like her. Indeed, that's what was causing her downfall. She sent me to see the General in her place.

My interview with de Gaulle lasted all of three minutes. He stood up behind his desk and welcomed me, asking in his famous tones: "And what can we do for our Josephine?" I explained the situation: Josephine's insistence on continuing what she viewed as her mission, the integrity that had made her refuse to accept a penny for her wartime propaganda tour, which she had considered a duty, her strong sense of honor. The General listened carefully. "I'll see what can be done," he said. Soon afterward I met with his private secretary, Monsieur Gallichon. We spoke at length. A way must be found to aid the Josephine Baker Foundation rather than Josephine herself, because I knew she would never accept a penny in her own name. Monsieur Gallichon sent me to see the director of a large private bank. He knew of a château in the Allier, in central France, that could be made immediately available to Josephine and her Tribe. I explained that Josephine had always tried to provide for her children herself by taking to the road, like any other performer. I also described her dedication to the concept of the College of Brotherhood and her insistence on constructing it at her beloved Les Milandes, in which she had invested everything. Perhaps there was another solution, then, one I had been toying with. Between engagements, Josephine went with me to see Gilbert Trigano of the Club Méditerranée. He seemed very sympathetic to the humanitarian aims of Les Milandes. Couldn't we collaborate with his group, giving it control of the business end and full administrative responsibility, while Josephine retained the château and enough land for her college? Josephine listened carefully. It was of course understood that our respective lawyers would work out the legal technicalities before anything was signed. I suddenly felt as if an enormous weight had been lifted from my shoulders. It looked as though Les Milandes might be saved. "What do you think?" I asked my wife. "He's very clever. No wonder he's been so successful." The lawyers got to work. There was a matter of percentages to be settled. Only one thing concerned Josephine: the fact that Les Milandes had been created for the children. If it was taken over by the Club Méditerranée, wouldn't her Tribe be cheated? It was explained to her that a system of trusts would protect the children until their majority and that she could retain full control over the château, the restaurant and the college grounds. . . . Josephine lapsed into a silence, which I knew meant trouble.

When we were alone, she exploded. "All those people and those lawyers care about is *money*. Trigano hasn't even bothered to come and *see* Les Milandes! He sent his business manager instead. It's nothing but business to him. I refuse to see business conducted at the expense of my children. Not just because they're my children—any mother would feel the same —but because they're even more! People have no right to try and cash in on a dream."

I attempted to reason with her. Many people believed that we had developed Les Milandes strictly as a business proposition. She shrugged. "We've created something where nothing existed before. Who'd ever heard of Les Milandes? We've sunk everything we own into the property in order to create a place for us and others to enjoy. But we just don't seem to be able to make a go of it." "That's because we're amateurs. And it's exactly why we need collaborators." "But all these people care about is profits. Where's the idealism in that?" "We simply can't go on alone, Josephine." "Then we've got to find help that is 'pure,' uncorrupted by business interests. Unfortunately the 'pure' usually don't have money! Still, if all the idealists in France donated whatever they could afford, we'd be saved. People are out to get me and Les Milandes."

We were at an impasse again. Josephine insisted on the impossible. This time I had not only failed to win her over, but in the process had convinced her that I was on the side of the "profiteers," the "impure." I had no choice but to leave. On February 20 I boarded the plane for Buenos Aires.

Alone in a Copenhagen hotel room, Josephine wrote:

All my life I have fought for my beliefs. My ideal is universal brotherhood, a dream I've realized at Les Milandes. My life, like that of so many others, is a constant struggle. I've placed my worldwide reputation as an artist on one side of the scale and human justice on the other. The choice is easy for me because I've always placed human justice above materialism.

I recently traveled to Mexico on behalf of Les Milandes. A representative of a California company visited me there to propose a film on my life. The pay was excellent, enough to solve Les Milandes's money problems, but the contract contained a clause stipulating that when the film was released I would have to go to Vietnam and sing for the GIs like certain other entertainers, including Marlene Dietrich. I replied that those performers were free to do as they liked, but that I categorically refused to go to Southeast Asia because I felt the war was wrong. I even went so far as to say that I might well lose Les Milandes when I returned to France, but that my integrity was not for sale. Needless to say, the contract never materialized. I went back to Les Milandes and the rest is public knowledge. . . . My last ten years have been a constant struggle with businessmen, lawyers, financiers.

Marc Vromet-Buchet: During 1967 things went from bad to worse. Water had begun leaking through the roof of the château, making ugly marks on the Oriental rugs. But Josephine doggedly refused to give up hope. Her work often brought her to Paris. On these visits she no longer went to hotels but instead stayed with friends. She was a frequent guest at my house on the Rue de Dantzig, where she and whatever children she had in tow would transform my living room into a dormitory. On these festive occasions Josephine seemed to glow. Some nights when she couldn't sleep, she would get up and make stew for the following day. She would bring not only her Tribe but also one or two dogs and cats she couldn't bear leaving behind. There was only one way to tell when she was angry. Whenever she was faced with one of her many insoluble problems, she began clattering dishes in the sink to hide her agitation.

The year 1968, one of violent upheaval in France, was particularly disastrous for Josephine. I was with her at Les Milandes on March 15 when Sylvain Floirat, the founder of the radio station Europe 1, came calling. That February the property had been put up for sale again, but at the last minute the auction had been postponed. There wasn't a moment to lose. Monsieur Floirat had been sent by mutual friends to look over the domain. He toured the hotels, the amusement park, the cabaret, the theater, until an exhausted Josephine told him to go on without her. She sat down to wait in the living room, near a table bearing an announcement of the forthcoming auction.

When his inspection was over, Monsieur Floirat proposed paying all Les Milandes's outstanding debts, which totaled 146 million francs, and granting Josephine the usufruct of the property. She didn't know what "usufruct" meant. Even after it had been explained to her she kept

repeating: "I don't understand. . . . I need time to think it over."
She retired to her office. The subject was closed.

Josephine: I needed 37 million francs, including costs, to stop the sale.
I asked a director of the Fiduciaire in Paris to find the money. He felt
that forty million was a more prudent sum since it allowed me to pay off
the 12.5 percent interest rate in advance. If I hadn't raised the money by
due date, the property would be sold. I now needed a total of 150 million
francs in order to pay back my debt and reimburse my creditors. . . .

I sometimes feel so tired. I remember one day last year when I arrived
at a lawyer's office, check in hand, in order to stop a sale. He immediately
telephoned all the creditors that the auction was off for the moment. But
he suggested that they continue to look for fellow creditors with whom
to join forces, because sooner or later the sale would occur. He sent me
on my way with the words: "It would be a real pity if you straightened
out your affairs. You're the best local client we've got!"

Jacqueline Cartier: France Soir commissioned me to do a story on
Josephine, whose plight had captured French hearts. She was billed to
reopen at the Olympia on April 3, 1968. Les Milandes was scheduled for
auction on May 3. Josephine would have to work fast!

The show business world was determined to save her by appealing to
"kind hearts" everywhere. Pathé-Marconi prepared a special record with
a plain white jacket to benefit operation *S.O.S. The World's Children.*
It was launched with a flourish over national television.

Each record sold at the Olympia bore an inscription penned by Josephine in red ink. They were bought up by the hundreds. *S.O.S.* summa-
rized Josephine's life in twelve songs ranging from "J'ai Deux Amours"
to "Hello, Dolly," which was her next project in collaboration with Bruno
Coquatrix: "But first I've got to rescue Les Milandes and the College of
Brotherhood," she told me. "Then in January we'll stage *Dolly.* I realize
I'm sixty-two, but Dolly was no spring chicken, either. Ginger Rogers
played her in New York and now they're doing the show there with Pearl
Bailey and an all-black cast. We want to try the same thing in
Paris."

The lines at the Olympia's ticket windows were so long that it was
decided to rebill Josephine there on May 15. By then Les Milandes would
be out of danger. Josephine never doubted this for a minute. "Forty-five

records were sold in my little village alone this morning! I just heard the news by telephone. In fact, sales are off to a fantastic start all over France. . . . Thank goodness for television. That's what has saved me. Did you know that Spain, Belgium and Germany want the record too? It's the general public, the little people, who are helping to see me through. They love and understand me." She was beaming.

Josephine left to tour Scandinavia with a light heart.

I found the following account in Josephine's papers. I can think of no better way to express what happened on that terrible spring day:

Friday, May 3, 1968. It's one-fifteen in the afternoon. I'm alone in my bedroom in Göteborg, Sweden, in the hotel where I am currently performing.

I'm sitting here sick at heart, waiting for a phone call reporting on the decision of the Bergerac tribunal in the Dordogne. Will Les Milandes be put up for sale at two o'clock or not? If it isn't sold forty-five minutes from now I can continue my fight for human rights on my domain and build my College of Brotherhood there. If the sale does take place, I'll work to purchase another home for my children. But first we'll head for the desert, with empty hands but full hearts. We'll construct our college on the sands. I'm determined to fight this through.

The minutes are crawling by. I keep looking at my watch. Each ring of the phone makes me jump. The forty-five minutes are up now. The auction has begun. It's two o'clock. I'm still waiting. Three o'clock, four. Still no word. It's five now and I just got a call from a Parisian journalist. That voice! *I'm afraid I've got very bad news. At four o'clock Les Milandes was sold for 125 million francs.*

Three years ago the domain had been assessed at 663 million, for the land and empty buildings alone! What a swindle! The château itself was valued at two hundred million. It had gone for twenty-eight!

A sudden sense of calm swept over me, like the quiet that follows a storm. Everything seemed frozen in place. I tried to speak into the telephone, but the shock had rendered me speechless!

In spite of the sale, Josephine continued her tour. I met her at Orly on May 14, on her return from Belgrade. "How about an autograph, Josephine?" First it was the customs inspector, then the porter; at the same time passengers pressed her to sign their plane tickets. She was all smiles, but I could sense her tenseness. The night before, at Skoplje, she had been in a train collision. Fortunately she had been riding in the last car, from which she emerged unhurt to help in the rescue operation. There hadn't been time to reflect on her own grave problems.

We headed at once for the Grand Hotel to collect Marianne, Moses, Luis and Jari, on vacation from their various boarding schools. Then it was off to the Austerlitz station and the train that would reunite us with the other eight children.

"I want them to have one last time together in the country," Josephine explained to Bruno Coquatrix. "But that means spending two full nights on the train. Try to be sensible, Josephine!" he begged. "It means a great deal to me, Bruno. Don't worry. I'll be back Thursday for opening night. I'm indestructible."

We sat up in our second-class carriage all that night. "*Maman,* have we really lost Les Milandes for good?" asked Moses. Josephine shrugged. "We'll talk about it tomorrow. Akio was at the auction. He'll explain what happened."

We arrived at Les Milandes at six the next morning through a mist tinged with gold. A friend brought her car to meet us. The countryside was magnificent, but I hesitated to say so. Josephine was literally drinking in the view through the car window. The property was closed off. We carefully pulled the gate shut behind us. "There are snoopers here night and day," our driver informed us. I was introduced to Margaret in the huge kitchen, where she was setting out steaming bowls of coffee. "My sister's tough as nails," explained Josephine. "We all are in my family. We never have toothaches, and if someone cuts into our stomach, we're back on our feet in three days."

There was a sudden commotion on the second floor: my young traveling companions had decided to wake up their brothers and sister with a flourish. Amid shouts and gales of laughter, Akio entered the room. So this was the eldest member of the Tribe: a tall, slim youth whose deeply circled eyes sparkled with intelligence. "You look ill, *cheri,*" remarked Josephine. He had attended the May 3 auction in his mother's place. "It reminded me of wild beasts attacking a defenseless animal," Akio said in a toneless voice. "I've never seen such unfeeling faces." Looking up at the ceiling, he asked, "Do you want me to quiet them down?" "No, let them enjoy themselves while they can. . . . But tell me what happened, *cheri.* I understood that the auction would be put off like all the other times because the money had been raised the night before."

Akio shrugged. "We all thought the sale had been postponed. The mayor of Castelnaud even said, 'If I'd known that the sale would take place I'd have bought the property for our municipality.' " Akio knew nothing more except that all the creditors had been alerted except one, whom it had apparently been impossible to reach. Since that single party had been unable to approve a postponement, it had been necessary to go through with the auction according to law. "How lucky for the buyers that the creditor couldn't be found!" Josephine remarked. She suddenly sounded exhausted. "The important thing, *Maman*, is that we're all together. We can live out our dream someplace else. It's a big world." Josephine squeezed her son's hand, then turning to me, said, "He's my eldest . . . the one I rely on. We're going to build my College of Brotherhood together."

The plans for the college lay on her desk. Josephine suddenly brightened. Straightening her shoulders, she shrugged her weariness away. "How is it possible for people of different continents to respect each other if education remains centered around differences between the races, things like skull configurations and skin color? Think of the effect this has on innocent young minds!" Then her expression changed. Turning to Akio, she murmured, "There's something else I don't understand, *cheri*. I asked Bruno Coquatrix to represent me at the auction and outbid any potential buyer. After all, he knows how well *Disk S.O.S.* is doing, that money is coming in, that I would somehow have raised the funds." "He wasn't there, *Maman*." I'll never forget the look on Josephine's face, her expression of utter amazement. "I don't believe it, Akio. I'm sure you're wrong." "No, *Maman*, he didn't come." Josephine fell silent, her eyes cold and grim.

After breakfast I was given the grand tour. "Some people talk about the château as if it were Versailles," Josephine said, laughing. "But once we're all inside, it's small." I asked her what she planned to do next. "I have no idea. There must be some way to appeal. It's unthinkable that the property was sold for a tenth of its assessed value."

After a gay family lunch around the huge kitchen table, Josephine helped the children with the dishes. It looked like a well-rehearsed ballet. Josephine dipped the plates into the big dishpan while some of the children stacked, others dried, one swept and another put away. In fifteen minutes the room was immaculate. The children ran off to play and Josephine and I went to town to get an official account of the sale from the clerk's office.

Before we knew it, it was evening and time to return to Paris.

The following night I joined Luis, Jari and Moses in a box at the Olympia. A dazzling Josephine dominated the stage. The show was *Paris Mes Amours* and when Josephine walked through the audience during her Gypsy number, the palm she read belonged to the ambassador from the Ivory Coast. At the end of the show, we all received a surprise. Josephine was awarded a plaque celebrating the two thousandth anniversary of the city of Paris. A spotlight raked the children's box. But as soon as the curtain fell, Maguy Chauvin literally whisked them away. They had to be back at school early the next morning. I found Josephine in her dressing room, changing wigs. "I'm absolutely exhausted," she sighed. I assured her that her fatigue hadn't showed on stage, then hurried off to call in my story. From the phone booth I saw her go sweeping by, resplendent in a green-and-gold djellabah, on the arm of the ambassador from the Ivory Coast. . . .

During the evening I had run into Bruno Coquatrix. "Why didn't you top the highest bidder at the auction for Les Milandes?" I asked. He pulled twice at his cigar before answering. "Isn't it a blessing, Jacqueline, that Les Milandes is no longer hers? If she had kept it, the place would have ruined her." And he quietly changed the subject. There was more than enough to discuss! The night before, rampaging students had occupied the Odeon Theater and they were now threatening national radio and television headquarters. In the chaos of May 1968, Josephine Baker's problems seemed secondary.

On May 22 I received a call from Josephine. "I'm turning over my case to one of the top French lawyers, Jacqueline. There's something fishy going on. I'm sure I've been betrayed."

Ten days later the Olympia was seething with excitement. Bruno had decided to open the theater to the students rather than have them occupy it by force. "Over my dead body," snapped Josephine. "I'm not budging. I'll occupy it myself, with the help of the staff."

On June 4 there was a parade "for de Gaulle" on the Champs-Élysées. Josephine and Akio were among the marchers. Two days later the wires hummed with the news of Robert Kennedy's shooting. I called Josephine. Her grief-stricken voice was unrecognizable. Kennedy's death had just been announced. "But it's better this way, isn't it, Jacqueline? If a man like that had been paralyzed or badly handicapped . . . Did you know it's through him that I finally got my American visa? Otherwise I'd still be 'undesirable' in the United States. My God, what a terrible tragedy!"

Josephine telephoned me two days later. "I'm about to leave for Bobby Kennedy's funeral with Akio, Janot, Jari, Luis and Moses. They're old enough to understand. Bobby's cause was ours and I want to be sure they know it. They've got to realize that one killing can't destroy an ideal. We'll follow the funeral procession." "That does it!" said Coquatrix wearily. "There go her earnings from the show."

On June 12 I called her at Les Milandes. She could barely speak. "And you're planning to perform at the Olympia tomorrow night?" "Of course," she croaked. "The stage is my best medicine."

She was back in Paris the next day at dawn. I hurried to her bedside in the Hotel Scribe, where she lay muffled in woolens. "The phone hasn't stopped for a minute," she said in a hollow voice. "Coquatrix is telling everyone that I have pneumonia. Ridiculous! It's from the air conditioning in New York. I'm hoarse, that's all. I'll be back on stage for Saturday's performance. I don't want Coquatrix to close down the theater, then blame it on me!"

On June 16 she was performing again, swathed in feathers, her voice good as new. She waltzed with a young man in the audience, stroked a bald head, sang along with the crowd, reintroduced a song from Liberation days called "Fleur de Paris." "Wait until you see my surprise," she had whispered earlier that evening. She had ordered little red, white and blue bouquets from a fashionable florist—I could hear Coquatrix already groaning about what it had cost her—which she tossed to the spectators. Her gesture was like an electric discharge, causing the audience to rise to its feet in a burst of patriotic fervor. There were tears and shouts of applause.

The final performance of *Paris Mes Amours* was scheduled for June 29. What lay in store for Josephine next? She distributed her bouquets among the crowd for the last time. A friend was waiting at the stage door to drive her to Les Milandes, which theoretically was no longer hers. "Don't worry. I haven't left there for good yet!" she assured me as she stepped into the car. Then she drove off into the darkness.

On July 4 I learned that Josephine had been taken to the hospital in Périgueux. She had suffered a stroke.

The months that followed were the cruelest that Josephine would know. Her recuperative powers were astonishing. Ten days after her stroke she attended Marianne's First Communion. The next week Akio underwent an emergency appendectomy. Josephine hovered over him until it was time to take to the road again. On August 17 she returned from Copenhagen to block a legal procedure which she didn't understand. She was still hoping that the sale, which she saw as a swindle, an injustice, sheer theft, could be reversed. She slapped a process server who ventured onto "her" property. She had become a tigress defending her young. The family camped out in one room. An eviction order was filed on October 7. Josephine was granted a delay, however, since evictions could not legally be enforced between October 15 and March 15. But from January 19 to January 22 all the furniture was auctioned off, netting a mere 26.5 million old francs instead of the expected 40. Josephine was ruined, dispossessed, hounded. Newspapers everywhere published a dramatic photograph portraying her crouching, grief-stricken, on the steps of her château, wrapped in an old blanket, a kitten on her knees, refusing to budge . . . an ageless woman whose face was distorted with exhaustion, bitterness and sorrow. She no longer owned a stick of furniture. People threw stones into her château windows. She was finally dragged out of her house with such force that her hands were injured from clinging with her considerable strength to the kitchen stove. Some of the men had struck her, and I suppose in striking this idol, this black Venus, they had satisfied some sordid need. Josephine had always believed in miracles: the only one here was that she had escaped alive.

She was rushed to the Périgueux hospital again.

I found the following letter, dated February 6, 1969, and addressed to General de Gaulle, among her papers: ". . . Not only did they seize my clothing, they took some of my documents, papers, etc., including some of your letters which were packed with the rest because I never thought the sale would take place and *I didn't take precautions.* . . . Everyone's out to get me. Your faithful Josephine, in spite of everything."

I also found a note written in Copenhagen, which I believe was Josephine's final cry for what she saw as justice. The words sprawled across the page:

"Josephine suspects no one but she must know the truth, both for herself and for the sake of those *who have trusted her.*"

CHAPTER 19

A New Start

Moses: When we left Les Milandes at the end of the school vacation, we were convinced that we would never see our château again. Still, in our heart of hearts, we hoped for a miracle. That came from living with *Maman.* We'd seen her move mountains so often. . . . "Not this time," Akio insisted. He knew best. After all, he was the oldest, the boss, the one *Maman* left in charge in her absence. Jean-Claude, Brahim, Mara and I, the family "tough guys," decided to knock down the cabin we had built in the woods. If *we* couldn't enjoy it, no one would! Armed with pickaxes from the toolshed, we set to work angrily. As the cabin fell to bits, so did our childhood.

Afterward we took a last walk along the banks of the Dordogne. . . . Here was where Jean-Claude had almost drowned. Fortunately Luis, a strong swimmer, had been there to rescue him. Over there was where a particularly sports-minded tutor, an Egyptian hired to teach us Arabic, had ordered us into the river for a quarter-mile swim after lunch one day. Someone told *Maman* and he was packed and gone by nightfall. One of many!

We continued on to the animal cemetery, where numerous dear friends lay. Then we wandered through the courtyard, the scene of memorable parties, including the wedding of one of our African servants. *Maman* had roasted whole pigs for the celebration. What a wonderful way to grow up! Jari, who knew his Bible, like all Protestants, explained that this must be how Adam and Eve had felt when they were banished from Paradise. . . . I kissed our little monkeys. I had helped raise them. When *Maman* had brought them back from South America they had been seasick all the way. (We later donated them to the Vincennes zoo and when I visited them there two years later they went wild in their cage. Julie and Makarios still remembered me!)

It was Marianne's idea to say goodbye to the trees. I'll never forget her standing there, arms tight around a scratchy trunk, in tears. How often we had scraped ourselves on their bark, broken their branches while climbing. They had given us gashes and falls in return, those rough playmates. Yet here we were, the four terrors of the "Baker clan," hugging our trees. . . .

We set up housekeeping on the Avenue Mac-Mahon off the Étoile in a two-room apartment rented by our faithful friend Marie Spiers. It was a bright, attractive place, but two rooms were quite a squeeze for twelve children plus Aunt Margaret, Uncle Elmo, *Maman* and assorted cats and dogs! Luckily Uncle Richard and his family had left Les Milandes long before.

Boarding school in Switzerland was out of the question now. We looked for schools in Paris, but the school year had already begun and it was difficult to find space. What did it matter? The important thing was to stick together, to rally around *Maman*. "It reminds me of those Vietnamese families they show on television sitting in front of their ruined homes," remarked *Maman*. "But it's not as serious for us. Houses aren't that important. It's what they stand for that counts. We'll build ours somewhere else." We each had our own idea of a possible site—including *Maman*. She still hoped to void the sale which had left us homeless. We heard constant talk about lawyers and the law. . . . Then one day the conversation changed to Monsieur Jean-Claude Brialy. "Who's that?" asked Stellina. "A movie star, silly," Jari explained. Soon afterward Monsieur Brialy visited the apartment. We liked him immensely. "I think he really wants to help," said *Maman*.

Jean-Claude Brialy: The moment entertainers strike it rich, they are bombarded with madcap schemes for investing their money. In my case this included possible ownership of a cabaret in the Opéra district called La Goulue. Ordinarily I wouldn't have given the offer a second thought. But my mind kept returning to Josephine Baker. I admired her tremendously, first as a born performer—a quality that appeals to hams like me —second as a unique, idealistic, extremely courageous woman. The fact that I barely knew her except on a hand-kissing "How do you do, madame?" "Good night, monsieur" basis was unimportant. I had followed the story of Les Milandes and knew that she had hit bottom. The word in show business circles was that Josephine was through. There had been too many "farewell" and "comeback" appearances designed to "save" Les Milandes. Now that she had lost the property, no theater would touch her. Yet for someone like Josephine, the stage was the only possible moral and financial solution. I arranged to meet with her to discuss a possible booking at La Goulue.

She was extremely skittish, which was not surprising considering the way she'd been tricked and cheated. Could she have time to think over my offer? she asked. It was clear that I didn't need the money; that I was beholden to no one for my success; that I owned a château; that I expected nothing from La Goulue; that my offer had no strings attached. She finally accepted. Opening night was scheduled for March 27, 1969.

"You'll never make a cent off Josephine Baker," I was warned. Paris is like that; quick to turn its back. Josephine had monopolized the limelight for too long. I approached a famous couturier about making her clothes. He refused. I tried another. No dice. It was the same with all the well-known names. A destitute Josephine was of no interest. I finally received a letter from a dressmaker named Jany Six stating that her seamstresses "were ready to work nights to offer Josephine a gown."

Josephine hadn't given up yet. "I'm going to nullify that scandalous sale," she insisted. "Les Milandes went for a song!" She would have to work fast; March 15 was approaching, the date when the eviction order went back into effect. On March 8 news reached Josephine in Paris that Les Milandes's new owner, profiting from her absence, had had a locksmith open the door of the château and was emptying out the building.

A frantic Josephine took the night train for the Dordogne, where, according to the newspapers, she climbed through her kitchen window, then barricaded the door after a brief scuffle with a man who had blocked

her way. The press went on to report that Les Milandes's new proprietor
had probably jumped the gun because of a legal action filed by an irate
creditor who felt cheated by the low price received for the domain. Since
it now seemed conceivable that the sale might be voided, the owner had
decided to strike while the iron was hot.

Josephine brought suit for illegal entry and refused to budge. Sunday
. . . Monday . . . Finally on Tuesday, when she opened the door to fetch
water, eight men pounced on her and dragged her outside.

France Soir filled in the details as follows in its March 12 edition:

[The assailants] were house-painters from Clermont-Ferrand. . . . Their employer
had promised them a one-hundred-franc bonus each if they managed to evict
Josephine. . . . Stationed near the site of the former monkey cage . . . a twenty-
year-old law student, the son of the new owner, directed the operation. . . . "The
law's on our side," he said coldly. . . . However, the public prosecutor of Bergerac
countered: "You have no right to carry out an eviction on your own." . . . The
youth's father . . . is legally responsible. He is subject to several counts: illegal
entry, assault and battery and duress, among others. The public prosecutor ruled
yesterday to reinstate Josephine on the premises. "You can return to your kitchen
now, Madame Baker," he said gently after she had spent more than seven hours
sitting on the steps in the rain. . . . A medical certificate notes "traces of
hematomas on the left forearm, marks on the arms and legs . . . impaired
breathing." Josephine Baker was taken to the Périgueux hospital last night.

Marie Spiers: On March 18 my husband Pierre telephoned me from
abroad. He was anxious for me to have Josephine moved from Périgueux
to a clinic on the outskirts of Paris. I was waiting at the Orangerie clinic
in Aubervilliers when the ambulance drew up. At the sight of Josephine
lying there ashen-faced behind her dark glasses, my heart sank. She appeared to be dying. The doctors ordered an electrocardiogram and a
transfusion. How could she possibly open at La Goulue in ten days?

As it turned out, Josephine left her sickbed in what seemed to be record
time, possibly due to her amazing instinct for survival. As soon as she
could speak, she dictated a message to be sent to all her friends, unknown
supporters as well as acquaintances. "Thank you for your letter, which
gave me great comfort in this time of trial and sadness. The hardest thing
for me to accept is that my fellow humans could hurt me this way. That
is why your letter means so much to me. My physical injuries will heal

with time, but my psychic and spiritual wounds go much deeper. It's always that way for those who really care and I've fought for human dignity all my life. Thank you for not forgetting the ideal of brotherhood, in which my children and I so profoundly believe." She had the letter printed, since it would have been impossible for a secretarial staff, could we have afforded one, to answer each message personally.

Ever since Josephine had fallen again on hard times, had tasted defeat and poverty, she had relied on my small dress shop. I had provided the street and theater clothes for her last few tours, a welcome change from the threadbare black fur coat the world's "most elegant woman" had been reduced to wearing. "But everyone knows that I'm broke," she insisted, "so who cares how I'm dressed in the daytime. What's important is to look dazzling when I perform." I can still see us poring over fashion magazines, working out designs. She knew just what became her, exactly how far she dared go. Nothing was too beautiful to wear on stage. I remember one white outfit edged with white mink. She wouldn't hear of artificial fur! Even my furrier looked astonished at such extravagance. I hasten to add, however, that although it took years, Josephine paid me back every cent.

"It's time to fit my dresses for La Goulue," Josephine announced from her sickbed on March 22. I thought she'd gone out of her mind and hastily phoned the doctor. "Returning to work is the best thing for her," he assured me. Before I knew it, she was surrounded with seamstresses, pins and gowns. It was the first time she had been out of bed since her hospitalization.

Five days later, right on schedule, Josephine was singing "J'ai Deux Amours" at La Goulue–Chez Joséphine before an elegant opening-night audience which included Anna Magnani and Françoise Sagan. She "changed the scenery," as she liked to say, by going from table to table, propelled by Jean-Claude Brialy. She had a word for everyone and the delighted audience remained until 5 A.M., celebrating Josephine's resurrection.

Things were also settling down on the Avenue Mac-Mahon. During the first desperate months, Margaret had been forced to come to my shop nightly and dip into the till for the next day's marketing money. But things looked much brighter now and Josephine often took time out to visit the shop, which was so cramped that when she curled up in the dressing room for a snooze, my astonished customers saw two bare feet protruding from under the curtains. A fifteen-minute nap was enough to revive her, a luxury it was hard to enjoy in the two rooms she shared with fourteen people, three dogs and two cats.

I was delighted to see her regain her love of life. She dressed almost exclusively in white now, in accordance with her mother's belief that after a certain point light colors are the most flattering. Combined with her new short-haired wigs and her perpetual sunglasses, the effect was devastating. "The only thing that concerns me is the way business is falling off at La Goulue," she confided. "The public is sick of Josephine. Poor Jean-Claude." She was more upset for him than for herself. What worried her most, of course, was Les Milandes. She still hoped to drive the abusive purchaser out and kept after her lawyers. But her efforts were in vain. On April 12 André Dirand, who had been managing Les Milandes for the past ten years, was evicted from Josephine's kitchen, where he and his German shepherd, Tintin, had been standing guard since Josephine's departure for the Périgueux hospital. The dream had ended. Les Milandes was through.

When the news reached Josephine, she picked up a note pad and began to write:

I prefer to remain silent for my children's sake, out of respect for my dream. But the truth will be known someday. In the meantime, patience. I'll show my strength and courage when the time is ripe. . . .

My beloved Les Milandes . . . I will never forget the first time I saw that sleepy little hamlet, covered with briers, without roads, electricity or water, tucked away in the hills, dreaming of the Middle Ages. My dear ones are buried there: my admirable mother . . . Pepito, who showed me the way, teaching me the few graces I know. He was my eyes, my wit, my ears. . . . It was here that I hoped to see my parents-in-law Bouillon end their days in peace. . . . It was here that my Rainbow Tribe got its start. I hope that in years to come my children will represent every point of view as well as all colors and religions, because that is where true freedom lies. My young ones haven't let me down. They are genuine brothers and sisters who deeply love one another. *The Rainbow Tribe has advanced us all a thousand years.* . . .

My head and heart are bursting with the need to spread happiness and joy. My ideal is so simple, yet so many people view it as a crazy dream.

Surely the day will come when color means nothing more than skin tone, when religion is seen uniquely as a way to speak one's soul; when birth places have the weight of a throw of the dice and all men are born free; when understanding breeds love and brotherhood.

I can't write my book just yet. I'll have to wait until my heart and soul and spirit are at peace. But time goes by so quickly and my life moves along at the same fast pace although my body, like everyone's, is slowing down. I can't do a tenth of what I should. . . .

Pierre Spiers: When I think of Josephine, three images stand out with special clarity:

—Josephine being greeted by a hundred or more black porters holding flowers as she stepped off a plane in New York.

—Josephine at a benefit performance at Carnegie Hall on October 14, 1963. Our baggage, containing all our scores, had been lost along the way. Jerry Mengo and I had had to reconstruct them at the last minute for full orchestra. To make things worse, Josephine liked to stop when the fancy struck her during the show and chat with her audience. Finally there hadn't been time to practice. You can imagine how nervous the musicians were. But thanks to Josephine's amazing showmanship, the performance went as calmly and smoothly as if it had been thoroughly rehearsed. The evening ended unforgettably. After the show, Duke Ellington's sister invited us to supper, where the Duke and Sammy Davis, Jr., played and sang for us. Josephine was moved to express her black heritage in a series of touching Negro spirituals. I look back on that evening as the most exciting and inspiring of my musical life. It gave me a true awareness of Josephine's real talent, so far removed from such show business bravura as the feather headdresses she carried off with her inimitable style. I recognized a real gift of music in her pure, melodious voice. . . .

—Josephine on tour in Holland. Martin Luther King had just been killed. His widow met with us to ask Josephine to assume leadership of the movement. Despite her impulsive nature, Josephine knew when it was best to look before she leaped. She and I discussed the offer for two days. The fact that King had been assassinated didn't frighten her. Her own beliefs subjected her to frequent menaces. I remember one time during a hospitalization for both a stroke and heart trouble, when she received an anonymous letter, mixed in with notes from well-wishers, saying that "plans were afoot to ensure her never leaving the hospital alive." When her doctor wanted to alert the police, Josephine assured him that it wasn't necessary, that she was used to threats, that one letter wouldn't keep her from getting the rest she badly needed in order to be back on stage the next week. It clearly wasn't fear of the possible danger involved in being Martin Luther King's successor that worried her; just the opposite. But I felt I must remind her of her responsibility toward her twelve adopted children. "You're right, Pierre, they're very young to lose their mother," and she declined the offer, carefully explaining why.

We were spending all our evenings at La Goulue–Chez Joséphine now. But times had changed since the days when earlier Chez Joséphines had packed them in. In the eyes of many, Josephine had become an elderly woman struggling for survival. Instead of making her bitter, this drove her to fight all the harder.

Jacqueline Cartier: On April 24, 1969, I visited La Goulue with my friend André Levasseur. He had the draft of a contract in his pocket. For several years now, André had been the official stage designer for the Société des Bains de Mer de Monte Carlo, whose yearly August benefit for the Monacan Red Cross, presided over by Princess Grace, was the event of the season. For 1969, Lavasseur was planning a ninety-minute full-scale revue. "Whom are you considering as the star?" the Princess asked Wilfred Groote, managing director of the Société. "Josephine Baker, Your Highness." The Princess, who had never seen Josephine perform, asked if she wasn't too old. André convinced her that on the contrary, only Josephine could carry off a show of this kind with real style. Jean-Claude Brialy, who had been let into the secret, would serve as master of ceremonies. André asked me to handle the promotion. . . . La Goulue was almost empty that night. I doubt that more than three tables were taken. But my feeling of gloom evaporated the moment Josephine stepped into the limelight. Superbly dressed and seemingly unmarked by the tragedy of Les Milandes, she performed with unequaled charm, as if the room were full.

After the show she joined us at our table, and André outlined the terms of the contract. "You mean it's for charity? For the Monacan Red Cross? In that case I can't possibly accept a fee." André explained that if the gala was a success, the revue would be given several showings before the general public. Therefore it was only fair that she should be paid. She finally agreed.

André had several meetings with Josephine on the Avenue Mac-Mahon in order to acquaint her with his plans and to work on the show. "I was very impressed with the dignified way they managed to live while confined to those two rooms. The children were neat and clean, the apartment immaculate. When I asked Josephine, dressed in a spotless white suit, if it wasn't too much for her, her answer was always the same. 'Don't worry, André. Can't you see how well we're doing? Everything's fine.' She never complained and I didn't dare to question her more closely. We limited our conversation to the revue. When I showed her the costume sketches, her eyes lit up like a child's. Out of gratitude for her support, the Société des Bains de Mer wanted her to keep what she wore in the show, I informed her. 'Oh, that's much, much too kind,' she murmured. We felt sure that owning the costumes would equip her to accept jobs elsewhere. If only we could help her get back in the saddle again! To me, Brialy and our friends, she was still la Baker, a unique, irreplaceable star.

"One evening I visited the Avenue Mac-Mahon for the last time, bringing the final costume sketches. Josephine's criticisms were extremely apt. She had an uncanny sense of the theater. We parted with the understanding that we would meet in Monte Carlo at the end of July to begin rehearsing. When I got home that night, I realized that I had forgotten to show her one of the sketches. When I rang her doorbell the next day, I was amazed to get no reply. A hasty consultation with the concierge produced the news that Madame Baker and the entire family had left that morning, bag and baggage; they were gone 'for good.' I was astonished and extremely worried. None of Josephine's friends knew where she had gone. As the days passed, I grew increasingly nervous. Princess Grace had put me in charge of the benefit. How could the show go on when its star had disappeared in a puff of smoke without so much as a word? After two long weeks I finally received a telegram: DEAR FRIEND SEE YOU AT FIRST REHEARSAL AS PLANNED YOUR JOSEPHINE. It had been sent from Barcelona."

André and I eventually learned what had happened. A few months earlier, a wealthy Spanish industrialist, Luis Rabajas, had decided to help Josephine by putting at her disposition a huge property in the resort town of Sitges on the Costa Brava. This revived her hopes for a College of Brotherhood. Rabajas had also offered her a ten-room villa where she could "come and relax" whenever she felt like it. Now that she was about to take a new and perhaps crucial step by performing in Monte Carlo, and at the same time plagued by a lack of funds with which to pay her rent in Paris, she had decided to hole up for a while.

But on July 25, right on schedule, she stepped off the train in Monaco with her twelve children, a dog and a parrot. The family were to be guests of the Société during their Monte Carlo stay. When she was asked if she preferred rooms at the Hôtel de Paris or the Hermitage, she replied: "How nice of you to give me a choice. I think the Hermitage would be best since you don't have to dress for dinner. That's more practical with the children."

Josephine threw herself into rehearsals with a stamina that eclipsed the rest of the dynamic cast. I was struck by the way she stretched out on the ground like a cat between numbers, her hands clasped behind her neck. She would then wiggle her feet and study them with total attention as if nothing else mattered. But at the words "You're on, Josephine," she'd be up on the stage in a flash. Rehearsals often lasted until two in the morning, even later toward the end. Afterward the entire cast would head for an all-night restaurant, the Tip-Top, where we laughed, relaxed and talked out last-minute ideas for the show while Josephine gobbled spaghetti. It would be daylight by the time we got to the Hermitage. "I sometimes wonder whether I don't enjoy rehearsals even more than shows," Josephine mused.

Josephine's gala appearance was preceded by a testimonial evening on August 5, featuring a showing of *Zouzou*. The film was lent by its producer, Nissotti, a Monacan by adoption, who could be seen daily, sunning himself on the beach near a tiny patch of earth on which he grew tomatoes. This delighted Josephine, who launched into one of her former hits: "Don't Touch Me Tomatoes!" What was she like to work with? I asked Nissotti after the showing. "Easygoing but stubborn. At one point she brought a stray puppy onto the set to play the part of a dog. 'It would be much simpler to hire a trained animal, Josephine!' I kept insisting. But she wouldn't listen. After twenty takes that mutt still refused to eat his chop like it said in the script. We tried everything—even sprinkling the meat with sugar." Josephine burst out laughing. "He looked like he needed the job! I named him Zouzou and he stayed with me until he died." I asked her if she had seen *Zouzou* again since filming it. "Not until tonight." "Don't you think you look beautiful?" "Beautiful? It's all a question of luck. I was born with good legs. As for the rest . . . beautiful, no. Amusing, yes." She returned to her hotel to exchange her evening gown for pants and see that the children got to bed. Then she returned to the Sporting Club for a lighting rehearsal. While André fiddled with the lights, we continued our conversation:

"Some people think that my troubles are over. I wish it were true. I still have to earn my keep. I may well return to Spain. They want three thousand francs a month for the little five-room apartment I've been considering renting in Paris. Think what I'd have to earn! Margaret is terribly discouraged. She wants to move to New York." The only glimmers of hope in an uncertain future were the revue, which would open in three days, and an eventual comeback in Paris. "I know I antagonized certain people by marching down the Champs-Élysées for de Gaulle in 1968," she confided. "Too bad. It's a pity that France, like the rest of the world, values money over allegiance." Talk turned to Les Milandes. "One day I'll bring the whole story out into the open. I'm going to write a book about what happened and let people judge for themselves." At dawn, as usual, we went out for spaghetti. . . .

A few hours later Josephine arrived at the shop of Madame Frieda, the dressmaker, for her fittings.

"Here's what your eighteen chorus girls will be wearing, Josephine," said André, pointing toward eighteen clumps of bananas. "And for you . . ." He fastened a band containing the feathers of five hundred royal pheasants about her waist. "And I'll really be able to keep these costumes, André?" "Absolutely. I told you the Société wants you to have them." Her eyes shone with the excitement of a little girl in front of a sparkling Christmas tree.

At last the long-awaited evening arrived. For once Finette, Josephine's miniature white poodle, was not allowed to mingle with the audience, which included Princess Grace, Maria Callas, David Niven, Gregory Peck and Ed Sullivan, seated at tables in the posh Sporting Club. The curtain rose, revealing a set done in various shades of pink and graced by chorus girls in feathers and diamonds. Jean-Claude Brialy walked onto the stage, thanked Their Highnesses and the public and introduced Josephine— who was nowhere in sight. Seemingly unperturbed, Brialy recalled the *Revue Nègre* of 1925, pointing out that Josephine had never missed an entrance in her entire career. Then, at the sound of a ship's siren, he launched into a description of the *Sirène des Tropiques*. Finally, after informing the crowd that he would do his best to fill in, Brialy was midway through a monologue when a voice called out from the back of the room: "Here I am! Here I am! I made it!" "You're late, Madame Josephine," Brialy said severely. "But the boat just docked," she replied. Although the stars of Sporting Club galas traditionally appear from the wings, Josephine, in white boots and a clinging white jump suit that accentuated her twenty-two-inch waist, hopped nimbly over the balustrade that stood at the rear of the hall and pushed her way toward the stage, jostling the diners as she waved her vanity case over their heads. "Sorry, but I keep all my scenery in here!"

The gala's audience is reputed to rank among the most disdainful in the world. Much of the crowd was prepared for an elderly has-been, marked by sorrow, and the impact of a stunningly youthful and beautiful Josephine bounding into the room as if fresh from the sea was like an explosion. The most world-weary spectators burst into applause and were still clapping when Josephine reappeared almost instantly, sumptuously costumed. I looked nervously down from my perch in the electricians' box, remembering last night's rehearsal. The wheeled staircase, which had arrived in the nick of time, had tipped forward with Josephine aboard. Only a stagehand's iron grip had prevented her from tumbling into space. Instead she had landed backward on her huge wheel of tail feathers, crying, "I'm like a stranded turtle! I can't get up alone with this on." "This" measured almost six feet across.

Dress rehearsal had been marked by another unpleasant surprise. When the ornamental torches were lit, they dripped resin all over the floor, transforming the stage into a skating rink. The corps de ballet toppled like matchsticks in the midst of their Russian number! It was necessary both to change torches and to have eighteen pairs of boots soled with rubber, requiring the services of shoemakers as far afield as Villefranche. Amid the general excitement, Josephine was the only one to maintain an "everything will be fine" attitude and an iron morale. When I passed her dressing room shortly before show time, she was praying.

The ninety-minute revue was punctuated by applause. "Not bad for a sixty-three-year-old, is it?" Josephine quipped between numbers. "But I watch what I eat." In her ten changes of costume, which were transparent in the proper places, she was every inch the dazzling la Baker, and at the end of the show the audience pelted her with roses from the floral centerpieces. . . . As far back as Monacans could remember, nothing like it had ever happened at the Sporting Club.

But to me, the most moving thing of all was the ovation Josephine received backstage from the crew and the remark I heard an old-timer make to a younger man: "Take a good look at that Josephine. You won't see her equal again!"

The revue was so successful that it not only played to full houses all week but was rebooked the following year. In August 1970 I joined Josephine and André in Monte Carlo. We met at the Café de Paris on the square because Josephine had insisted: "I don't look stylish enough for the Hôtel de Paris." She was wearing a bare-sleeved white linen outfit and a snug little wig. Her long nails were carefully varnished and her waist as slim as ever. "Not bad for sixty-four, is it?" she said in her familiar way, then ordered spaghetti bolognese and two bottles of beer. "Last year I felt terribly tired . . . no, I *mean* it! But this year I'm rarin' to go! I found this marvelous new song in Italy, André. We've *got* to add it to the show. And that means a new gown as well!" André explained that there were only five days left until show time and that Madame Fevrier, the feather dresser, was on holiday. Without Madame Fevrier, Josephine reluctantly agreed, nothing could be done. "But surely you'll agree that there's always room for improvement, André! Besides, styles change every year. I don't want to look outdated." André reassured her that her costumes had all been done over. With a sigh of relief, Josephine began humming her Gypsy song: "I'll give you happy endings and sell you a dream." "What about you, Josephine? Do *you* ever dream?" "Me? Never. I don't have the time."

A few months later I learned that Josephine was planning to found "a community of four hundred young people from around the world" on the island of Ventotene, off Ischia.

Jean-Claude Brialy: The Monte Carlo show had worldwide repercussions. Once again Josephine found herself swamped with offers. She was not only back in the saddle, as André and I had hoped; she was galloping forward.

Josephine found the atmosphere in Monaco so warm and supportive that she began to consider settling there. With Princess Grace as fairy godmother and the help of the Monacan Red Cross, she found a villa at Roquebrune, perched on the rocks. Her friends closed ranks around her, with Nissotti guaranteeing the bank loan. Josephine and her brood had found new shelter. Stellina now went to school with Princess Stephanie, who was the same age. In order to pay for the villa and raise her children, Josephine would have to continue working, but she was the first to admit that she couldn't imagine retiring. I was able to follow her travels around the world, thanks to her frequent letters. I had become her thirteenth and oldest child—in fact, I sometimes felt older than Josephine! Nothing better expresses her warm heart than the following fragments:

Dear Jean-Claude:

Since I last saw you I've been in Buenos Aires on a week-long work trip. I took Jari along. It did me the world of good, because although I am aware of my obligation to keep the children in school, I miss each and every one when we're apart. For example, three weeks ago I was in Tel Aviv, where I put Moses into a kibbutz. He'll be there for two years. I know it's the best thing for him, but it breaks my heart to have him so far away. I can't tell you how *sad* I am, Jean-Claude, to be separated from my son. Next year Akio and Janot will be going to Japan and I know that will make me suffer too. . . .

October 23, 1970

My dear Jean-Claude:

It seems like ages since I heard from you. . . . I'm just back from a three-week trip to Mexico. . . .

The older children are beginning to worry me. But I suppose that's normal at eighteen. . . . I imagine you'd agree. . . .

I'd like to take this opportunity to tell you once again how much I appreciate everything you've done for me: the cabaret, the Monte Carlo show . . . and to thank André too, sought after as he is by people with much greater talents than mine. . . .

Thank you too for all the meals you gave me. . . . Those peaceful evenings at your house were infinitely precious to me! You know how low my morale was then. . . . Love and kisses from Josephine and her Tribe, who love you very very much.

Oslo, November 11, 1972

Jean-Claude dear:

I was both delighted and deeply touched to hear your voice on the

phone yesterday. When I think that with all you have to do you took the
time to call! Thank you.

You mustn't get upset, because there is nothing to do at this point but
wait until the time comes to begin electroshock therapy for my heart. As
I've told you, I'm doing everything I can to get myself into the proper
shape by sticking to doctors' orders. The best thing is not to think about
it. We can't control our fate. All we can do is hope for the best. . . .

That was Josephine: generous, loving, sensible.

Marianne: I remember 1971 as the year we all went to Rome for an
audience with Pope Paul VI. *Maman* liked taking us places, but I was
frightened to death of her driving. One day on the coast road, for example,
she was driving so fast that a motorcycle policeman chased us to a stop.
"Oh," she exclaimed, with her most charming smile. "Did you want my
autograph? What's your first name?" He handed her his ticket book in
stunned surprise, she signed with a flourish and we were on our way.
. . . Another time, on a narrow inland road, we found ourselves nose to
nose with an enormous truck. *Maman* got out of the car and shouted at
the burly driver that it was up to him as a gentleman to back up. Just in
case, she told me to find a policeman. When I returned with the officer,
she was up in the cab, seated beside the trucker. They were exchanging
snapshots of their children and swigging wine out of a bottle. . . . Then
there was the day at the Étoile in Paris when *Maman* abandoned her car
in the midst of a traffic jam and handed her keys to a policeman.

Moses: Maman would always get up early to write. She began by
answering her mail. My most treasured letters from her are the ones I
received in the kibbutz, although it's only since her death that I've
realized their true worth.

My little Moses:

I hope you received my last letter, scolding you for your conduct. Your
behavior could seriously affect others. . . . You know perfectly well why
you were sent to Israel: to soak up your people's history and become a man
worthy of the name Moses.

Nevertheless, you're beginning to act exactly the same at the kibbutz
as you did at home. . . . You simply must understand, Moses, that you'll

be staying there for two years. And not as a tourist. You've got to work just as hard as the others. You've got to use some self-discipline. There's no use trying to pull your usual tricks, because no one will pay attention. You absolutely *must* show some of the brotherly spirit that I believe in so deeply.

Please try to settle down and do as I say!

All your brothers and sisters send a big hug and so does your mother, who loves you.

But since she was angry, the letter is signed "J. Baker."

Two weeks later I received the following:

Dear little Moses, my darling son:

Maman is simply thrilled with your last two letters. If you continue this way, *cheri*, everything will be fine. Try to start the new school year with good faith and determination. Perhaps I'll visit you at Christmas with Marianne if the Kibbutz permits it. All your brothers and sisters send you a delighted hug and lots of brotherly love.

And this time the signature read in her ample hand: "Your proud and loving mother."

Akio: On April 18, 1971, *Maman* was on tour in Argentina. I was asked to receive an important public-service award in her name. One fragment of my acceptance speech particularly pleased me: "Setbacks have not and will not shake her deep faith in Universal Brotherhood." The phrase almost spoke itself, because plans for a College of Brotherhood had gained new momentum thanks to Maguy Chauvin. The proposed site for the campus was now Yugoslavia.

In October we received a telegram from a Professor Livakovic saying that *Maman*'s proposal had been adopted unanimously by the Šibenik town council and would be the subject of a special meeting in Zagreb the following week.

As the oldest child and the one who had been most closely involved with Les Milandes's tragic end, I begged *Maman* to take every precaution. She assured me she would. The Josephine Baker Foundation, with headquarters in Geneva, possessed all the necessary guarantees. We bombarded *Maman* with questions:

"Where will the Citadel be built?"

"On an island."

"Is there electricity in the area?"

"No. It reminds me of Les Milandes when I first arrived. But the Yugoslav government plans to bring in power and a Dutch friend has offered to do the installation free."

"Will we have a park like at Les Milandes?"

"An even bigger one, *cheri*. I'm hoping to call in a famous Japanese landscaper. And we'll contact the finest nurseries all over the world."

"What will the campus look like, *Maman?*"

"Perhaps a cross between Signor Fedrigolli's plans and those of a Danish architect, Anna-Marie Bremer, whose work I like. I thought we could stage an international competition for a statue to be placed in front of the Citadel."

"A big one, like the Statue of Liberty?"

"Hardly, *cheri*. Šibenik isn't New York. And I want it to glorify youth."

"How will people get to the island?"

"I absolutely *must* get in touch with a shipowner."

"Onassis?"

"Why not? He's in Monte Carlo often enough. What I'll do is charter a boat to carry students and visitors back and forth between Šibenik and the Citadel."

"What will you name the boat?"

"How about *Brotherhood?*"

"That might sound ugly in Yugoslav. An international name would be better."

"What about *Josephine?* That's international," Moses, Brahim and Marianne shouted.

We all burst out laughing. *Maman* had never looked younger. She told us that the authorities in Šibenik had already promised to install telephone service, build roads, provide water and drainage facilities . . . that she had already requested a ninety-nine-year lease, to be on the safe side . . . that our house would be located at the end of the property, and that all incoming money from any book she might write or any musical comedy or film about her life would go to the Citadel.

"What about Roquebrune, *Maman?*"

"We'll sell it."

But Monsieur Nissotti would hear none of it.

"You can't put Roquebrune on the market, Josephine. It's not fully paid for yet. As guarantor I'll never permit you to mortgage it."

Maman fell silent. But as soon as we were alone again, she resumed her discussion of plans and arrangements.

"There will be a museum, sculpture, paintings. . . . But the most important, of course, will be the college itself, where people will learn to live together in true brotherhood."

And we began to dream of paradise again.

A doodle from Denmark (collection of the author)

CHAPTER 20

Triumph

Jo Méhu (showman): For more than thirty years, Lucien Bertaux was Josephine's costume designer. I particularly remember the models he created for the show I staged at New York's Roxy Theater in 1951, a superproduction featuring white columns, draped red velvet, props made of genuine silver, crystal chandeliers, a mock-up of the Place de la Concorde and a finale in which Josephine appeared in a cloak made of sixty-six feet of satin and trimmed with fifty-five pounds of pink fox. Her jeweled headdress was equally sumptuous, causing Bertaux to comment: "Only two women in the world could carry that thing off: Josephine and Cleopatra." When Josephine telephoned Lucien from Stockholm in November 1971 and consistently got no reply, she alerted mutual friends. After several unsuccessful attempts of their own, they notified Bertaux's concierge, who found him dead. Josephine immediately asked me to pay Bertaux's widow money due on a model, adding: "Time's flying by for us all. Only talent is permanent."

We missed Bertaux terribly as we prepared for Josephine's four special appearances at Carnegie Hall. The revue, scheduled to open on June 5, 1973, was billed as a jubilee—commemorating Josephine's fifty years as an entertainer. Two days before show time, the black producer Jack

Jordan gave her a sixty-seventh-birthday party, complete with a huge cake, at the Terrace Room of the Hotel Plaza. One young reporter asked Josephine to take off her tinted glasses. "Can't you wait until after the show?" she retorted. When another journalist asked what she fed her twelve children in her Monacan villa, she replied, "I step out into the forest, catch a few monkeys, skin them and cook them up!" Despite her flippancy, Josephine was well aware of the importance of her New York appearance. When the curtain rose on opening night, revealing a portly matron, some of the spectators must have thought it was Josephine. In fact, the performer was seventy-eight-year-old Bricktop, named at sixteen for her flaming hair. By 1924 she had conquered Paris and gone on to share the late twenties with Josephine.

Bricktop recalled old times at Bricktop's Club in Montmartre, then introduced a slender, radiant Josephine, wearing a flesh-colored body stocking sprinkled with diamonds. "Not bad for my sixty-seventh birthday, is it?" quipped the star, then, patting the amazing ostrich-feather construction she wore on her head, continued: "And I've brought my own Eiffel Tower." The crowd went wild. Josephine received nineteen curtain calls and was begged to encore every song from "I'm Just Wild About Harry," which dated back to the days of *Shuffle Along*, to "Hello Dolly." The management was finally forced to call in the fire department to restrain the mob so that Josephine could leave the theater without being crushed by her fans. La Baker was front-page news the next day. "She looked terrific for a thirty-five-year-old," observed the *Daily News*.

After her Carnegie Hall appearances Josephine requested booking at Harlem's Victoria Theater, where few of the twenty-five hundred spectators had seen her before in the flesh. A legend now, she utilized each of her triumphs to publicize the College of Brotherhood, discuss her recent visit with Marshal Tito, report on the island the Yugoslav leader had put at her disposition, and promote the Josephine Baker Foundation. "I'm terribly happy," she confided. "New York's at my feet again." She would now devote all her strength to winning back Paris.

Mara: By the time I was fourteen, I was the only boy in the family who hadn't visited his homeland. Now that Janot and Akio had returned from Japan and Moses was back from Israel, *Maman* decided to take me to Venezuela, which I had left in her arms at the age of two months. During the plane trip, we had a serious talk. I would be seeing my family, *Maman* explained. "If you decide you want to stay with them, *cheri*, believe me, I'll understand." La Chinita airport was mobbed. *Maman* asked me to go down the stairway first, and as I slowly descended the steps, the crowd burst into shouts. I suddenly found myself hemmed in, engulfed. "It's your father; it's your father," cried *Maman*, as a tall man in a poncho smothered me in his arms. I was swept up by a swarm of people, all of whom seemed to be cousins. They gave me a special drink to celebrate my welcome, while some of the crowd sang and others danced the chicha right on the runway, to the beating of drums. I was stunned but delighted. It was true, then; I was a real Indian *guajiro*. I could tell from the faces around me. I had their features, the same black hair. . . . There were journalists too, of course, waving their microphones. I could speak French, English, Italian and a little Spanish, but I didn't know the *guajiro* dialect.

We must have met almost every person of note in Caracas during our whirlwind stay, including the President of the Republic, Dr. Caldera, whom we called upon in his palace. When *Maman* wasn't acting as an ambassador for UNICEF, she was promoting her prospective College of Brotherhood in Yugoslavia or discussing the twelve members of her Rainbow Tribe. Then of course there were *Maman's* gala stage performances. . . . Wherever we went, we were followed by a flock of my tribal brothers.

Our visit ended all too soon. "What have you decided to do, *cheri?*" *Maman* asked softly. "Do you want to remain with your people?" I looked her square in the eye. "When you brought me to France I was sick, wasn't I? I vaguely remember my nurse Hélène quoting the doctor as saying I wouldn't have survived in the jungle. It's thanks to you I'm alive. Why would I want to leave you?" *Maman* gave me a big hug. At times she was strong as a man. Before boarding the plane, I told an inquisitive journalist that after studying medicine in France, I planned to return to Venezuela and serve my people. Then I bade my many relatives goodbye. In spite of their obvious poverty, I couldn't help being shocked at the way they kept badgering *Maman* for more and more money. "You really can't blame them, Mara," she explained. "They're desperate. The Indian people were once proud and wealthy. Those we should resent are the people who reduced them to their present state of degradation. . . . The world is motivated by self-interest; that's why our family's actions today and the way you children behave after I'm gone is so important. The dream that brought you together must never die."

"After I'm gone . . ." When people are there at your side, especially if they're as lively as *Maman*, it's hard to believe that it isn't forever. But I was suddenly faced with the painful truth one day in July 1973 when *Maman* didn't return to the Copenhagen hotel room where Brahim, Koffi, Noël and I were waiting. Friends arrived instead with some sort of flimsy story. We not only didn't believe them, but Brahim, the oldest among us, shouted, "Let's try the hospital." Sure enough, *Maman* was there. She had suffered a heart attack and didn't know us! Acquaintances took us in hand. I remember asking to stop at the first church we saw after leaving the hospital. "Brahim and Koffi too?" asked our astonished friends, knowing Brahim was a Muslim and Koffi a fetish-worshipper. They obviously didn't understand *Maman*'s dream! Yet to us it all seemed so simple.

Eight days later, *Maman* was back on her feet, and within a month she was in Israel, attending that nation's twenty-fifth birthday celebration. People had come from all over the world for the occasion. Nureyev danced, Leonard Bernstein conducted, Pablo Casals and Isaac Stern played and *Maman* sang. The festivities were held outdoors in old Jerusalem. A photograph arrived at Roquebrune showing *Maman* and Golda Meir falling into each other's arms. An attached note in *Maman*'s familiar scrawl read: "Never forget for a minute that *she's* the star."

Maman loved to write. "It's the best way to speak your soul—if you have one," she used to say. When she learned that Ted Kennedy, Jr., had lost a leg she was deeply upset. "We've got to send him a letter," she insisted, "wishing him courage." The next day, December 16, 1973, the note was ready to mail. Tears came to my eyes as I read it. *Maman* had explained to young Ted that his leg had been taken from him because it had become so weak and useless it could no longer run like its mate . . . that such separations are always cruel but that many of us are forced to sacrifice one or more parts of our bodies, or worse, part of our family . . . that she and her Rainbow Tribe greatly admired his bravery.

Jari: I followed *Maman*'s comings and goings around the world through the frequent letters she wrote to my boarding school in Montreux. She had to keep working in order to pay off her debts. Each of her letters began by expressing her sadness at being away from her family, then went on to outline her latest plans: she wanted to raise the roof of our villa and make the house more comfortable by creating several small apartments. The top floor would be transformed into a cabaret so that she could do most of her performing at home. "Any volunteers to run the restaurant-cabaret are welcome," she informed us.

On her return to Roquebrune, *Maman* wrote me that "even Marianne would be better off with *Papa;* you are at an age when a father's supervision is not only advisable but indispensable." She worried about us constantly: "But I know in my heart and soul that I've done the best job I could," she insisted. "The rest is in the hands of fate." In a subsequent letter she said it appeared that only Noël and Stellina would continue living at home. Although this grieved her, she went on, surely it happened to all parents in time. After all, what could be more natural than to want to live your own life? "We older people felt exactly the same way once. We've simply forgotten." Her next letter, while expressing concern for her Tribe, bubbled over with excitement about a new turn in her professional life. André Levasseur had asked her to star in another Monte Carlo Red Cross gala. This time the show would be billed as *Josephine's Story.* "Just what I've dreamed of for years. And Jean-Claude Brialy will be my partner. What could be better?"

André Levasseur: We were all tremendously excited about the show as rehearsals began. Josephine seemed younger than ever. "If we're a hit in Monte Carlo, maybe we'll make it to Paris," she reflected. That was her secret dream. She was burning to win back the city she adored but which had spurned her ever since she had sided with the powers that be by marching down the Champs-Élysées in June 1968. Still, as things had turned out, the regime was still very much alive and so was she! But Josephine's critics wasted no time. Although she had been a sensation at the 1969 Sporting Club gala, that had been *five years* earlier, they snapped. Besides, another barbed tongue informed me, "After a certain point every year counts twice." All I could do was shrug. At sixty-eight, Josephine was more dynamic than our youngest dancer. The chorus line watched her open-mouthed and by the end of the third rehearsal adored her. Jean Moussy, whom I had asked to choreograph the show, had wondered what he could possibly do with a sixty-eight-year-old woman, but he didn't worry for long. Inspired by Josephine's presence, the show had an extraordinary warmth from the start, an even more intimate ambience than that of the 1969 gala. Were we all subconsciously thinking that this was our last chance; that we'd have to win now or never? "Never . . ." What a frightful word! Looking at Josephine brought different words to mind: "again" . . . "always." She seemed more indestructible every day!

This time we knew we had the full support of Princess Grace. She was not only convinced of Josephine's talent, but now that Josephine lived in Monaco had approvingly watched her raise her Tribe and fight for her ideals. And the Princess had another reason for backing Josephine. That July had marked the inauguration of a new Sporting Club. To ensure its success, the Société des Bains de Mer had booked Sammy Davis, Jr., for the gala opening. Sammy's acceptance had had several strings attached, including the services of a yacht during his stay. He had also proved to be extremely unpredictable. His last display of temperament had occurred the night of the show. As the moment approached for him to step onto the stage before an audience so full of titles they could not be tallied for sure, it was learned that Sammy had left—on the yacht! Josephine, swathed in a handsome diaphanous feather-trimmed coat, had risen from her seat and saved the evening by offering to sing. The Princess was extremely grateful.

As rehearsals continued, Josephine bloomed in the congenial and cheerful atmosphere backstage. She was highly amused by this musical history of her life, narrated by Brialy. I had reservations, however, about the rapidity of the costume changes. "Aren't we rushing you, Josephine? Wouldn't you like more time between numbers?" "No, no, no! The show has to keep moving. Like this!" And she beat out the measure with her fist, gradually increasing the tempo. . . .

There were many familiar faces in the audience that turned out for the Red Cross gala on August 8, 1974. But this time the stakes were much higher than simply pleasing the glittering crowd. Among the spectators sat Jean Bodson, managing director of the Bobino Theater. The success of tonight's performance would determine whether or not the show went to Paris. At curtain time, the atmosphere was electric, both backstage and in the hall. During the prologue, Josephine was drawn onto the immense stage of the Sporting Club in a carriage, magnificently dressed in 255 yards of tulle embroidered with mother-of-pearl and studded with camellias. As she drew up before a set depicting the Hôtel de Paris de Monte Carlo, where forty-six dancers in dress clothes, cast as headwaiters and beaux, stood waiting, I sensed that the evening was ours. Jean-Claude had prepared an opening text which touched us all deeply: "I know I should address you as *vous* out of admiration, but I'm going to say *tu* because I love you. . . . Thank you for being here, Josephine. Thank you for all that you are. . . . You have been called the Black Pearl, the Ebony Venus, the Panther . . . pick the name you like best. You have been wife and mother, a unique personality fashioned from dreams. Thank you, Josephine, for your spontaneity, your intuition, your courage, your tact, your tenderness, your sense of beauty, your respect for the public and your passionate devotion to peace and liberty everywhere. You are a constant surprise, touched with magic yet deeply human. You are a legend, but the most moving tale of all is your own life story. Fifty years ago your star rose in the Paris sky. It sparkles here tonight in Monte Carlo's blue heavens. . . ." The applause was deafening. When the show ended an hour later, the stage was strewn with flowers. Josephine, moved to tears, whispered: "This time it's Paris for sure, André!" The next day headlines in *Nice-Matin* announced: A MILESTONE IN THE HISTORY OF MUSIC HALL.

It wasn't that simple, though. Apart from Bodson, no one in Paris believed in Josephine, and we felt that the Bobino was too small to house our lavish show. Fortunately Bodson agreed to act as co-producer if we could find larger quarters. We immediately thought of the Champs-Élysées Theater, where Josephine had made her first Parisian appearance, but it was booked solid. The Casino de Paris, which she had graced so often, would have been ideal. But Monsieur Varna was no longer there. Still, Roland Petit, the new director, gave us reason to hope. In the meantime, Josephine had to go back on tour. She sent us rave reviews of her engagement at the London Palladium, but when I showed them around Paris I was met with: "Yes, but the English love old-timers." Was it possible that one of Josephine's two loves, Paris, could forsake her this way? It seemed unbelievable. While Jean-Claude and I waited for Petit's decision, Josephine wrote to us from Stockholm, from Tel Aviv. . . .

Dear Jean-Claude:

I've been expecting word from you and André for days concerning possible new developments. I can't tell you how impatient I am. . . . I'll be in Stockholm until September 12, in Valence on the 13th, 14th and 15th, and home on the 16th. . . .

Jean-Claude Brialy: Letters such as this prove the strain she was under.

She also asked me to enroll Mara and Brahim in a Jesuit school in Paris, since she seemed certain she'd be working in the capital. That way they could prepare for their studies in medicine and journalism. Unfortunately, after much deliberation Roland Petit turned us down. Surprisingly, Josephine was the one who comforted *me:* "Of course you're disappointed after all the effort you made to find a producer in Paris. But you mustn't take it too hard. Don't forget, we can't control destiny." Her favorite phrase. And to prove that all was well, she gave me a rundown on the latest news of the children:

"You certainly can congratulate yourself on the good influence you've been on the Tribe, Jean-Claude. *My* Jean-Claude has decided to go back to school and pass his baccalaureate. Then he'll go on and study film-making. It means private lessons, but the expenditure seems worthwhile since it's for his future good. Akio and Luis have left home and moved into a studio apartment. Mara and Brahim are studying hard. Jari is still at hotel school in Switzerland. Janot and Koffi are working. Noël is at Saint-Nicholas. Stellina is in London, which should do her a world of good, and Marianne is about to begin secretarial school. . . . What a threesome you and André and I make! But we really ought to share our trials and worries. May I visit you in Paris? I'll only take two or three hours of your time. And while I'm in town I'll get a checkup from my doctor."

It was October now. We were trying to work out a deal with the Mogador Theater. Its management "simply adored Josephine Baker," but Josephine was forced to leave for Johannesburg, Durban and Cape Town before anything was signed. And in fact it never was. The Mogador wouldn't risk a penny on Josephine. Once again Bodson offered the Bobino. At the same time Josephine wrote me a despondent letter from Tel Aviv: "Moses has just informed me that he plans to marry a chambermaid at the hotel where he is waiting on table. What a terrible mistake to marry at nineteen, knowing nothing of life! Would you have time to drop a firm note to Mara? It seems he is skipping classes in favor of soccer. And Marianne has left secretarial school. . . ."

Moses was married on December 14. His mother was not present. On Christmas Day, Josephine wrote informing me of various offers she had received from America proposing to film her life. "We've been negotiating for over a year, but there's a lot of blah-blah involved!" She was still suspicious about the loss of Les Milandes and asked one of our lawyer friends to provide her with accounts of sums received in her name at sale time—money she had never seen. It was time to clear up this matter. In early February she wrote to me from Italy. She was busy working on the new songs for the show but concerned about Akio, who had left for Argentina to join his father. As usual, she was preoccupied with her dual responsibilities as entertainer and mother.

André had now completed adapting *Josephine's Story* for the Bobino stage. Since there was obviously not enough performing space for our forty-six dancers and two full orchestras, he compromised on twenty-nine dancers, ten live musicians and Pierre Spiers. The rest of the orchestration would be dubbed. He also shortened the show's name to *Josephine,* and instead of delivering a running narrative, I would simply introduce the first few performances. Ironing out the final contracts involved several painful meetings during which Josephine, in a slim, severely tailored suit, impassive behind her dark glasses, sat listening while lawyers representing the various opposing interests haggled as if she weren't there. The problem was how to cover the show against possible illness on the part of its star. Josephine's age and delicate health were openly discussed. Not a single insurance company was willing to take the risk.

As we were leaving one of those humiliating sessions, I remember trying to play down its ugliness. "Don't worry, Jean-Claude," Josephine murmured. "I knew it would be this way. But I've been thinking. It seems to me that André, you and I should start our own company. After all, I won't be performing forever. But I could still be useful in the management end. *If* our Bobino show is a success, of course. Everything depends on that. . . . You'd serve as chairman and general manager and André would act as producer. We could create the kind of revues and musical comedies that Paris loves. After all, Parisians have the best taste in the world, don't they? And everything André does is marvelous. We'll give Paris back the prestige it's lost in this era of blue jeans and permissiveness. . . . I'm also hoping one of the film deals will come through. That should pay for a country place or a little town house that I could turn into a museum bearing my name. That way I wouldn't be completely forgotten. If all goes well, I'll stay at the Bobino another three months, then I simply *must* spend six months in England and six more in the States. What I can earn in those twelve months abroad would take years of effort in

France. The managers of the London Palladium and New York's Palace Theater will be there opening night. I *must* finish up my career with enough money to guarantee my future."

The conversation turned to Josephine's various projects: her records, her book, the film, a possible musical comedy. No, the insurance companies' position hadn't upset her too deeply, she assured me. ("You have to put yourself in their place. After all, I'll be sixty-nine in four months." In fact, although her checkup had been satisfactory, Dr. Thiroloix had prescribed a treatment for her heart.) What *had* wounded her deeply, however, was the disdainful attitude of the various Parisian theaters. When we arrived at the Bobino, which was redecorating its façade for the show, she shook her head. "Let's face it, Jean-Claude. I'm returning to Paris through the back door." "How can you say that, Josephine? The minute you walk in, it will become the main entrance."

Marie Spiers: As rehearsals continued, Josephine seemed to smell success. Her doubts slowly vanished. At first she lived with me and I frequently accompanied her to the theater. I also recall some wonderful evenings we spent alone at my piano while Josephine went over her songs. The show was now an hour longer than in the Monte Carlo version. It included a trio of comics whom Josephine liked immensely. She was also very fond of the troupe of dancers and I dreaded the moment when she would issue them a blanket supper invitation with her usual generosity. To forestall this, Jean-Claude Brialy alerted the restaurants around the Bobino. Otherwise Josephine would have squandered all her earnings on others before the first curtain had risen. . . . As opening night approached, Josephine seemed more vigorous than ever. In addition to her rehearsal schedule, there were recording sessions and fittings to attend. She still found the energy after supper to visit cabarets. Mixing with others stimulated her. Her mornings were spent with real estate agents, looking at houses that could also serve as museums. She wanted to move back to Le Vésinet, and I had difficulty persuading her that if she was performing in the middle of Paris and living in the suburbs she would lose a great deal of time on the road. I finally found her an apartment on the Avenue Paul Doumer, near mine. It was spacious enough to house the children— though it seemed unlikely that they would all return at once. But she refused to listen to reason. Finally I said, "You're going to hurt my concierge terribly, Josephine." She looked at me, aghast. "Why?" "Because she spent tremendous time and effort combing the neighborhood for me. She was so proud to have come up with something just a few buildings from here! Oh, well, forget I mentioned it." Later that morning, as we passed the concierge's loge, I noticed Josephine glancing inside. Within an hour she had telephoned my shop. "Have you signed for the apartment yet?" "Of course not, Josephine. You said . . ." "What are you waiting for? Do you want someone else to snap it up?" Fortunately she loved the place on sight. "It's true. It's big enough for everyone." But the little back chamber bothered her. "I don't like that room, Marie." "It's the quietest place in the apartment. Perfect for sleeping." "Maybe so. But it smells of death."

Jacqueline Cartier: Seventy-two hours before J Day, passers-by gathered at the doors of the Bobino, attracted by the frenzied music inside. Rehearsals were in full swing all over the theater. Dancers were practicing tap steps in the corridor. A children's chorus was swaying to the strains of a Louisiana melody. In the foyer, upholsterers were transforming the somber blue walls into a vivid red, while workmen inserted thousands of little reflecting glasses into columns and outlined the balconies with mirrors. Mastermind André Levasseur's worktable, covered with models, dominated the stage. His technical staff was grouped around him. "Come with me. I've got all sorts of things to show you," Josephine cried, pulling me into the wings. "They're laying carpets everywhere to keep our four hundred costumes spotless, especially the all-white outfits and the gowns with feathered trains." The Bobino had been completely made over for Josephine's appearance. An entire corridor had been transformed into extra dressing rooms and what had once been a huge closet was now a rose-colored makeup room. Josephine pulled me onward past two hundred pairs of dancing shoes and a row of feathered headdresses three feet high. Two dressing rooms had been converted into a tiny suite for Josephine, complete with a day bed, which of course she never used.

Josephine was in rehearsal clothes: pants and a sweater. Her figure was pencil slim, her voice like bronze. "I feel fine. Marvelous. Although I recently heard one of the troupe grumble: 'Everyone knows she was born in 1871 and is really a hundred and four!' " She had been rehearsing since ten that morning and it was now eight at night. Rehearsals would continue until midnight. To cut down on travel time, André, Josephine and the Bobino's young director, Jean-Claude Dauzonne, had booked rooms at the nearby Sheraton Hotel. "Do you know how long I've known Dauzonne, Jacqueline?" Josephine asked with a smile. "Since he was a child. Gabriel Bouillon was a friend of his father's and once took us to visit the family house in Enghien. Jean-Claude was three then, with the same incredible green eyes he has today. And here he is my director. He's changed a lot more than I have."

The stage manager walked by pushing two baby carriages, and a jeep was rolled onto the stage, from which Josephine would sing some of her prewar songs in uniform. "We absolutely *must* have some cane-shaped barley sugar," she exclaimed. "Do you know what I mean, André? To distribute to the crowd when I sing my sugar cane number. They'll love it." The famous hairdresser Alexandre swept in, followed by an assistant carrying a three-foot-high wig as if it were a gigantic wedding cake. It would be worn with one of the four costumes Josephine would appear in during the nine-minute finale. "Why don't you lie down a minute, Josephine?" André suggested. "We have a few dance numbers to run through." "No. I can only relax on stage or in the audience." She flopped down into a seat next to mine. In a minute or two I felt a sudden weight on my shoulder. It was Josephine's head. She had dropped off to sleep like a child.

"But she *is* a child," remarked Brialy. "Resilient, enthusiastic, playful . . ."

Forty-eight hours before J Day, Josephine slipped a note into Brialy's pocket: "Always remember the faces some people made at the thought of my comeback! Always remember the glimmer of hope in the eyes of those who wished me success and the frowns of those who hoped for my downfall! You've been at my side all the way, with a smile on your face and a kind word to say. I know you're afraid for me. But I'm no longer frightened. It's all in the hands of fate. Will it be heads or tails?"

It was heads.

The first performance of *Josephine* was held for the readers of *France Soir.* A down-to-earth, simple audience. They gave her a standing ovation. The date was March 24, 1975.

But Josephine was not convinced. In her usual wary way, she asked

Marie and Pepito Abatino's niece Lélia, who had come from Sicily to stay, to station themselves at the theater exit and study the crowd's reaction. They returned to report that the only adjectives they had heard were "Fantastic!" "Incredible!" "Marvelous!" . . . "Your readers are very kind," Josephine told me. "But I can't help thinking that the show could be even better." As usual, she was her own severest critic. Perhaps the dance contest she held with the audience dragged out the evening. André agreed. "And what's more," she added, "it burns up a lot of my energy without adding much. We've got to be flexible. Let's cut the whole sequence."

The next evening the theater was filled to the bursting point. And the applause at the final curtain was louder and longer than ever. There wasn't a single free seat in the crowd; the Bobino made a policy of launching its shows before a paying audience. The critics would be invited to the April 2 performance and a gala was scheduled for April 8. But within twenty-four hours of the first show, all Paris knew that *Josephine* was a hit. "I've never seen anything like it, and I doubt I will again," commented Brialy. A whole new generation was discovering the fabulous star. To other spectators, teary-eyed with nostalgia, Josephine recalled their youth, and seeing her there, lively, vibrant and happy, gave them a new lease on life. At the end of every performance the crowd rose to its feet, shouting, *"Merci, Joséphine!"* and the theater remained lit for an hour after the show since the backstage area was too cramped to accommodate the crowd of people who were forced to wait for their Josephine outside. . . .

We celebrated Easter in high spirits. Josephine received a group letter from the children. Luis had got married while Josephine was opening at the Bobino, but the fact that she couldn't attend the ceremony was unimportant. What counted was that everyone was happy and each child contributed an affectionate word: Mara, Marianne, Koffi . . . everyone except Akio, who was far away. On April 2 the critics confirmed *Josephine's* success. After the show, Brialy invited the entire cast to supper at his stylish restaurant, L'Orangerie, on the Île Saint-Louis. That Sunday evening, April 6, Guy-Louis Duboucheron, a mutual friend, gave his weekly party in his beautiful apartment on the Place Vendôme for Josephine and the Bobino cast. Josephine adored Duboucheron. "With all those jewels he wears, he looks like a Renaissance prince," she remarked. Josephine, radiant in a white jump suit, was in particularly high spirits that night in spite of having given a matinee and evening show. She laughed, ate with her usual gusto and did the samba to a record fresh from the Rio carnival. It was 4 A.M. when she finally danced her way to the elevator.

By Tuesday, the night of the much-awaited gala, the show was already booked solid for a month, and London and New York had submitted offers. "Next Monday, when this gala business is over, let's get together with our lawyers," Josephine suggested to André and Jean-Claude. She itched to move ahead, to found her company, settle her contracts and begin a new life as quickly as possible. "At my age, there's no time to lose."

Jean-Claude had been alerted that a telegram might arrive from the Élysée Palace. Indeed, when he entered Josephine's dressing room on the evening of April 8, the wire lay on the dressing table beside a pile of other messages and a good-luck rabbit's foot. Josephine didn't dare to open the envelope and handed it to Brialy. "All in the proper time and place, Josephine," he remarked.

The Bobino gala was even more emotional than the one in Monte Carlo. The little theater radiated warmth and the air rang with applause. A smiling Josephine sang:

> Good evening, Paris,
> It's been simply ages;
> Do I look too outrageous?

"You look fantastic! Marvelous!" the audience shouted.

> Older perhaps,
> But that doesn't mean
> That I'm leaving the scene.

Each of her numbers brought renewed applause as she sang on and on in a voice that ranged from resonant to velvety to the merest whisper:

> When I first sang "J'ai Deux Amours"
> I meant a love that lasts *toujours*.

I tried to analyze her charm. It came from within. Suppose another performer could match the way she modulated her voice, moved, wore a motorcycle outfit or simple raincoat with the same flair as a spangled sheath; suppose another had her natural gifts . . . elegant hands, a supple body. Josephine would always have her soul besides.

At the end of the show, Jean-Claude Brialy read the telegram from the Élysée:

IN TRIBUTE TO YOUR LIMITLESS TALENT AND IN THE NAME OF A GRATEFUL FRANCE WHOSE HEART HAS SO OFTEN BEATEN WITH YOURS, I SEND YOU FOND WISHES, DEAR JOSEPHINE, ON THIS GOLDEN ANNIVERSARY PARIS IS CELEBRATING WITH YOU. GISCARD D'ESTAING.

The audience burst into roars, tears and laughter, beside itself with emotion. In spite of the dazzling stars and celebrities that filled the hall, all eyes were fixed on Josephine. She had won Paris back with a vengeance!

The theater exit was mobbed with bystanders craning their necks to catch a glimpse of Sophia Loren, Alain Delon, Jeanne Moreau, Princess Grace . . . and finally Josephine herself. She was wearing a lacy gown which managed to be both modest and revealing and a turban frothy with veiling. In spite of the Princess's presence, it was Josephine who received the royal welcome.

The festive crowd moved on to the elegant Hotel Bristol, where Jean Bodson was giving a supper for three hundred people. Anxiously I searched Josephine's face for traces of fatigue. But she looked fresh and happy between her two faithful escorts, Levasseur and Brialy, who had never ceased to believe in her. An enormous cake was brought in, marking this fiftieth anniversary: 1925–1975. As she stood there hand in hand with Princess Grace, I couldn't help wondering at the strange ways of destiny. Perhaps the friendship of these two Americans symbolized the coming of a better world. . . . It was four in the morning when Josephine said her goodbyes, walking from table to table with a word for everyone. Where were the cynics now who had predicted that she would never be able to walk down a ramp again?

After the next night's performance she still showed no signs of exhaustion. I joined her in her dressing room while she pulled off her wig and combed out her sparse hair, grimacing with pain. "You can't imagine how that hurts, but I have to get rid of the kinks in order to tease it properly. Otherwise these huge things don't stay in place." "These huge things" were jeweled wigs holding towering sprays of feathers. Josephine's dresser sponged off her streaming body with eau de cologne. Once Josephine had stopped pulling at her scalp, her face grew drawn. She studied herself mercilessly in the mirror. She had never had a face lift. ("With my heart, do you think I'd risk anesthesia?") "Just give me a minute, Jacqueline, and I'll get myself together." Pulling on a fluffy little wig, she added dark glasses, a pair of earrings and a scarf knotted at her throat. Emerging from her dressing room the picture of casual elegance, she asked, "Where are we going for supper?" Brialy, André and Dauzonne exchanged glances. "How about Chez Michou?" Josephine suggested. No, not tonight, they protested. They were tired. "Tired? Young people are no fun anymore!" Josephine said sharply. They suggested going across the street to a small café where the dancers were eating. "And here I got all dressed up to go to Chez Michou! Oh, well . . ." She sighed. Josephine ordered her favorite, spaghetti, and a glass of beer. It was a pleasant, simple meal. Since it was André's umpteenth night on the town, he went home early. Brialy soon left too. Dauzonne took Josephine home. As she was leaving the café, she waggled her finger at the troupe with the words: "Next stop London, my friends. And then . . . New York!" The dancers cheered. When Jean-Claude Dauzonne left her at her apartment door, it was two o'clock in the morning.

That Thursday, April 10, 1975, Marie Spiers was surprised not to receive Josephine's usual eight o'clock call. But there seemed no cause for alarm. After all, Josephine had a great deal of rest to make up after the strain of the last few days. Indeed, when Marie called the apartment at nine, Lélia told her that Josephine was still sleeping. At eleven Lélia stopped by Marie's shop to pick up Josephine's plane tickets for Sicily. "She's still in bed. I heard her snoring," Lélia reported. At three Marie called again. Josephine had an appointment with the press. She'd never be ready on time. Lélia replied that Josephine was still snoring and that she was unable to wake her. Marie instantly called Dr. Thiroloix, closed her store and hurried to the Avenue Paul Doumer, where she met Brialy and Levasseur, who had also been worried to learn by telephone that Josephine, who usually slept four or five hours, was still in bed. What Lélia had taken for a snore was a rattle. Josephine was in a coma. She lay in bed in her flowered nightgown, surrounded by newspapers which were still making news of her triumph. She must have been reading them before drifting off. . . .

Josephine was rushed to Salpêtrière Hospital by ambulance.

At eight that evening I stopped by André's apartment to get the latest news. I found him prostrate with grief. "Thiroloix says there's nothing more to be done. And that it's better this way." He choked back a sob. "Can you imagine Josephine in a wheelchair? I'm about to leave for the hospital. Jean-Claude feels he *must* attend Charles Trenet's opening at the Olympia tonight. Incidentally, Jacqueline, the Bobino has issued a statement saying that Josephine is taking a few days' rest. We've all agreed to say nothing further. Otherwise the hospital would be mobbed."

I too was expected at Trenet's performance. Flash bulbs exploded as photographers crowded around Brialy's front-row seat. I could guess what Jean-Claude was telling them. "No, nothing serious. She'll be good as new in a day or two. The excitement was too much for her." Our eyes met.

Later that night André called from the hospital. Josephine's condition was unchanged. She had not regained consciousness.

By five o'clock Friday afternoon the doctors had given up hope. André called from Salpêtrière, asking me to join him there to help ward off the press, who were arriving in ever-increasing numbers. I had an important call to make along the way and at the home of my hostess, a prominent Parisienne, ran into Princess Grace. André had told me that she had sent a telegram, which he had not had time to answer but which had touched him deeply. I knew I could tell her the truth, and did. The Princess turned ashen and asked at once, "May I go with you to the hospital?" We slipped away together. "She's such an amazing woman," Grace murmured during our car ride. "I've had a chance to get to know her since she's been living in Monaco. I've seen the way she's raised her children and stuck to her beliefs. She's been so brave all her life. I never found the proper time or place to tell her, but the first time I ever saw her was at the Stork Club that famous night. I'd never heard of her, but my escort explained who she was. I remember admiring the way she was willing to risk a scandal —and asking myself if I would have had her courage!"

We entered the hospital through a back door, where Roger Ragoy, André's assistant, stood waiting. He guided us through a maze of corridors and elevators in order to avoid the photographers, who were everywhere. We stopped in front of a tiny room with an open door. I glimpsed a priest inside giving extreme unction. Josephine's breathing was horribly labored, but even on the threshold of death she seemed to be fighting with her usual gallantry. Her sister Margaret, who had just arrived from Roquebrune, looked on with seeming disbelief. Brialy had not yet finished his day's filming, but many of the cast members from the Bobino were there, their faces twisted with pain. There were other friends as well, struck dumb with sorrow. Two black nurses joined us and crossed themselves. Princess Grace knelt to pray beside André.

On Saturday morning, April 12, 1975, at half-past five, Ragoy telephoned. Josephine had abandoned the fight. She was dead.

Later that morning André conferred with Margaret about the funeral arrangements. Above all, Josephine's death must not be turned into a circus. It must reflect the star's own dignity. He questioned Margaret about her sister's religious affiliation. "She's Catholic, of course," snapped Margaret. André explained that he had been unsure because Josephine had expressed a desire to go to Israel twenty-four hours before opening at the Bobino. "I like to pray there before important events in my life." André had convinced her that the trip was impossible unless the show was delayed, but that on the first possible occasion he would make the trip with her since he had never been to Jerusalem. "What fun! We'll go together. Just the two of us. We have a date for after the gala. . . ."

By nine that morning flowers were pouring into the hospital. The gates had been closed to keep out the curiosity seekers. We didn't want a picture of Josephine on her deathbed, no matter how beautiful she looked in final repose. She must be remembered as her vital, triumphant self.

The funeral procession left Salpêtrière on April 15 at noon and threaded its way across Paris. It arrived at the Church of the Madeleine by detouring past the Bobino, where the marquee bore the word JOSEPHINE in bold letters. Bystanders added their bouquets to the flower-laden cars in the procession, which could barely make its way through the dense crowd. A motorcycle escort was needed to clear the path. The road was lined with sorrowful onlookers, but the throng at the Place de la Concorde was especially striking. The Rue Royale was literally banked with Josephine's enormous public. They had come, they were there, impressive in their dignity and silence. The Place de la Madeleine was covered by a tide of quiet mourners.

In the huge church, packed to capacity, many members of last week's gala Bobino audience sat grief-stricken. The entire troupe of the Bobino, including the stagehands, sat behind the managers, the young dancers' faces swollen with tears. Jo tried to comfort the children.

The service was also that of Lieutenant Josephine Baker. The coffin, followed by a bearer carrying Josephine's decorations, was saluted by twenty-four flags representing various branches of the military. Many public authorities, ministers, generals and ambassadors were in attendance. The funeral was of almost national scope, decorous yet crowded with spectators. Still it was a deeply personal occasion. Next to the President of the Republic's wreath lay roses from *"Papa* and the children," a heart made of flowers from Brialy and Levasseur, and a Star of David fashioned out of roses from an anonymous friend, honoring Josephine's personal attachments and fight against racism. . . .

Suddenly the poignant notes of "Sonny Boy," which Josephine would sing no more, rose from Pierre Spiers' harp. Then, after Mozart's *Requiem* was performed, Pierre sat down at the Madeleine's huge organ and played as never before the melody that had linked Josephine to Paris for a lifetime: "J'ai Deux Amours . . . My country and Paris." The little song solemnly filled the vault, then moved upward and beyond.

On Sunday evening, November 7, 1976, the Variety Club Foundation of New York presented a *Special Tribute to Josephine Baker* at the Metropolitan Opera House in Lincoln Center, New York City. The purpose of the various Variety Clubs is one dear to Josephine's heart—to help the world's orphans.

The program, with Princess Grace of Monaco and Jacqueline Onassis as honorary chairmen, and the supper afterward at the opera house, made for a brilliant evening. Thousands of Josephine's friends and admirers were there, looking their strikingly glamorous best. Among the famous narrators and performers were her devoted friend Jean-Claude Brialy, two of her sons, and nonagenarian Eubie Blake, who was one of the first people to recognize the young Josephine's talents.

Josephine would have loved the festivities. In fact she did. She was there.

Index